Al-Mutanabbi Starts Here

Edited by Beau Beausoleil & Deema K. Shehabi

Contributing Editors:
Sinan Antoon
Summer Brenner
Julie Bruck
Jordan Elgrably
Susannah Okret
Persis Karim
Rick London
Dunya Mikhail
Bonnie Nish
Maysoon Pachachi
Rijin Sahakian
Zaid Shlah
Louise Steinman
Sholeh Wolpé

Project website:
http://www.al-mutanabbistreetstartshere-boston.com/

Jaffe Center for Book Arts:
http://www.library.fau.edu/depts/spc/JaffeCenter/collection/al-mutanabbi/index.php

Al-Mutanabbi Street Starts Here
Edited by Beau Beausoleil & Deema K. Shehabi
© 2012 PM Press
All rights reserved. No part of this book may be transmitted by any means without permission in writing from the publisher.

ISBN: 978-1-60486-590-5
Library of Congress Control Number: 2011939672

Cover designed by Tania Baban, based on a broadside printed by Suzanne Vilmain for the Al-Mutanabbi Street Broadside Project
Interior design by briandesign

10 9 8 7 6 5 4 3 2 1

PM Press
PO Box 23912
Oakland, CA 94623
www.pmpress.org

Printed in the USA on recycled paper, by the Employee Owners of Thomson-Shore in Dexter, Michigan.
www.thomsonshore.com

Contents

To Carol Pierce — (and the OUTING LIBRARY!) — in honor of your great love of books. 2017 [signature] p. 118

I. THE RIVER TURNED BLACK WITH INK

Introduction

Sometimes the weight of our own silence becomes completely unbearable, until we cannot take one more day of reading about the blood, bone, and ash.

And then the moment comes when we recognize that this distant landscape is our own, and that we must walk through it.

On March 5, 2007, a car bomb was exploded on al-Mutanabbi Street in Baghdad. More than thirty people were killed and more than a hundred were wounded. This locale is the historic center of Baghdad bookselling, a winding street filled with bookstores and outdoor book stalls. Named after the famed tenth-century classical Arab poet, al-Mutanabbi, this is an old and established street for bookselling and has been for hundreds of years. It has been the heart and soul of the Baghdad literary and intellectual community.

The connection between the booksellers and readers on al-Mutanabbi Street and the booksellers and readers here is very simple and direct. We all share the belief that books are the holders of memories, dreams, and ideas. I felt, as a poet and bookseller here in San Francisco, an urgent need to keep this singular, tragic event in our consciousness, because it has such deep historical and cultural implications, for us, here in this country, and for the people of Iraq. To this end, I decided to create a coalition of poets, artists, writers, printers, booksellers, and readers.

I had two basic goals. The first goal was to have those involved in the arts respond to this targeted attack. A response that would consider the various underpinnings that made up the fabric of al-Mutanabbi Street: a street that held bookstores, a street that held both Shia and Sunni, a street that indeed welcomed all Iraqis, a street where people felt relatively "safe" as they walked, browsed books, bought stationery, arranged for printing, or sat in the Shabandar Café. These same people somehow believed that this place of knowledge and history "protected" them from the encroaching chaos.

Besides seeking to gather more dead, the car bomber and his cohorts were attacking the thoughts and ideas latent in each book, trying to also kill the notion that someone might be free to say something not sanctioned by them. It didn't matter if that idea was in a children's book, a book of philosophy, a memoir, poetry, or perhaps even more dangerous, a blank notebook.

My second goal was to try to close the distance between al-Mutanabbi Street and similar "cultural streets" here and around the globe. I want people to understand the commonality that exists between al-Mutanabbi Street and any street that holds a bookstore or a cultural institution. I want people to understand that a carefully chosen attack like this should be seen as an attack on us all.

I have felt that concentrating our attention on this one car bombing, on this one day, on this one narrow winding street, would reveal many things to us and perhaps also help us to see the bond we have with everyday Iraqis. These are the Iraqis who get up each day and work to live, Iraqis whose lives are altered forever by being in the wrong place at the wrong time: while on their way to work, to school, to the market, just sitting in a café, or picking up a book to read on al-Mutanabbi Street.

I have come to feel that wherever someone gathers their thoughts to write towards the truth, or where someone sits down and opens a book to read, it is *there* that al-Mutananabbi Street starts.

As much as this anthology celebrates al-Mutanabbi Street and helps others understand what it means to the Iraqi cultural community, it is also a lament for those who were killed and wounded that day, and by extension, on all the streets and days before, and days after, even this very day, as I write these words.

Al-Mutanabbi Street has reopened, although many booksellers were killed, and many of the survivors left the street; still books are being displayed and sold again, and the gutted Shabandar Café has been made new (the owner lost many family members in the blast). And, today my friend Maysoon Pachachi writes to me, "We will see how long it will take for al-Mutanabbi Street to get its soul back."

One might say the same about our own country, as well.

I have always wanted the Iraqi cultural community to know that we would not let them endure all that has happened in silence. Al-Mutanabbi Street starts in many places around the globe. Everywhere it starts it seeks to include the free exchange of ideas. We must safeguard that.

These are our words.

Al-Mutanabbi Street starts here.

—**Beau Beausoleil**

Preface
Al-Mutanabbi Street in Baghdad: When Books Take You Captive

Muhsin al-Musawi

When writing or speaking of al-Mutanabbi Street, one cannot make a mere reference to a street in an urban center, not only because it has long been recognized as the consortium par excellence for booksellers, scribes, and bookstores in Iraq, but also because of its long history. Al-Mutanabbi Street's lineage dates back to the urban district of scribes of Abbasid in Baghdad (762–1258 CE), and it challenges our knowledge of the genealogy of culture and the resilience of an industry that has been resisting destruction. Samuel Kramer's monumental study of Sumerian and old Mesopotamian writing, as the oldest and earliest in the world, consolidates an Iraqi tradition which is as much a celebration of writing as of fertility and love. However, this celebration is always challenged and confronted with powers of destruction and death. In Sumerian poetry war and destruction were metonymized as storms, callous, devastating and ignorant. In Kramer's eloquent translations of poetic tablets, we are met with the impetus of passionate narratives and pleadings anchored in a sublime human yearning for peace and a life of plenty. Writing itself is a celebration of this will to live, for only through recuperation, reproduction, fertility, and love can a human society survive in joy.

Mesopotamian writing is a testimony to this longing and struggle. Although Baghdad is new in comparison to these ancient traditions, it inherited this love for writing and documentation upon its establishment in 762 CE, and sustained it through the city's cultural growth. The area around al-Mutanabbi Street itself was the old Abbasid district of scribes' markets and booksellers' stalls and shops. At that time it was probably adjacent to Darb Zakha, or Zakha Alley, where there were then cultural and educational institutions and schools. It was part of a large and thriving district of many alleys that were usually referred to as Suq al-Warraqin (Scribes' Markets). The renowned bibliophile al-Nadim (died 998 CE) made eloquent mention of this market, which Ahmad Ibn Tahir, the celebrated Ibn Tayfur (died 893 CE) had already documented in his book on the history of Baghdad. The jurist Ibn al-Jawzi (1200 CE) would write later his book *Manqib Baghdad* (*Baghdad Attributes*) in which he counts these markets among the city's landmarks. These shops numbered in the hundreds according to later scholars, like Ahmad Susah and Mustafa Jawad (died 1969) who reproduced the Abbasid map of Baghdad. Perhaps it is difficult for contemporary readers to imagine the extent to which the book industry thrived during that period. Books were produced in almost unlimited numbers. Especially after the emergence of the paper industry in Baghdad (the art of papermaking having been reputedly transferred through some Chinese travelers or captives), books were available in abundance. Scholars with many students could get hundreds of copies of their books. The demand was unabating. But during the civil conflicts between the two contending caliphs, the sons of Harun al-Rashid, some of these markets suffered. Their greatest loss took place in 1258, with the Mongol invasion of Baghdad, which led to enormous destruction of libraries and intellectual life in particular. Historians wrote extensively about this loss and the invasion was always referred to as the "great destruction" when "books of knowledge were burnt." Ibn Khaldun (1406 CE) summarized these accounts in his history, recording how the enormous quantity of books thrown in the Tigris changed even the color of its water.

As the unique witness to and evidence of civilization, Baghdad's book center was always a challenge to warmongers and destructive forces. Wherever its industry thrives and expands there is evidence of good life. Indeed, the history of the Scribes' Market in Baghdad is unique historical evidence, a compelling itinerary, of Iraq's journey through periods of struggle between prosperity and stability and the forces of evil and death. Baghdad groans under invasions and criminal destructiveness that leave the city in mourning, before picking up again to outgrow loss and celebrate life with songs of jubilation and enchantment. Scheherazade is never tired of narrating the tales of young men or barbers who speak of their reading and books. A book is a repository of knowledge and the custodian of tradition.

Almost every significant prose writer in the Abbasid period wrote something about the value of books. Al-Jahiz's monumental epistle on books is well known among scholars and readers in the classical Arabic tradition. So were the writings of Ibn al-Muqaffa (died 756 CE), Sahl Ibn Harun, Ibn Qutaybah (died 885 CE), and others. But more important was then the celebration of books in the titles of many of these authored epistles or studies. It has become a tradition since the first century of Hijra (622 CE) to have "The Book of…" as part of the title. Thus, we have *The Book of Horses*, *The Book of Anecdotes*, etc. This sumptuous celebration of the book industry is also a record of Baghdad's expansion, prosperity, and wealth.

Less than forty years after its establishment it was the largest city in the
known world at that time. Books only testify to this life of replenishment
and exuberance. Among the best sites in ancient Baghdad was the library
belonging to the Mustansiriyya University (constructed 1233 CE), which
was close to the markets and had an excellent collection of books. One
of its resident teachers was the blind Zayn al-Din Ali Ahmad al-Amidi
(died 1314 CE) during the reign of the Mongol Sultan Khazan Khan, the
grandson of Helagu (Halaku), who was responsible for the destruction of
Baghdad. There he invented his pre-Braille system of reading and writing
for the blind. But the school suffered neglect and even destruction during
that time and throughout the Ottoman period. The street was called
then al-Akmak Khana (the public bakery). Early in the twentieth century,
the place witnessed some revival. After being subsumed into the gov-
ernmental quarter during the British occupation, some of its old cafés
were revived, along with restaurants and bookshops. The government
quarter was called al-Qishla after the tall and lonely minaret whose top
has become ever since an enormous nest for birds. The name suggests a
populated area, as government headquarters had made it the center of a
very busy place. That area witnessed the crowning in 1921 of King Faisal
the First as the king of Iraq under British rule.

Among individual booksellers from al-Mutanabbi Street's more
recent history were Abd al-Rahman Efendi (1890), Mulla Khidayyir
(1900) and his son Abd al-Karim, who later owned Mishriq Bookshop
(Oriental Bookshop). He was followed by Numan al-Adami (1905) with
his Arabiyya Bookshop, then Mahmud Hilmi (1914) with his famous
Asriyyah Bookshop (Contemporary Bookshop). Shams al-Din al-Haidari
had his Ahliyyah Bookshop (The Native Bookshop), which was the first
to get Franklin's books published. The famous Husayn al-Fulfili, with
his many anecdotes, had his Zawra Bookshop named after the original
epithet of Baghdad (1932). Around the same time, Muhammad Qasim
al-Rijab bought the historical house of Saib Shawkat on the right side
of the same street. It became the Muthanna Bookshop. The renowned
book industrialist made this bookshop the first to get Orientalists' books
published and circulated in Baghdad, Beirut, and Cairo. He established
also the Muthanna Club in Adamiyyah District, facing one of the king's
palaces on the eastern side of the river. The Club was the meeting place
for Iraqi nationalists. It was also the butt of criticism as the meeting place
for pretentious seekers of power in Iraq of the 1930s. Mahmud Jawad
Haidar had his bookshop, al-Marif, on the right side of the street, the
same side where Ali-al-Khaqani had his Najah Bookshop (later changed
into al-Bayan Bookshop, which produced a famous journal published
in Nejef). Abd al-Hamid Zahid inaugurated the auction for books, and

had his bookshop on the right side, as the Bookshop of Abd al-Hamid Zahid. He was among the leaders of the popular revolution of 1920 in Iraq against the British occupation. Abd al-Rahmad Hayyawi established the Nahdhah Bookshop. I got my book *Bourgeois Themes in Poetry* through his bookshop and had many conversations with him. His son Najah took over after his father's death, and was followed by his brother Muhammad. The latter lost his life in the deliberate explosions in the street in 2007, which were meant to destroy the book industry center. At the corner of the street that connects to Jadid Hasan Pasha Street, and the Qishla Quarter, there was the famous Shahbandar Café (Shah Bandar). It was established in 1917 by Muhammad al-Khishali. His three sons were also killed in those explosions. To the left of the street and branching out of the governmental quarter is the famous Sarai Marketplace, a market that is reserved for booksellers, scribes, and stationery stalls, along with a few scattered artisans whose professions and occupations are inherited from their fathers and grandfathers. Thus alongside bookshops you may come across a shoemaker, or an art and cover designer.

In this historical geographical survey, we might get a glimpse of a thriving center of an active cultural life, but we need also to recall that Fridays in particular are the days when people have their holidays after a week of work. There they go to search for a book, a secondhand publication, an old issue of a journal, or a banned document. We should not be surprised to come across some security personnel in plain clothes, and you need to be alert to the whispers of the bookseller who may entrust you with this piece of information so that you will be on guard lest you get in trouble. Between free expression and censorship there is always a struggle and conflict and the street is the place where this is played out. Indeed, political parties were bent on planting some of their young sympathizers there to distribute a pamphlet or to spread a word. Many of these young men were also captured by the security office during the 1980s under Saddam Hussein's reign to suffer long imprisonments or death. Al-Mutanabbi Street and its companion the Sarai Book Marketplace were the lungs through which the city breathes its cultural presence, a pulsing place of life and educational activity, where booksellers know authors and avid readers by name. The Street grows into a symbolical space, for it brings the past and present into sharp relief and nevertheless conveys haunting or comforting messages.

The association in name with the great poet Abu al-Tayyib al-Mutanabbi (died 965 CE) could be a random choice by a bookseller, or by the Baghdad urban planners who needed, early on in the century, to put names to streets. As the street had a few booksellers after World War I, it might have invited the worthy name of the great poet. But the poet was famed, too, for celebrating poetry, his own poetry, above everything else. In a famous verse, he enlists the pen and the notebook or scriptoria along with the horse, the night and the wilderness, as the spaces and means that bear witness to his valor and power. That verse is as follows: "The horse, the night, and the desert know me/and the sword, the spear, the paper and the pen." No wonder, then, that al-Mutanabbi lives up to his name and his challenge, surviving attacks and resisting failure and death. Between the epistles on books and their merits, the use of the word *kitab*, or book, in the titles of thousands of books since the seventh century, and the stupendous growth of the book industry testify to a thriving cultural life and civilization. Whenever there is such a growth there is good life, reproduction, activity, and love. Epistolography (the art of writing and studying letters, particularly in the public context) grew between the eighth and the twelfth centuries, not only as testimony to a growing statecraft, but primarily as a rising respectable profession whose professionals have to be aware of many fields of knowledge. Books are the repositories and inventories of traditions and scientific explorations. The epistolographer was then the model for the knowledgeable person. They were first scribes before growing into their stately profession. Perhaps none among them could have left these scribes' markets unvisited or unsolicited. Many well-known authors who exercised great influence on the rest of the society emerged, after all, from the book markets of Baghdad, Basra, and Kufa in Iraq before the thriving of Cairo and Damascus.

While drafting the preface to this commendable volume as a tribute to the street and its symbolic value, I cannot help recollecting the topography of the street, its shops, the haggard and pale faces of booksellers, their humor and tales, and their effort to grow into publishers, though most were unable to be larger than what they were: devotees of books whose struggle could get a few books published for a few select authors. To go to al-Mutanabbi Street means to spend hours, ending up also in Kabab al-Ikhlas restaurant on the right-hand middle of the alley branching out from al-Rashid Street. You may end up eating some *kubba* from a vendor at the corner of the Sarai Book Market. Usually you get lured to have tea from the same vendor or, if you are lucky and left with a few pennies, you may settle in the Shabandar Café or a neighboring restaurant. There you can have a look at what books you have bought. It is rare to trust your colleagues, who are on the lookout for new books, too, and may well end up stealthily taking one of your new acquisitions. The love of reading was a notorious habit among Iraqis before the encroachment of ignorance that accompanied occupation. But even if you stop going there, al-Mutanabbi Street will live in your memory, with its bustle, whispers, humidity, and unexpected encounters. You may leave al-Mutanabbi Street or the Sarai

Book Market, but they will never leave you; hence they take you hostage, but with a difference. As a reader and lover of books you perhaps cherish this captivity.

This anthology, *Al-Mutanabbi Street Starts Here*, celebrates this exquisite relationship between the book and the reader, humanity and culture, writing and life and love. It is a tribute to a street that grows into a large and archetypal symbol and spatial metaphor for books. Situated in Baghdad, the city of the Arabian Nights, and in the oldest civilization that brought humanity to learning through writing, al-Mutanabbi Street is a call for all to regain Baghdad's cultural luster instead of letting it fade in violence, greed, exploitation and corruption in a wicked trajectory of dictatorship, invasion, occupation, and comic but dangerous puppets.

I. THE RIVER TURNED BLACK WITH INK

The Bookseller's Story,
Ending Much Too Soon

Anthony Shadid

Washington Post, Monday, March 12, 2007

It was a summer day in 2003, when Iraq was still filled with the half-truths of occupation and liberation, before its nihilistic descent into carnage. Mohammed Hayawi, a bald bear of a man, stood in his shop, the Renaissance Bookstore, along Baghdad's storied al-Mutanabbi Street.

On shelves eight rows high rested books by communist poets and martyred clerics, translations of Shakespeare, predictions by Lebanese astrologers, a 44-volume tome by a revered ayatollah and a tract by the austere medieval thinker Ibn Taimiyyah. Dusty stacks spilled across the cream-colored tile floor, swept but stained with age. In those cramped quarters, Hayawi tried to cool himself with a fan, as perspiration poured down his jowly face and soaked his blue shirt.

We had met before the American invasion, and nearly a year later, he almost immediately recognized me.

"Abu Laila," he said, using the Arabic nickname taken from the name of a person's child.

He then delivered a line he would repeat almost every time we saw each other over the next few years. "I challenge anyone, Abu Laila, to say what has happened, what's happening now, and what will happen in the future." And, over a thin-waisted cup of tea, scalding even on this hot day, he shook his head.

A car bomb detonated last week on al-Mutanabbi Street, leaving a scene that has grown familiar in Baghdad, a collage of chaotic images, disturbing in their brutality, grotesque in their repetition. At least 26 people were killed. Hayawi the bookseller was one of them.

Unlike the U.S. soldiers who die in this conflict, the names of most Iraqi victims will never be published, consigned to the anonymity that death in the Iraqi capital brings these days. Hayawi was neither a politician nor a warlord. Few beyond al-Mutanabbi Street even knew his name. Yet his quiet life deserves more than a footnote, if for no other reason than to remember a man who embraced what Baghdad was and tried to make sense of a country that doesn't make sense anymore. Gone with him are small moments of life, gentle simply by virtue of being ordinary, now lost in the rubble strewn along a street that will never be the same.

After his death, I thought back to our conversation on that summer day. As he often did, Hayawi paused after an especially vigorous point and dragged on his cigarette. He ran his hand over his sweaty cheeks. "Does this look like the face of 39 years?" he said, grinning. He then knitted his brow, turning grimmer. "We don't want to hear explosions, we don't want to hear about more attacks, we want to be at peace," he told me. He always had dark bags under his limpid eyes, whether or not he had slept. "An Iraqi wants to put his head on his pillow and feel relaxed."

Independent Thinker

Hayawi had worked at the bookstore all his life. His father, Abdel-Rahman, opened it in 1954, and after he died in 1993 his five sons inherited the business, keeping a portrait of the patriarch, in a Russian-style winter hat, hanging on the wood-paneled wall. Over the years, Hayawi and his older brothers would branch out. They owned other shops on al-Mutanabbi— Legal Bookstore and Nibras Bookstore down the street—along with a business that sold Korans across town.

His family was Sunni Muslim, but Hayawi played down its importance to his sense of self, and he lived with his wife and young son, Ahmed Akram, in a predominantly Shiite neighborhood. He took pride in his independence, in being someone who celebrated the gray areas, a reflection of the best of what the intellectual *entrepôt* of al-Mutanabbi Street was supposed to represent.

We first met as I wandered into his shop before the invasion, when Saddam Hussein was still in power in 2002. As usual, he was unshaven, and even then, he seized the opportunity to talk. "Iraq's invasion of Kuwait was wrong," he told me quite boldly—a blasphemous idea at the time.

But years later, he was unable to understand the American obsession with Iraq and Saddam. "Why the crisis after crisis?" he asked. "For weapons of mass destruction? We don't have any. If we did," he declared, "we would have fired them at Israel. A war simply for Saddam?"

After the invasion and the government's fall, Hayawi described himself much as other Iraqis did in that first uncertain year: as neither for Saddam nor happy with the Americans. He was angry, of course—at the chaos, the insecurity, the lack of electricity.

"The American promises to Iraq are like trying to hold water in your hand," he told me in one conversation. "It spills through your fingers."

But he was never strident; he was filled with a thoughtfulness and reflection that survival in Iraq rarely permits these days.

Hayawi resented the occupation but voted in the elections the United States backed. He was a devout Muslim, but feared the rise of religion in politics. In his bookstore, once-banned titles by Shiite clerics, imported from Iran, vied with books by radical Sunni clerics, among them Muhammad Abdel-Wahab, the eighteenth century godfather of Saudi Arabia's brand of Islam. Profit may have inspired his eclectic mix, but Hayawi also seemed to be making a statement: al-Mutanabbi Street, his Baghdad and his Iraq would respect their diversity.

He was always a proud man. Every so often, Hayawi would repeat this story: he was driving to Syria on business in his yellow Caprice and was stopped at a U.S. checkpoint, manned by two Humvees, outside the Euphrates River town of Ramadi, in Western Iraq. Through a translator, one of the American officers, clad in camouflage and dusty from a desert wind, began to ask him routine questions.

"'What are you doing here?' the soldier asked."

"I said, 'What are YOU doing here? You're my guest. What are you doing in Iraq?'"

"He laughed and he patted my shoulder," Hayawi recalled.

Bookstore Retreat

The doorway of the Renaissance Bookstore was a border, in a way. Outside were the sirens of ambulances and police cars. Gunfire was common. Horns blared in two lanes of traffic, one more than al-Mutanabbi had been built for. Inside Hayawi went about business as he had every day since he inherited the shop from his father.

The last time I saw him, in 2005, he was sitting behind his desk, sipping a cup of tea that cost 10 cents, a pack of Gauloise cigarettes next to it.

As he did every morning, hour after hour, Hajji Sadiq, the money changer, ambled into the bookstore.

"What's the rate?" Hayawi bellowed.

"I won't tell you unless you're going to buy," Hajji Sadiq answered.

Hayawi waved to friends passing along the street outside. An elderly woman stood at the door, asking for alms. Vendors entered offering everything from books to beach towels.

The day went on, in the rhythm of a life that now no longer exists. Two Kurdish booksellers came in, bringing a gift of honey from Sulaimaniya in the North. They greeted Hayawi in Kurdish, then the conversation continued in Arabic. Hajji Sadiq returned, quoting an exchange rate that had barely changed. The electricity cut off, with no one seeming to notice. Customers from Balad in the North told of the situation there, as did visitors from Basra in the South.

By afternoon, the electricity came on and a water pipe was brought out. Sweet-smelling apple-flavored tobacco smoldered.

"Life goes on," Hayawi told me that day. "We are in the middle of a war, and we still smoke the water pipe."

Literary Loss

Al-Mutanabbi Street always seemed to tell a story of Iraq.

Its maze of bookshops and stationery stores, housed in elegant Ottoman architecture, was named for one of the Arab world's greatest poets, a 10th-century sage whose haughtiness was matched only by his skill. The street was anchored by the Shahbandar Cafe, where antique water pipes were stacked in rows three deep. On the walls inside were pictures of Iraq's history: portraits of the bare-chested 1936 wrestling team, King Faisal's court after World War I and the funeral of King Ghazi in 1939.

In its heyday, this street embodied a generation-old saying: Cairo writes, Beirut publishes, Baghdad reads. But under the U.N. sanctions that followed Iraq's invasion of Kuwait in 1990, isolating it from the world, its stores were lined with magazines 20 years old, obsolete textbooks and dust-covered religious tomes that seemed more for show than for sale. It became a dreary flea market for used books, as vendors sold off their private collections in an attempt to get by, and Hayawi and his brothers eked out a living by selling religious texts, works of history for university curricula, and course work in English, what he called a passport.

In the months after the invasion, al-Mutanabbi Street revived into an intellectual free-for-all. There were titles by Mohammed Baqir al-Sadr, a brilliant theologian killed, as the story goes, when Saddam's executioners drove nails into his forehead. Shiite iconography—of living ayatollahs and 7th-century saints marching to their deaths—was everywhere. Nearby were new issues of FHM and Maxim, their covers adorned with scantily clad women. On rickety stands were compact discs of Osama bin Laden's messages selling for the equivalent of 50 cents. Down the street were pamphlets of the venerable Communist Party. As one of the booksellers once said, quoting a line of poetry by al-Mutanabbi, "With so much noise, you need ten fingers to plug your ears."

Al-Mutanabbi Street today tells another story.

When the Mongols sacked Baghdad in 1258, it was said that the Tigris River ran red one day, black another. The red came from the blood of nameless victims, massacred by ferocious horsemen. The black came from the ink of countless books from libraries and universities. Last Monday, the bomb on al-Mutanabbi Street detonated at 11:40 a.m. The pavement was smeared with blood. Fires that ensued sent up columns of dark smoke, fed by the plethora of paper.

A colleague told me that near Hayawi's shop, a little ways from the now-gutted Shahbandar Cafe, a black banner hangs today. In the graceful slope of yellow Arabic script, it mourns the loss of Hayawi and his nephew, "who were assassinated by the cowardly bombing."

The Washington Post, © March 12, 2007.
All rights reserved.

A Man in Love with Knowledge

Mousa al-Naseri

My name is Mousa al-Naseri. I was born in Baghdad in 1964. From 2001 to 2007, I worked as a sales representative for an Iraqi wholesale merchant of stationery items and imported office supplies. Most of my work was on al-Mutanabbi Street, but I also had customers on other historic streets such as Souq al-Sarrai. The nature of my work was walking down the streets, presenting the inventory of imported stationery goods and office supplies to the owners of the bookstores and stationery shops. Every day, I walked down the alleyways and the streets for hours checking on the supplies and taking orders from my regular customers. I carried with me, besides my selling skills, two big plastic suitcases filled with samples of the inventory. What I couldn't carry with me, because of its weight or size, I wrote on a long, detailed list.

On a regular workday, I started my day showing my goods to the shop owners on historic al-Rasheed Street, where the beautiful statue of the famous Iraqi poet, Abdul-Ghannai Maarouf al-Rusafi, stands. Then, I walked straight down to al-Mutanabbi Street. The stationery shops are spread out along the two sides of the street, which I estimate to be around 300–400 meters long. Sometimes, after finishing those long strenuous trips, I took a short rest at the old and famed al-Shabandar coffee shop, and I would sip a cup of real Baghdadi tea, *istikan chai*. The al-Shabandar was always filled with the essence of poetry and intellectual discourse. I often found myself listening to a discussion of literature or politics while enjoying my tea. I would then rush back to my work, spending another two or more hours offering my goods to the rest of my customers on Souq al-Sarrai. After finishing Souq al-Sarrai, al-Rasheed Street, and al-Mutanabbi Street, earlier in the day, I headed back to the office. On the way back, I passed by al-Shabandar coffee shop again; continuing, I would head towards a few more shops that sit near *al-qushla*, another beautiful historic building where I do more work with the shop owners. This stop concludes the strenuous part of my long day. However, the last part of my work is to go back to the warehouse where I started the morning, to put together the orders I collected during the day. I make sure these orders go out to the customers that same day. Finally, my workday is done, only to start the whole journey again the next morning!

I didn't work with books on al-Mutanabbi Street, but books had a great impact on my life. Influenced by the famous Arabic saying: "In this world the book is my best companion," I chose the book to be my closest friend, a friend that I never abandoned. In addition, I was a PhD student. I had my Master's degree in history and I was writing a dissertation entitled "The Freedom of Expression and its Development in Islam until the Ummayyad Period." Unfortunately, I didn't get to finish my graduate degree due to my sudden departure for the United States. By the end of 2007, I had left my work as a stationery-goods sales representative on al-Mutanabbi Street in order to work independently as a wholesale merchant in the same business of stationery and office supplies. I began to look for a storage area on al-Mutanabbi Street for my new business. I worked hard to find both a place for my project, and a partner to work with me, a person who was willing to take on this new endeavor with me. We worked together until it was time for me to move on. I left everything and came to America.

Al-Mutanabbi Street, which is in the center of Baghdad, is located between al-Rasheed Street and al-Maydan area. Considered as the intellectual marketplace for the Baghdadi people, it is a place where books of every genre and subject matter flourish. The market is most active during Fridays and holidays when book lovers and seekers flock from all corners of Baghdad and neighboring cities to grasp the book they came looking for. Also, most of the students of the Iraqi colleges and universities come to this street looking for books in their area of interest or for research. This book market is regarded as an outlet for the Iraqi thinkers, intellectuals, and literary people and as a center to meet and talk. It is a place for those who have a thirst for knowledge. Al-Mutanabbi Street is also a place that has many libraries and historic buildings such as the famous al-qushla building, which I mentioned earlier.

This street had the greatest impact in shaping my love of literature and knowledge. Since I was a child, I was fond of visiting this street from time to time, looking to buy a book or two. After reading them, I would go back to sell them and buy new books with the money I got. I will always remember a special trip to al-Mutanabbi Street during 1978. I was looking for a book recommended by some friends. They said it is a great read, but it is prohibited from circulating openly. The book was none other than the famous *The Prince*, by Machiavelli. I was really anxious to read that book. I tried really hard to get it, but I failed. Nobody would sell me the book;

they were all afraid I would inform on them. When I became a graduate student, I considered this street as my savior. I walked the street often, looking for special books and reference material that I would need later for writing my thesis and dissertation. After the looting and burning of the public and the university libraries during the events of 2003, it was nearly impossible to find the books I needed.

The mere experience of walking down that street and spending time with books and book lovers made me value the intellectual and cultured part of myself. In addition, it was there that I would meet some intellectual colleagues, who, like me, felt the gap that separated us from what was happening in the Arab and international social, political, and literary world. During its three-decade regime, the Ba'ath party blacklisted books. So, we used to gather on al-Mutanabbi Street to look for those editions that had just made the blacklist, searching secretly so the government wouldn't find out about us.

The act of terrorism on al-Mutanabbi Street, in spring 2007, was a catastrophic event, by any measure. A vehicle of evil was parked on a corner of al-Mutanabbi Street. The horrifying explosion altered the meaning of al-Mutanabbi Street. It destroyed a vast part of its historic buildings, killing innocent workers and shoppers, and burned thousands of books. Miraculously, I survived that incident, since I used to walk down that street for hours every day. I was about thirty meters away from the place where the explosion happened. I still remember passing close by the spot where the car was parked many times that day. One of my customers, Ali, called me, asking me to supply him with some stationery items. His shop was in one of the buildings that were destroyed. Ali also survived the explosion. I lost friends who are impossible to forget: stationery merchants, booksellers, and bookstore owners. I especially remember Mr. Adnan, the owner of Adnan Bookstore, who helped me tremendously during my graduate years. He lent me great books and reference material that I needed for writing my Master's thesis. I also remember all the losses that the bookstore owners had to endure. It was a disaster in every sense of that word. However, the biggest loss were those innocent souls who died on that street; many of them were the head of a family, many worked on al-Mutanabbi Street, and others were just passing by while looking for a book. The owner of the historic al-Shabandar coffee shop lost four of his sons and one of his grandsons. I had a friendship with one of those sons.

I state here that whoever did this horrific, criminal act on al-Mutanabbi Street, which took lives or injured some of the best educated and intellectual youth . . . I say, they live in a ditch of their own ignorance and darkness. However, they failed, for they don't understand who the Iraqis are, nor Iraqi history and culture. A history that goes back 7,000 years.

They don't know or understand the Iraqis' fondness for literature, knowledge, and books. We must not forget the famous saying that is repeated by every intellectual Arab, "Egypt writes, Lebanon prints, and Baghdad reads."

My brother was also working on al-Mutanabbi Street, as a door-to-door stationery supplier, when the explosion happened. He left everything and ran in search of me, wondering if I was dead or alive. He was running from place to place, bewildered and overwhelmed, asking everybody if they had seen me. And, I was, simply, in the same condition, doing the exact same thing. This tragic incident still fills my heart. It will dwell with me for a long time. My memory of it distresses me: the memory of friends and colleagues who are gone; heaps of valuable and old books that were burned, damaged, and scattered everywhere; the memory of the dismay and horror I saw on every face, that day.

The great efforts to restore this street mends my soul and gives me patience; it assures me that this deeply rooted street will come back one day, to continue its intellectual and cultural role, to be a river that serves thinkers, scientists, and intellectuals.

I worked for a little more than a year (2005–06) with NPR, in their office in Baghdad. My job was translating news from the local Iraqi and Arabic channels. I also translated officials' statements and speeches. From 2007 to 2009, I worked as a journalist and translator for a French news agency in their office in Baghdad. Similar to my previous job, I translated news in regard to Iraq that was broadcast on Iraqi and Arab channels. I also accompanied foreign journalists, helping them translate from Arabic to English, some of the news and the stories they were working on. In regard to my move to the United States, I submitted a request for immigration with the International Organization for Migration (IOM). I was interviewed many times. Eventually, my immigration application was accepted.

Translated from the Arabic by Afaf Nash.

For al-Mutanabbi Street

Naomi Shihab Nye

"... books and stationery, some still tied in
charred bundles, littered the street."

A single sentence which mesmerized one mind for hours
will not be seen again, in that edition,
will not be seen tucked into the bookshelf
of the friend we will never meet,
on the street we will not know.

What blows to pieces
goes fast. They'll give it names—
successful mission, progress in security.
What lingers long—quiet hours reading,
in which people were the best
they hadn't been yet,
something was coming,
something exquisitely new,
something hopeful anyone might do,
and the paper flicker of turning.

The Last Word

Deena Metzger

There will come the time
before the last word will be spoken,
when the dead will listen
to learn what their fate will be,
what destiny the last word will fulfil,
and every word that ever was spoken
in that langue will be gathered
into one.

The harsh judgment of chance and
circumstance will be rendered
as the entire cannon will be weighed
against the skin of sheep
and the bodies of trees.
Each word against each life
without pity. And everyone
who had ever spoken
will have to come forth
and claim their words
and what became of them,
how they served the living
and how they served the dead.

One way or another, whether
"Praise," or "Damnation,"
nothing will be redeemed
and the great prison house
of language will fall,
and bury the last speaker
for there will be no one left
to do it in the mother tongue
to which she was born,
the one that held and rocked her
in its melodies and rhythms
its beauty and cruelty.
All words will go, as empires must,
into dust. This has been written so many times,
but we never believe we will die out,

die out by our own hands,
and by our own words,
by what we have sworn
by what we have spoken.

The Grief of Birds

Sam Hamod

there is the grief of birds
not out of your hand, but in
the eyes
glazing as they do
when the moon
tells you even that
is not enough, to love
someone so completely
that you give up yourself
and all those you hold dear
to leap into the arms, the
heart of someone
who is less than the moon,
less than the rivers,
but whose love
blossoms each and every morning

Al-Mutanabbi Street

Lutfiya al-Dulaimi

Before I was born on al-Mutanabbi Street, I was no one. I could deny the documents that made reference to my birth on a particular day of the year or a certain province of the country. I was a mere small woman without a place in this world. Then I was born on al-Mutanabbi Street the day my first book was published—A *Passage to the Sadness of Men.* I had discovered as a girl of nine the richness of the story through 1,001 *Nights* in a room that girls were forbidden to enter, and I was determined to become the contemporary Shahrezade. This young girl had no future, except perhaps to become a woman set aside to live a pointless life among quiet, forgotten women. But Shahrezade, the first woman to use the magic of imagination to narrate the tales of the East, plucked me out of my time and visited upon me the spell of dreams and tattooed a shining mark on my forehead, setting in place my destiny, as had the gods and goddesses of old: go to the place of books. You will be one of those women who narrate stories, one of the daughters of Shahrezade.

Thus, that first narrative sealed my fate and gave me over to the enchantment of the tale. Yet in contrast to Shahrezade's salvation through stories, the contemporary tale and the narration of stories would eventually expose me to death at the hands of terrorists, because I was a woman, and an Iraqi writer living in a land that was ransacked in 2006. The extremists had decided to cut out this woman's tongue, to decapitate her, but she escaped death and gave birth instead to another in her series of offspring.

I'll never forget the day I carried the manuscript of my first book to the al-Jahiz Printers located in one of the side streets off of al-Mutanabbi Street. I keenly followed the production of the book, visiting the printer every day, then spending the rest of the day browsing the bookshops scattered around al-Mutanabbi Street, buying stacks of books, and finally returning home at the end of the day bearing my treasure trove. When I collected the first copy from the printers, I swaggered vaingloriously down that street, possessed by the feeling that I had become on that day a new person, and I walked, drunk with pride, toward al-Rasheed Street, bearing my one true birth certificate in this world. I was possessed by a spell at the thought of being a writer walking down al-Mutanabbi. I can remember that I was wearing a short purple and black dress. That was 1970. I was very skinny then, and I feared that the wind might take advantage of my excessive lightness and exhilaration to blow me away. When news of my book's publication spread, my writer and journalist friends came to al-Jahiz Printers on al-Mutanabbi Street to pick up their copy and congratulate me on the birth of a new work, whose two godfathers were al-Mutanabbi, the greatest of Arab poets, and al-Jahiz, our most skilled prose stylist.

We All Come from There

No writer or poet from Baghdad, or any other city in Iraq, lacks a piece of a memory from that venerable street of books and bookshops, the Modern Bookshop, the Nahda Bookstore, Al Ma'arifa Booksellers, Al Muthanni, and others. Who among us had not been enticed by the magical stacks of books on the pavement and in carts, or walked awestruck, browsing titles and sniffing the scent of the pages? Who among us could forget the pleasure of buying new books in the 1970s, or banned and Xeroxed books in the '90s during the period of sanctions? Fridays were like holidays to commemorate the gathering of friends and the purchase of new books in al-Mutanabbi Street. That street was a paradise for readers and writers, an enchanted gateway for the passerby to approach the treasures of a culture. It was a market for wordsmiths and stationers, a place for the most extreme celebrations of the mind. It had a place of luminous distinction in the memories and dreams of its visitors. It encompassed the calamitous losses bequeathed by a history of defeats, rulers, and brutality. It was the domain of poets, writers, traders in manuscripts, and booksellers, seekers of fame, and yes, spies listening intently to the whispers of the intellectuals. (In the '90s, it was even subject to raids by security forces.) Banned books that had been copied and produced surreptitiously were published there, and those driven mad by the cruelty of war would wander up and down, reciting classical poetry that made fun of the dictator or yelling out mock news broadcasts that tore through the silence of the writers, who stood by petrified at how the brutal regime might respond.

The Fall of the Attestations of Books in al-Mutanabbi Street

I decided to set one of my stories in al-Mutanabbi Street, based on its special role in our cultural life. I called it "The Eclipse of the Attestation of the Book," a title that played with the multiple ironies of a time when intellectuals were embargoed and made hungry to the point that they sold their books in this street to be able to afford bread for sustenance or medicine for a child with leukemia during the sanctions years of the 1990s. I made the main character a lover of books who lost a part of his memory whenever he sold a portion of his immense library in response to the repression of the regime. His name was Birhan, which also means "attestation," and his plight recalled that of the philosopher al-Kindi, whom the Abbasid Caliph sentenced to prison and fifty lashes because of his writings and ideas, even though he was older than sixty.

Finally, Birhan sold the last of his remaining books in al-Mutanabbi Street, so that his memory was completely erased, and he left the street shattered and aimless to wander the ancient neighborhoods and alleyways of Baghdad. At first, the censors wouldn't allow it to be published, but I wrote a new section about the sanctions in which the protagonist discovers the horrors the country was facing during his wanderings through the backstreets of the city, until the piece became a short novel. Friends printed it secretly using a photocopy machine, and we distributed a hundred copies to friends in al-Mutanabbi Street. We had dared to challenge the repression of culture by the authorities. Later, a proper publication of it was done in Spain, and then repeated in Ramallah, Palestine.

Al-Mutanabbi Is Murdered Twice, First as Poet, Then as Place

After the catastrophe of the brutal explosion on the street of culture, I still imagined myself there. I reflected constantly upon the days we'd spent in the street. My friend, the poet Dunya Mikhail, and I would go there on Fridays to buy books—both the banned and the unbanned. I could see myself walking there among the smoke and the wreckage, treading lightly over the wounded dreams of poets and novelists. I stood by myself and cried, and the smell of burning books engulfed me. Heat from the ashes formed a layer on my face. I saw myself in the midst of darkened, burnt-out shells of the bookshops, listening to the sporadic coughing of a few remaining booksellers or regular customers, and I blubbered uncontrollably over the shocking scene that seemed to me straight out of Ray Bradbury's *Fahrenheit 451*, a book that had prophesied all the way back in the early 1950s what thought and culture are being subjected to right now by sanctions, prohibitions, and burnings, and in the face of consumer culture, media's intrusion into human life, and the rise of intolerance and terror.

A poem rang in my ears, one written by al-Mutanabbi, who was killed for being a poet, and when the street was dedicated in his name, it came in the sights of hardened killers and the idea police—those terrorists who are frightened to death by books and culture. They had announced their hatred for thinking and enlightenment, and their pursuit of every single writer, journalist, and artist that might possibly pose a threat to their backward assertions and their ideology that proclaims they alone possess the single and impregnable absolute truth. I heard the great classical poet Abu Nuwas, as he walked next to me, recite an elegy for our burning, occupied city, as he stammered drunkenly: "Weep not over renown; weep only for this."

And the road wept along with him, the columns in al-Rasheed Street, the ashes of al-Shabandar Coffeehouse where the writers had escaped the solitude of their craft, the carts, the bits of pavement, the burnt tiles from buildings, the books turned into scattered scraps of pages, the bookshops turned into piles of trash, all wept, and in the midst of all this weeping, cries ascended from the dead, the victims of the word. We could hear distinctly their plaintive wails amidst the flames, those who loved the book, even unto death, whose fate was connected ultimately to its fate.

Al-Mutanabbi Street, which had flourished through its words, poems, discussions, and debates, had become a path for ghosts, reigned over by a catastrophic silence and the smell of death. No longer did the coffeehouses ring out with the clamor of their regulars, arguments of the poets, mirth of the domino players, or the zeal of its disputants. No longer did the hawkers of books cry out and spit on the hot, dust-covered pavement, while they announced the availability of a thick manuscript or a rare book from the eighteenth century. There was no one to utter a word, no song to emerge from the Um Kalthoum Coffeehouse on the corner of al-Rasheed Street that was traversed by al-Mutanabbi, none of the rhymed prose of Yusuf 'Amr, nor songs by Fairouz ... nothing to be heard in the street, except the roar of the flames and the suppressed cries of those buried under black mounds of debris, the sellers burned to death alongside their *diwans*, novels, and philosophical books, indiscriminate destruction of bilingual, reference, and spiritual books. The otherwise total devastation was punctuated only by limbs, and flames, and the cries for help of the victims emerging from the midst of the smoke.

The Street of the Books Horrifies the Murderers
"There is no glory in this land, except in death; books are a drug that distracts people from heaven." Thus say the murderers and the *jihadis* from the Stone Age, as they malevolently promote ignorance of tradition and thought, and spread death through their barbaric justice to the poet, the novelist, the writer, the historian, the bookseller, or the ordinary woman who has come to buy a dictionary or encyclopedia; to the romantic, who walks dreamily reciting a love poem, set upon offering it up to his beloved that evening, and the author of a story negotiating a new printing of his book with his publisher.

They all died among the 130 victims, each of them passionate lovers of the book, killed in the street of the books, with no coffin but the ashes of the tale, and no funeral music except the crackling of the flames.

And Abu Nuwas leaned on my shoulder and repeated: "Weep not over renown; weep only for this." But I whisper back: "Don't forget that books and libraries have been burned thousands of times over the course of human history, not least in 1933 in Berlin, the day the Nazis celebrated in a central square amidst the beat of marshal music and chants of soldiers, and although the burning of books in al-Mutanabbi Street won't be the last, books will persevere, and libraries and bookstores will flourish, for the beauty of books does not die, and al-Mutanabbi Street is a Phoenix that will be reborn from the ashes, O Abu Nuwas. Indeed, I'll meet you here one day soon, for I have made a vow to a man who loves me in a foreign land, that we will meet on al-Mutanabbi Street. We three will drink a toast together to al-Mutanabbi and to our new books in the al-Shabandar Coffeehouse. Do not forget our date, my dear Abu Nuwas."

Translated from the Arabic by Hosam Aboul-Ela.

An excerpt from this essay was printed as a broadside by Nick Smart for the Al-Mutanabbi Street Broadside Project.

Occident to Orient

Zaid Shlah

I

but I wanted to know you,
what progress I could find there,
show you snow, proffer bushels
of snow, white—and no apricots;

I wanted you to sound lovingly,
mahogany *oud*, because I had
come all this way, and my ship
leaves tomorrow—

resolutions drawn up from
the other side of the ocean
argue for the aesthetic of a girl
with eyes like plums, black
and sad,

and as the drums begin
to beat, the taste of anise
on our tongues,

almond shells left on
the Persian rug,—this
Arabic, I find, is easy

2

I saw her, the cotton rags
about her, torn—her shoes barely
covering her tiny feet

and I wanted to save her, to
run out and steal her, shelve
her in some ivory room, away
from all this ugliness—

put her there, keep me here,
and this is my wanting, she feeds
me with the hunger in her belly,
and tomorrow, being a foreigner,
I must return back home

3

in a picture above my headroom
I enter every night, dark, with music
from the Orient

her body waiting on
the bedroom floor; my entrance,
her greeting, unmoved—

I remove thigh and chest from
its linen and cloth container, sip Ceylon
chai from an austere cup, which I have
removed from her silk & gold

my hand well within her grasp,
Napoleon's sweep and brash brigade,
not taken—

and I would sleep
for a time—this seraglio
for a headroom;

would, that you
and I had this, and
nothing more,

I might take
you, for my bride

4

words like feathers I have plucked
from your mouth: cardamom, *zahferon*,
u sukar; and what about the labyrinth
negligee you whirl,

and the giants you placate, is this
mine or yours to bear? still, there is no
rationale,—

hips, arms and thighs, palms over
Baghdad continue to sway, breasts sweeter
than dates—arak, white, in delicate glass
the Caliphate, and all the Arabian horses
could not stop us, almond green eyes, green
and given to dance, given to us, given; and all
you are is dance

This poem was printed as a broadside by John Cutrone & Seth Thompson for the
Al-Mutanabbi Street Broadside Project.

Ways to Count the Dead

Persis M. Karim

**"Keeping track of the Iraqi death toll isn't the
job of the United States," a student said, "and
besides, how would we count the dead?"**

Take their limbs strewn about the streets—
multiply by a thousand and one.

Ask everyone in Baghdad who has lost
a brother. Cousin. Sister. Child—to speak
their name in a recorder.

Go to every school, stand
at the front of the class, take roll;
for every empty desk, at least two dead.

Find every shop that sells cigarettes—
ask how many more cartons they've sold this year.

Go to the bus station and buy ten tickets—
offer them free to anyone who wants to leave.

Go see the coffin-maker. Ask how much
cedar and pine he's ordered this month.

The dead don't require much. They don't speak
in numbers or tongues, they lie silent

waiting—to be counted.

This poem was printed as a broadside by Jill Hearne for the Al-Mutanabbi Street Broadside
Project.

Al-Mutanabbi Street

Ayub Nuri

Although I was born and raised in Iraq, I had never seen Baghdad until after the fall of Saddam Hussein's regime in 2003. I was a Kurd from Halabja, a town in the de facto Kurdish region that split from the rest of Iraq in 1991. Because I was a Kurd and had worked with Western media and aid organizations, I would have put myself at risk of imprisonment or even death had I tried to visit Baghdad before 2003.

Several days after Saddam's statue was brought down by American tanks in central Baghdad, I arrived in the city as a journalist. To me everything was new, the city, the people and their stories. One of the new things that I discovered was a place called al-Mutanabbi Street, which was in the heart of one of Baghdad's oldest neighborhoods. Al-Mutanabbi Street was a book market where there were shops on both sides of the street. The shops had books shelves that covered their interiors from the floor to the ceiling and from the front of the shop all the way to the back, but what was unique about those bookshops was that they displayed most of their books on low wooden and iron tables out in the street. The bookshops were part of a number of old buildings and they had some of Baghdad's unique architecture, with long pavements stretching in front of them and pillars supporting the front ceilings of the shops.

Al-Mutanabbi book market was most popular on Fridays because Friday is a holiday in Iraq. After my first visit to al-Mutanabbi, I fell in love with it, and I made sure to visit the street every Friday. I would start at one end of the street and walk down all the way to the other end. I would not skip a single bookshop and as I reached the end, I would return on the other side and check all the books on display. It was not only books that the shops on al-Mutanabbi sold; there were also magazines, computer software, and music CDs for sale. The market usually opened in the morning and went on until late in the afternoon. It was bustling with customers of all ages and gender; there were young and old, men and women coming to buy books and magazines or to just leaf through books that they liked. Among the bookshops, there were also a number of small-scale printing houses where they printed booklets, wedding invitation cards, and business cards. I had my first business cards made in one of the printing houses on al-Mutanabbi. There were also several stationery shops on the street where they sold school utensils, wrapping papers, and photo albums. I bought unique photo albums there and took them to my family as presents.

For some years, I was a big fan of Agatha Christie's crime novels and I read many of them. Unfortunately, I couldn't find any of her novels in Iraqi Kurdistan and I read her books only in Persian, which I bought in Iran. One Friday, as I was walking on al-Mutanabbi Street, the title of an Agatha Christie book caught my eye. I immediately picked up the book and asked the shop owner if he had more of them and to my delight he had twenty-seven. I took out money to buy them without regard to cost, but at that moment I was with an American journalist friend of mine, Elizabeth Rubin, and seeing the extreme joy on my face, Elizabeth bought all the books and gave them to me as a present. That occasion really increased my attachment to al-Mutanabbi Street.

Al-Mutanabbi was located between al-Rasheed Street on one end and the Tigris River on the other. On al-Rasheed Street there was a juice store that was famous in all of Baghdad for its traditional raisin juice, and I made sure to stop by that store and drink a huge glass of sweet and iced raisin juice whenever I went to al-Mutanabbi. At the other end of the street, there was a teahouse called al-Shabandar. Whenever I tired from walking among the books, I would go to the teahouse to sit on one of the wooden benches and drink tea. Intellectuals, poets, writers, and artists used to come to that teahouse to catch up with friends and talk about their own worlds. There were old pictures of Baghdad and other parts of Iraq on the walls of the teahouse combined with people's voices. The sounds of traditional music and cigarette smoke had always occupied the interior.

On Fridays, so many people were visiting al-Mutanabbi that at times you wouldn't be able to walk through the packed crowds who all stopped to pore over books, dictionaries, or posters of new political and religious leaders of the country. This crowd had provided a suitable ground for pick-pockets. One day, I went to the street with an American and a British jour-nalist. As I was trying to navigate my way through the crowd, I noticed that something was pulling my satellite phone from my belt. I looked down and it was the hand of a pickpocket trying to steal my phone. I immediately warned my American and British friends and told them to take their phones off their belts. They both did so, but a few minutes later the British man shouted, "Ayub, they stole my wallet." He had his wallet in his hip pocket and one of the pickpockets had stolen it.

Al-Mutanabbi Street was a place for everybody. The educated elite of Baghdad came to the market to buy and read books. Poets, artists, and retired people came to the teahouses nearby to see friends on the weekend. Students came to the market to buy their school materials and others came from cities and towns all over Iraq to buy books. I went to al-Mutanabbi almost every Friday to take a break from one week of work, and I found pleasure in leafing through so many new books that had come to the surface in Iraq after the fall of Saddam's regime. On display on al-Mutanabbi Street, there were books that had been printed in Iran, in the Arab countries, and in the West. Iraq's new political groups presented themselves to Iraqi readers through books and posters. Authors, subjects, and ideologies that had been banned for almost thirty years by Saddam's regime all flooded al-Mutanabbi Street, and I could see the excitement in the faces of those who came from different backgrounds to quench their thirst for books and information. But unfortunately, insurgents and fanatics couldn't stand the new colors that emerged on al-Mutanabbi, and they tried to turn everything black by bombing the street.

Qasida
My Father Spoke at Funerals, Ways to Raise the Dead

Marian Haddad

My very Baba spoke in panegyrics…like you, Al Mutanabbi;
Baba learned the Psalms in the lower grades. This is how they taught
then; he held a love for sound and reason, the ability to speak
in front of crowds. Generations carry voices. Yours at our helm—

strong; spirited. Lyric and capturing crowds. Baba did this, too,
even when he spoke of land he harvested. He could not stay settled
in school. His own mother losing a husband. Father, the only son
left in Syria, not far from Damashq, where you learned your own

words and the words of others; unlike you, Baba had to leave
the page, trade it in for the *rufish wa'l fess*…tilling the ground,*
growing orchards of village apples, vineyards that covered
his earth; Baba did not forget the words—took whatever chance

chance brought him to speak—to write each aleph down
on spiralled sheets, head bent under the orange light of his living—
he'd lose the self in dark corners where he sat above the books,
reams he'd written on the dead—or the living. Next morning,

he'd call us in to hear: Um Abdallah, Ta'aay, come, eager for ears
that would listen. This is what we do, Baba, what we learned from you
and Al Mutanabbi, the gift of speaking. How words break hard ground,
able to chisel a way into rock, water wearing down a stone. Speak loud

enough, each of you, to wake the dead; Baba, there, standing in front
of crowds, here, in this America, carrying his language and the lyric
of his birth. He did not know the walls of schools past twelve, yet
the history of words worked its way down. Cannot keep us out.

Even in fields. Words live beyond walls. No spirit can break a voice.
Even if walls have fallen, even if—there is no place to speak, no row
of shelters for books, libraries, song. Baba, before you died, you uttered,
word for word, in classical Arabic, King David, the Psalmist,

---

* *rufish wa'l fess*: pick and shovel

Urhumnah ya' Allah, kumma atheem rahimtekk. Have mercy on us,
oh God, for great is your mercy. Ninety years old and almost giving up
the body, you never lost the letters, alone there in the dark, thinking
no one was listening, just you, the *qasidas*, and the poetry of your mouth.

Girls in Red on Page One

Sarah Browning

Still clotted with sleep I retrieve
the paper from the porch.

So often children on page one
are laughing, learning new rhythms

of Brazilian Capoeira—tipped
in red sashes one against another—

or rolling Easter eggs
on the White House lawn.

In that slow-drawn moment
of waking, as I scan the Post

in the hallway, I think these girls too
are in that open red joy only children know.

But no—it's a Baghdad
city block, school girls

torn, their faces open
not laughing but gashed, open.

What idea, what god,
what future

what temple, what word
is worth these girls?

Tell me, this morning
in my red bathrobe:

how will we answer these girls

Al-Mutanabbi Street

Eileen Grace O'Malley Callahan

"Those who did this are like savage machines, intent on harvesting souls and killing all bright minds." —Iraqi poet Abdul Baqi Faidhullah, quoted in the *New York Times*

"Papers from the book market were floating through the air like leaflets dropped from a plane. Pieces of flesh and the remains of books were scattered everywhere." —Iraqi poet Naim Daraji, quoted by the Associated Press.

There will be no more confusion after the bomb explodes—

No more wandering, no more side alleys, no more multiple ways to turn;

No more tobacco shops, no more magazine vendors, no more newspaper racks or book sellers' stalls built hard against each other on either side of the narrow, crowded street;

No more decision led by whim and fancy about which shop to enter;

No more welcomed entry into slanted light and shadow; no more dust motes or crumbling pages; no more mildew; no more musty smell in the still, hot air;
No more teasing arguments with your old friend, the bookseller, about which book to buy;

No more teasing laughter about the hand-written note found between the front cover and the marbled end sheets of a pre-1914 atlas;

No more sudden discovery of a long out-of-print book of Persian poetry, a copy of which was once given to you by your lover;

No more sudden start of remembered beauty, as though the lost beloved had kept her promise and just now met you on the street;

No more sensuous feel of the book's soft papers made from the grasses nearest those towns whose names you remember from your own interior maps: your parents' home, your childhood;

No more hand-carved wooden blocks of prayer; no more secret poems of Sumerian kings; no more Gilgamesh, no more Inanna, no more minarets or domes embossed in copper & deep black inks long before these tinctures were ever refined in Europe;

No more printers; no more printing; no more engravers, no more engraving; no more paper, no more papermakers; no more calligraphers, no more binders; no more secret alphabets of animals and trees; no more Abulafia, no more Kabalah; no more Conference of the Birds; no more Ibn-Arabi; no more algebra; no more writing; no more astounding medical knowledge first brought to Europe by way of the Spanish Moors; no more Romani codes, no more hand-painted gold initial letters; no more fantastical alphabetical beasts; no more tooled inlay of dark brown and blood-red leather incised on the cover of the book you're holding now;

No more astonished reading of the poet's work, no more first-time knowing; no more wandering inner delights of meaning's multiple senses unraveling in your mind; no more intimate occasion of a first reading as language gathers its power and breathes its life into your soul;

No more stepping out into the afternoon heat with the book's promised pleasures now held inside the cup of your hand;

No more walking down the street to the cafe for a bowl of thick black coffee with sweet cream and argument and talk;

No more languages to puzzle, no more street-market Arabic, no more street-market French; no more Assyrian, no more Armenian, no more Azerbaijani; no more Persian, no more Aramaic, no more Turkish, no more Turkamen; no more Iraqi Baghdadi Arabic, no more Afro-Asiatic Baghdadi; no Kurdish, no Italian, no Middle Eastern Romani; no German, no Spanish, no Afghani, no Russian, no Portuguese, no Lebanese; no more muddled, inflected English with the oddly shifting taste of hidden syllables on your tongue; no more dictionaries, no more translations, no more crazy ocean of words swirling inside your head in the noise of the café; no more sweet drinks of heavy liqueurs; no more black coffee, no more infinite cups of tea; no more pleasure in the sounds of words well-tuned in all the twenty-five languages spoken in Iraq; no more shouting and arguing and teasing in all the languages spoken at once in the lazy hot afternoon of a Baghdadi;

No more decisions to make, no more books to buy, no more covers to touch, no more pages to turn; no more words, no more poems, no more stories; no more secret etymologies of love and time; no more wandering, no more laughing, no more teasing and nothing left to argue—

Only the heat remains, still shimmering at dusk on the stones of the long, narrow, winding street of Al Mutanabbi now blasted into hell, leaving behind dirt and anger and grief and revenge and a hundred thousand bits of books and ink and paper and letters and blood:

Everything is simple now: clear, emptied out by the deafening noise.

Abridged Qasida for al-Mutanabbi Street

Roger Sedarat

"There happens to be a great symmetry in Arabic that binds
the words for 'writer' and 'book' in a single sound. Book is
kitab, writer, *katib*, and the difference is little more than a shift
in stress when the words are spoken." —Phillip Robertson

What literary discussions brewed over tea
Here in the alley named al-Mutanabbi.

At the Shabandar café one could see
Poets become their books of poetry.

Though each one had its own identity,
Ghazal couplets shared the same legacy.

(Resisting narrative set the lines free
To run beyond the book-cased bindery).

Fans stalled. The lack of electricity
Threatened to warp the good stationery.

Writers kept writing, readers reading, the
Booksellers maintaining community.

Here eponymous al-Mutanabbi
Could rest, assured of his great prophecy.

Bam! No words for the bomb that suddenly
Injured hundreds and killed at least thirty.

With courage, turn to living history
Before "what is" destroys "what used to be."

"So strong is my voice; the deaf can hear me,"
The poet said on his Bedouin journey.

Know that the mighty Tigris near this street
Roars back to words of that great Iraqi.

Arabic equivalents of "A, B,
C," shame terrorists' illiteracy.

Al-Mutanabbi Street

Elline Lipkin

"The world is full of paper. Write to me." —Aga Shahid Ali

Fire in July as the days flame up,
one hour's red heat
      pressed against the next
      crowding late summer till it loosens its hold.
The mountains a smoulder lining the distance,
while blue flame now
outlines everything that can't be touched.

Inside the book, the page is a body,
the text a stamp that bites the blank,
      a scatter of words dressing the light,
as letters breed inside the cut rims, seeping
to print their shapes inside the patient palm.

The weeks will lean against fall's rush of months,
      a calendar working to crest its edge,
while words brush and flame
      once unbound from books,
      a pyre of hollowed bodies, spines still smoking,
      sending a lightning flash that will stalk
the reader through the next page found.

This poem was printed as a broadside by Heidi Barlow for the Al-Mutanabbi Street Broadside Project.

Fragment, in Praise of the Book

Meena Alexander

Book with the word for love
In all the languages that flow through me,
Book made of leaves from a mango tree
Book of rice paper tossed by monsoon winds
Book of pearls from grandmother's wrist
Book of bottle glass rinsed by the sea
—Book of the illiterate heart—
Book of alphabets burnt so the truth can be told
Book of fire on al-Mutanabbi street
Book for a child who wakes to smoldering ash
Book of singing grief
Book of desire glowing as light pours through.

An Ordinary Bookseller

Esther Kamkar

Not the hanging gardens of Babylon,
but a book in each pocket,
a garden to carry, he said.
His dusty stacks are in flames.
The smell of burnt flesh and burnt paper,
swallows the alley in grief.
Down the hill Tigris
writes another chapter
and binds with its memory.

What Prayer

Robert Perry

What prayer will make
the sign marked Baghdad
on the road between Damascus
and Aleppo seem ordinary

When the doctor is killing the patient
and the inalienable is made
strange and macabre

What amount of forgiveness
can be drawn from the Caravaggio light
that cut across Paul's face
on that very road

As suddenly as the sacred conversation
of al-Mutanabbi Street's ancient river
of books and ideas was stopped
by an explosion of fire

The dark fire that makes
the ordinary impossible

The mad king Fear and his lackey
Denial rule our hearts

Without hope?

Who can say?

Marianne Moore in Baghdad

Gloria Collins

He swims through her fish poem:
the water drives a wedge of iron
in his ocean-less room, his parched city.

"I study the poetry of Miss Marianne Moore,"
he emails our English Department.

His English is thin as a palm frond,
but dynamite grooves, burns, and
hatchet strokes are clear enough.

He writes: "today my brother is shot dead."
He reads by lantern light: bespattered jelly fish,
crabs like green/lilies; and submarine/toadstools …
images that soothe his heart, far from the sea.

"I study the poetry of Marianne Moore
for my Master's degree," he writes us.
Others must not know this, how he sits
on a rug, back curved, head bowed over a book,
how he eats and breathes her words,
drinks her metaphors, mixing them with his own.

He writes: "while I discovered the *salpiglossis* that has
spots and stripes, while I smelled the sea air and heard
the seagulls and brushed cat-tails from my face,
my uncle … a bomb … in the marketplace."

He recovers lettuce, slightly battered,
two bruised apples, someone's squash,
four unscathed eggs nestled in newspaper, imagine,
but not a trace of his uncle's body.

He studies the poetry of Marianne Moore,
seagulls, lobsters and whales, waves
of words he doesn't entirely understand but loves:
the lines draping the page in morning-glories or moon-vines;
the friendly nouns, the salt marsh grass and black sweet-peas,
and her cats, so much like Arab cats.

He reads the poems out loud while his mother makes tea,
verses mingling with mint-scent, street dust, his own humid
breath, the ash of his relatives and friends.

The al-Mutanabbi Street Bombing

Brian Turner

(In memory of Mohammed Hayawi)

In the moment after the explosion, an old man
staggers in the cloud of dust and debris, hands
pressed hard against his bleeding ears
as if to block out the noise of the world
at 11:40 a.m., the broken sounds of the wounded
rising around him, chawled and roughened by pain,
while a young man runs past, shrieking
at the unspeakable, a water-pipe still in his hands
as he runs with its tube and mouthpiece
bouncing like a goose with a broken neck.

The buildings catch fire. The cafés.
Stationery shops. The Renaissance Bookstore.
A huge column of smoke, a black anvil-head
plumes upward, fueled by the Kitah al-Aghani,
al-Isfahani's *Book of Songs*, the elegies of Khansa,
the exile poetry of Youssef and al-Azzawi,
the religious tracts, manifestos, translations
of Homer, Shakespeare, Whitman, and Neruda;
these book-leaves curl their darkening tongues
in the fire's blue-tipped heat, and the long centuries,
handed down from one person to another, verse
by verse, word by word, that wisdom of the ages—
it rises over Baghdad for all to see,
a fire made to shut out the sun.

☙

As the weeks pass by, the sunsets
deepen in color over the Pacific. Couples
lie in the spring fields of California,
drinking wine, making love in the lavender
hues of dusk. There is a sweet, apple-roasted
smell of tobacco in the air. When the lovers wake
at the break of dawn, there in a field of lupine,
they find themselves lightly dusted
in ash, the poems of Sulma and Sayyab
in their hair, Sa'di on their eyebrows,
Hafiz and Rumi on their lips.

In Perpetuity

Gloria Frym

The early bird with tinsel in her beak. This is how time passes and parents make their little nests. No longer a user of certain hygienic products, one now must supply one's child. The blood of love to come. Spring hovers close by. Nights shorten, buds dream. There seemed to be a break in the violence and now it will begin again. All is calm, all is bright just before the advance. Will any of the boys pick up a gun or will blast come from overhead, pilotless bombers bearing no bullets. One can now expect to be a veteran of many wars in one lifetime. No more yours and mine. Those who witness, those who drop in the markets, those who fly apart like blazing flower petals, those whose legs are blown off dancing, those who read in between the lines, on the front lines, hiding behind the fictional, stuffed with the emperor's stuffing, slicked with the sheik's grease, all concocted by the CEOs and their Pinocchio's. They know ruin never ends.

Against the Weather (for al-Mutanabbi Street)

Owen Hill

after a while

they will run out of bombs

meanwhile agents of art

face a time and a place

may as well arrange

the books on the shelves

all things otherwise

will grow old and rot

may as well distribute

universals of general applicability

time to sweep the streets may

as well flutters of paper still loaded

with charge shards of poems

you could hardly pick them up or

lay them down

may as well read a little marx

a little lorca start

in the middle

or close to the end

whatever's around

dust reshelve and open

the doors again

This poem was printed as a broadside by Roger Snell for the Al-Mutanabbi Street Broadside Project.

Dead Trees

Yassin "The Narcicyst" Alsalman

I've seen him straddle the sides of books in his lust for a literary climax on days like this, unable to satiate the fruits of his mind. Dreams lived through me so vivid he could swear he was Hammurabi at night, seeking refuge in Inana rubbing his sore body till his muscles were as fluid as the Euphrates. Al-Mutanabbi Street was his red light district slowly eyeing the wisdom that was into the knowledge that be, now. So far to go, he thought to himself, so fast the past. Nothing remains under his gaze in these dark days, as the concrete carnage remains burning a hole in his soul. Blood splattered on the walls of his old city, paper soaked in the tears of divinity. It only rains in his brain, the sun scorching his skin like a sinner staring into the eyes of the devil. What used to be lay no more. The Knowledge that was is today torn to shreds, where the market was once a circle of thought it remained nothing but that, a thought. A memory. A dream.

Beautiful it was to see the sky so blue, until the hue of brown sculpted its clouds like a heavenly desert engulfed by the flames of hell. Burn Baghdad Burn, he mumbled under his shortness of breath, accentuated by the soot and dust particles that strangle his being. Hamoodi was diagnosed with lung cancer under seven months ago. The doctor gave him a year to live and no cure. Hospitals remain bare from the days of Sanctions, unable to satiate even the hope of a common cold let alone the despair of terminal illness. War was his theatre; I was his intermission.

And he holds me so close to his heart, as the last remaining member of his family, wheezing into the days that he wished he saw beyond him. I brought him such joy, he never would give me away to any other man, never allowed me to leave his sight. I sat by him as he got rid of words, phrases, paragraphs and pages. Prose could not convey his love, so he rid himself of it all. Religion was no savior to his apostate, so he cherished every penny it brought him. Fiction was too far from his reality to even grasp, so he sold every lie back to the public. And I was left by his side, stroking his musings like no other could. He would learn me inside out in our ten years together; flipping over me and touching my every corner with the passion that no lover could caress, no imagination could create. I was his forever. He spoke to me, studied my disposition, took me and never put me down, sweeping me off my abridged temperament. Our love a pious creation. The day we met was written in the history books of life. Laying between God and science, I was a treasure to him, an escape from the harsh summers of solace and pain. As the growth in his lung was burgeoning and feeding on his heartbeat, Hamoodi had no idea that what was happening inside him mirrored the state of his nation. As Iraq was pillaged and mortared, he was still in his orbit, no longer growing with the moon cycle, regressing into the universe of his bad habits. I came to him a hypnotizing epic, an enchanting story, a myth for him to believe. Our saga long lived, our romance undying. On our way home, we stared back at each other though he could not see my eyes masked by the cover of my lore. You are a legend to me, he said so softly, a memoir, the jezebel of my saga, the tale I would have passed down to my children if they had existed.

The day our home was shattered came as swiftly as our love. The morning blared light in his eyes and heat in his body. Although he had heard my fables many a time, he made me repeat to him what was of our historic connection. And each time, he would smack his knee in disbelief at how perfect everything fit together. A perplexing puzzle it is. This was also the first day that Hamoodi coughed blood onto my face, wiping it so amorously he forgot that his insides were tearing him apart. He cared not for himself, torrid in his admiration for my eternal frenetic attention. Devout in his piety to what I will always be. The burst came ever so unexpectedly, searing my skin and throwing me to the other side of the road out of his hand. As pages flew around us, Hamoodi awoke dizzy and disoriented, looking for me without checking if he was hurt at all. Finally finding me, he looked around and saw what was left of his workplace and haven of knowledge. Crispy bodies lie immobile in their passing, souls fueling the fires of burning Qurans, biographies deleted by the hands of his own brothers and sisters. This war brought nothing but despair and violence. "The pages of my life no longer hold you together my love," said Hamoodi, salesmen of your mind and beliefs. Al-Mutanabbi Street was the lover he never tended to when she was around and lost all hope in her returning to him on this summer swelter of the Shaytan's doing. Nothing was ever as it seemed.

He walked the street, back and forth, daily, clutching me and shaking his head in disbelief for months on end. Mother nature had finally turned her back on father politics. He cheated her out of their pact and bond and Hamoodi finally realized he doesn't believe in anything anymore. He slowly retreated from our relationship, and finally, from himself. I would watch him slowly pace around his sheltered home in Hay Jihad, looking for peace in his madness. He could not accept that he was dying, leaving all that he had learned behind him as an invisible ghost. Why? he thought to himself. He cursed himself for his lack of faith, he cursed God for the lack of presence; the invisibility that was the divine grip on all that was written in its glory and suffering. In his last days, he would not move from his bed, wheezing his discontent into the air as a cloak of darkness, the sheath of his soul uncovered and falling to the pits of damnation. I don't want to die was the only words muttered to himself, ignoring me completely, leaving me to be an empty widow, a lore untold, a fabrication, the lie of our century. The cancer was not killing him alone. The loss of al-Mutanabbi Street his sarcophagus, the final blow to his shattered body.

Hamoodi died with me gazing at his spirit floating around the room, the greenish hue of his animus protruding from every orifice in his body. I wondered who would find this lonely man that used to be and imagined watching him decompose into nothingness before the discovery of his bones were left to be ravaged by the cancerous air around us. He left me a relic. Without you Hamoodi, I am but a poorly written present, an undiscovered goldmine, an untouched artifact, a wounded past and a distant future.

Nothing is what it seems and will ever be the same. No one will ever know me, or read me the same again. I have been deleted from your mind. And your mind has deleted me from our kind. I am all but a closed history. I am your book. I was.

Elegy for al-Mutanabbi Street

José Luis Gutiérrez

Here—as in the center of a clearing—purity
trembles—and we pass by . . .
—Gennadiy Aygi, "Phloxes in Town"

i
Melodious dissonance inherit this
our song.
It is never enough
in our capaciousness
to sustain
dismantled evidence:
dead stars by eyes unseen.
As on al-Mutanabbi Street you and I meet
and take shelter in the sanctuary of language.
In our steaming cups a galaxy of tea and cardamom
swirls and scents the crisp air as somewhere faraway
the riparian night delivers a soft palinode.
Your voice is dreaming rivers,
a tidal convergence
from the diurnal scalp to the nocturnal spleen,
your breath lifting my words from deep sleep.

ii
On al-Mutanabbi Street the rubbled remains
of bookstores and cafés amid pliable hierarchies of light.
These are the palisades of my grief.
Yet another Great Fire has scourged our city.
Springs aphasia
the ineluctable savagery of your
touch.
The marbled tongue of our most stolid breath balancing syntax.
This cordite weather wears your absence like rain.
. . . echoes of a memory I can't readily trace.
In between breaths,
another life, dreaming itself awake.

iii
Let the Book of Memory
hold no memory but one.
In Baghdad today
al-Mutanabbi Street has been destroyed.
Scheherazade: it was here I first learned her name.

The Letter Has Arrived

Sargon Boulus

You said
that you were writing as bombs were falling
eliminating the history of ceilings
obliterating the faces of houses
You said:
I write to you as God
allows these to write my fate
and this makes me doubt that he is God
You wrote saying:
Were it not for my words;
—These beings that are threatened with fire—
I would not live.
After they leave
I will retrieve my words with all their splendor
as if they are my white bed
in the barbarians' night.
Every night I stay up in my poem until dusk.
You said: I need a mountain, a station.
I need other humans.
And then you sent the letter.

Translated from the Arabic by Sinan Antoon.

Al-Mutanabbi Street

Peter Money

You were there and now you're
gone, a breath inside the kiss of a girl,
the flutter of a feather off the bird just there, frond
flaps the book shut, covers a molted interior,
& the voice of friendship stranger over the phone,
still, here, witness this book, molecule handed
in a street where the characters held & bent shape, and still,
we walk, using the only words we have, canes of
the thin fingers of our paler age
put to use—absence's lovers
restored their cage in antique letters
& come against all destruction.

Voices Surround & Fade: The Hooded One

Peter Money

What seems a narrow---- —
Where ability ends---- —
A hope dwindles---- —
Faith burns---- —
So much
is the errant light
in a dark
corridor
----and we are
here, reading.

A Letter to al-Mutanabbi

Sinan Antoon

You were right Sir
your words are still wings of light
always carrying you to us
(sometimes carrying us to you)
and your name is a green tattoo
on Baghdad's tired face
your street a forehead
of a body beheaded every morning.
Just another chapter
in the saga of blood and ink
you knew so well
I cannot lie to you
I'm quite pessimistic
we are still etching
on the walls of this cave
which is thousands of years long
signs we keep reinterpreting
and myths about a future world
where we don't devour one another
where the sun is friendly
and the seas cannot inherit our fever.
Some of us are digging
a deeper grave
about to embrace us all
they, too, have their engravings,
maps, philosophers, and books
We can only keep dreaming
of a shore for the wind
and dig wells
in the dark
with nails of silence and solitude
we will weave an ocean out of ink
for our myths
and out of words a sail
or a shroud
vast enough for us all.

Every book is a well
around which we sit
and drink to your health
try to live
like you did
with death and after it!

Escape from al-Mutanabbi Street

Muhammad al-Hamrani

For part of my life, I worked as a bookseller on al-Mutanabbi Street. In the early 1990s, I was well-known for buying the libraries of writers who were besieged by hunger because of the sanctions. Despite the difficult circumstances, I was able to save a large amount of money and managed to buy a bookstore in the middle of al-Mutanabbi. I called it al-Rahman Bookstore. Many thought that the name had a religious reference, but the name Rahman was mine. My mother gave me the nickname *Rahhumi*. But on al-Mutanabbi, everyone called me "Misery Man," because I smoked so much and used to tell all those painful stories about being in the army. Many customers came to my bookstore to discuss books. Often, I'd have to summarize a book's ideas in order to facilitate the sale.

After Saddam's regime fell and the death squads spread into the narrow alleys around al-Mutanabbi, no one was buying books anymore. As fear and random killings mounted, books became an unprofitable commodity. It seemed that every morning we would find the corpse of one of our friends. So as not to join my friends who had been murdered for unknown reasons, I sold my bookstore and started working at *al-Nur* newspaper, which was owned by a liberal who had returned to Iraq after the war.

A few days into my new job, I received threats from unknown parties after I published a story about families displaced for sectarian reasons. These threats did not faze me and I began to report on how some women were being raped in prisons. Most were too timid to name their assailants and would only allude to what had happened. But I did anger the government when I wrote: "Salma Abbud was arrested because she was carrying an automatic weapon under her *abaya*. Her automatic weapon was confiscated, and she was taken to prison. There, they forced her to take off her clothes to make sure she was not wearing a bomb vest. Salma Abbud, in her thirties, was carrying her brother's automatic weapon. He'd been in a death squad, and had been killed, and all he had left his family were his weapons. She said: 'We had no food at home, because the local shopkeeper had left the neighborhood, since he was from another sect and had been threatened. I was on my way to the market to buy half a kilogram of flour and five kilograms of rice.' But when she was arrested she was taken to the police station and was accused of being a terrorist. The policeman who had searched her entered her cell at midnight and took her to a nearby small room. He told her that her body was enchanting and seductive. He turned off the lights and forced her to have sex with him."

When the police learned of this article and people started to talk about it, an arrest warrant was issued for me. The editor-in-chief of my newspaper insisted that these were the stories that make newspapers sell. He asked me to keep writing them and to make the readers experience death and rape. "Write, even if it's imaginary," he told me. He said that what is taking place in our country is so unbelievable that you could make things up. Anything you invent will have its equivalent in reality!

Days later, I was riding a KIA bus home along an elevated expressway, when I spotted a gigantic American Apache helicopter hovering above the rooftops. It resembled an enormous terrifying insect. I watched the propellers that looked like swords in war. Birds fled from the noise and the women on the rooftops below us were hugging their babies. Suddenly, a missile was launched from one of those rooftops and the Apache helicopter exploded. I expected the fire to rain on our heads, but the helicopter must have been farther away than it appeared. I asked the driver to stop. We were in Camp Sara, a predominantly Christian neighborhood. I looked for my camera and voice recorder, but I had left them on my desk at the office. I had a few pens and a notebook—all I needed for a quick story like this one. Police and ambulance sirens wailed. I walked down the street, dreaming of my powerful front page story. I even started to plan the layout, photographs and captions. Smoke covered the area and more Apache helicopters appeared. American soldiers were getting out of their Humvees, walking slowly and pointing their automatic weapons at everyone in sight. I walked down a narrow alley and saw an old woman with a crucifix around her neck, smoking. "Did you see how they shot the helicopter down?" I asked. "Which one?" she answered, "the one that had Abd al-Salam Arif?" I said, "Arif? He died a century ago!" I left her mumbling to herself and walked until I was under the expressway. There was a cemetery there, covered in mounds of garbage. Stray dogs and cats were rummaging through the trash. A fast-moving pickup stopped next to me and two men got out and pointed their weapons. One of them said: "Get in, you dog!" He pulled me inside by my shirt. The truck held five other men sitting with their hands on their heads. The masked men kept their weapons pointed at the men's heads. As the truck zigzagged through the streets, I gathered that the armed men belonged to the group that shot down the Apache. The truck was heading towards the old al-Rasheed Camp road and then turned towards a long dirt road in an agricultural area. Houses and trees disappeared. I thought they were going to kill me, so I snuck my hand into my bag, took out my press ID and threw it out of the window. One of them saw me and asked me what I had thrown away. He struck me with his automatic weapon. I lied and said that it was my fiancée's photo and that I didn't want anyone to look at her. He warned me not to move again. The truck drove on for about ten kilometers before we started to slow down. The road ended near a big house on the banks of the Tigris. As soon as the truck stopped, a group of men came out of the house and started to drag us inside to a room. They emptied our pockets. One of the men kept looking at me. When they knew that three of us were from the other sect, they executed them before our eyes. They took their cell phones, rings, and money and told the driver to dump the corpses into the Tigris. The man who had been looking at me approached and asked: "Aren't you a bookstore owner?"

"Yes, I have a bookstore on al-Mutanabbi."

"I used to come to your bookstore."

"Now I remember you. You were the one who read a lot and who used to sit at the round table surrounded by friends."

"Nope. I used to buy books quickly and leave. I didn't have any friends."

"Oh, yes, bro, I remember you."

Of course, I didn't remember him at all. I had never seen him, but I explained to him how much I loved readers and bookstores, and that I had photographs taken with all the writers, artists, philosophers, clergymen, and madmen who stopped by the bookstore.

All of a sudden, he frowned and said:

"Which sect?"

"I am not Muslim. I'm Sabaean."

"And what the hell are you doing here?"

"I was walking to my fiancée's house and the masked men forced me to get into the truck."

"You mean the fighters!"

"Yes."

The masked men released the men—who turned out to be from their own sect—and kept me alone. After hours of discussion between the man and his friends, I sensed he was having trouble convincing them that I should be set free. Before sunset he came and told me what they had decided: "Brother, the group wanted to kill you because you are not against the Americans, but I explained to them that you are a good man with a conscience, and that I'd once seen you tear a picture of Bush to pieces. I told them, he reads Islamic books even though he is not Muslim. After listening to my explanation, the leader decided to set you free, but only after breaking your right hand and left foot. Then, you will be thrown out on the main road leading to the city center."

"Yes, I agree and am ready for whatever you want, but I don't want to die."

I remembered my editor's words: I was now living in the imaginary world he'd spoken of. Oh, if he only knew what was happening to me, he would abandon journalism and become a grocer! A masked man asked me to sit in the indoor courtyard of the house. He produced a big piece of iron. The masked men surrounded us with their weapons. The masked man put my hand between two bricks and struck it with the iron. I cried and fell, writhing in pain. The others gathered and started kicking my foot and then they put me in the car. I was crying like a baby and touching the parts that hurt. The young man who saved me said: "Before you leave the car, remember this favor! I kept you alive."

After this incident, I decided to flee Baghdad. I had come to hate journalism and decided to look for a place with no sectarian battles. Perhaps I could find an explanation for what had happened to me, and to the people around me. All I wanted to do as I left Baghdad, and the killers from various neighborhoods and various sects was to go back into history. I wanted to leaf through its pages and inhale the scent of yellow leaves and look back at the crimes drawn with ink on our land whenever a colonizer walked on it.

Translated from the Arabic by Sinan Antoon.

into the lizard's eyes

Lilvia Soto

When they were expelled from Paradise, Adam
and Eve moved to Africa, not Paris.
Sometime later, when their children had gone out
into the world, writing was invented.
In Iraq, not Texas. —Eduardo Galeano, "A Walking Paradox"

I touch the glasses I brought from across the ocean,
choose the one with the blue-shadowed white blossoms
that fits just right in my drowsy hand.

As the sun rises over the pecan groves,
in my adobe house in Casas Grandes,
within walking distance of the rammed-earth buildings
abandoned more than a thousand years ago
by the original settlers of Paquimé,
I rub the last dream off my eyes
and touch the gold-rimmed tea glass
I bought in the Albayzín,
Granada's Moorish quarter.

Looking out at the autumn sky, yellow grass, naked trees,
I stare at the lizard that comes every morning
to gaze at me as I drink my coffee
and prepare for the day's writing.
The steaming milk with espresso warms my hand,
and I touch, across the window pane,
the lizard's pulsating belly,
feel its beating heart,
its tiny, powerful, beating heart
that vibrates her elongated body
and brings her to my window
to start my writing ritual.
As we stare at each other,
her amber gaze stirs old memories.

The sun sets over Sierra Nevada
while in a whitewashed building along the Darro River,
I sit on a large embroidered cushion

on the floor of a teashop
around a small marquetry table,
holding a shimmering glass,
drinking sweet Alhambra Dreams,
savoring honey-dripping cakes,
listening to Carmen tell Anna, Jennette, Duke,
the young Americans studying with us in Seville,
about the Alhambra's Nasrid architecture,
the ceiling of Salon of Ambassadors that represents
the seven heavens of Muslim cosmogony,
the Patio of the Lions,
the fountains and terraced gardens,
the pomegranate trees, the jasmine fragrance,
the stories of Zoraya's doomed love,
of the 32 massacred Abencerrajes,
of Napoleon's attempt to blow up the red fortress,
of the spot, el Suspiro del Moro,
where the last Moorish king cried
the loss of his Al-Andalus kingdom.

Sitting in one of the cafés in the portals around Jardín del Centenario,
half-listening to Mate and Aída talk about the changes
Coyoacán has experienced through the years,
I look across and see the palace of the Spanish conqueror
who tortured the last Aztec king,
and hear the blind organ-grinder
playing María Bonita,
the same Agustín Lara tune
I used to hear sitting on my bedroom floor,
peeking through the blinds
at the old man winding his hurdy-gurdy
on the corner of our apartment building
on Marsella Street.

I drop a coin in his bucket
and make my way through the alleys
formed by the book-fair stalls
in the center of the plaza,
stroll through the rows of tables laden with
new and used books, sheet music, language programs,
magazines, CDs of classical music, indigenous instruments,
love ballads, political protest songs,

poems read by their authors, sung by others.
I touch old favorites—
El llano en llamas, Visión de los vencidos,
Elogio de la sombra, El ojo de la mujer,
El silencio de la luna,
Los versos del capitán—
leaf through new ones,
touch the pages,
some still uncut, some crumbling,
look at the old photos,
the handwriting of letters and manuscripts,
run my fingertips over the faces, the words,
the white spaces,
Soul-Braille of the lover of poetry,
hear the melodies, the rhythms, the breath,
hear the breath of my favorite poets.

I touch their breaths and their voices,
and my heart shrinks
remembering the ones I will not hear,
the ones I will not touch,
the voices silenced by the bombs
that killed and injured dozens
and destroyed the ancient buildings
of al-Mutanabbi Street,
the historic center of intellectual and literary life
in the cradle of my civilization,
for what I love is mine,
even if I have not seen it,
and now, never will.

Of course, those bombs aimed at the love of the word,
at the word of protest and the syllables of love,
exploded first, not in the street of The Poet,
but in the hollow heart of the bomber.

I hear the explosions,
and I touch the flames,
the smoke, the soot, the ashes.
I hear the explosions,
and I smell the blood,
I smell the red blood spurting and the black ink running down
the booksellers' row towards the Tigris.

I hear the explosions,
and I touch the grief,
for the dozens killed and injured,
for the evil that stokes a sick man's hunger for destruction,
I touch the grief for the attacks on our civilization.

I hear the explosions,
and I touch the fear of the intellectuals and the writers
forced underground,
exiled from al-Shabandar Café, from Al-Arabia Bookshop,
from the Modern Bookstore, from the Renaissance Bookstore,
from their meandering alley of dilapidated Ottoman buildings,
exiled from their Friday rituals of buying books,
discussing politics, reading poetry,
drinking their sweet tea from shimmering glasses,
smoking their sweet-smelling tobacco
from silver, crystal, gilded, or colored glass hubble bubble pipes
through the silver mouthpiece they carried in their pocket,
in case someone else had defiled the amber mouthpiece
with their lips.

I hear the explosions,
and I touch the anger of the writers and intellectuals
who wander the world
exiled from their booksellers' row,
from their writers' sanctuary,
from their traditions,
from their book-loving country.

I touch the gold-rimmed tea glasses,
the ornate, antique pipes with their amber mouthpieces,
the sorrow,
the ashes,
the silence.
I touch the silence and the fear.

And, then, on a smoldering Roman August morning,
when breathing becomes difficult and clay could bake on the sidewalk,
I touch hope.

Across a Vatican glass case,
I touch the triangular shaped symbols
made by a stylus on wet clay
that was later baked into a rose-colored
inscribed and sealed envelope
for a dark grey cuneiform tablet
from the Old-Babylonian Period,
circa 1700 B.C.
I touch a pink tablet, Number IV of the Poem of Erra
from the New Babylonian Period,
circa 629–539 B.C.
I touch a grey cylinder divided into three columns
celebrating the reconstruction of the Temple of the god Lugal-Marda.
It dates from the New-Babylonian Period, reign of Nabuchadnezar II,
circa 605–562 B.C.
I touch a legal document from the Ur II Period,
circa 2100–2004 B.C.

I touch mankind's first writing,
invented in Iraq over 5,000 years ago,
and I know that no bomb will ever destroy
man's need to leave a written record
of his sorrows, of his loves,
of his triumphs and losses,
of his enduring struggle to construct a world of respect,
respect for humans,
respect for the clearest manifestation of the human.

Back in my adobe house,
near the rammed-earth city abandoned
more than a thousand years ago,
for reasons we don't understand
because their builders left us no written history,
Eduardo Galeano reminds me, from Montevideo,
via a Buenos Aires internet journal
that a few centuries after the invention of proto-cuneiform
in Mesopotamia,
mankind's first love poem was written, in Sumerian,
by Enheduanna, daughter of Sargon, King of Akkad,
and high priestess of Nanna, the moon god.
Her poem of a night of passion between Innana,
goddess of Love, Sexuality, and Fertility,
and the shepherd Dumuzi,
was written on wet clay.
Her hymns to the goddess
are the first poems written in the first-person
and signed by a poet conscious
of her relationship to the goddess.

Looking into the lizard's eyes,
watching her soft, pulsating belly,
I touch faith,
faith that in Mesopotamia, Uruguay,
Tenochtitlán, or Texas,
in the end will be the word,
the human word of lament,
the human howl of injured justice,
the weeping of sorrow,
the cry of desolation,
the whisper of compassion,
the invocation of the truth,
the proffering of forgiveness,
the melody of love,
even if it has to be scratched on scorched earth.

After Rumi

Janet Sternburg

Every morning
(each of us)
wakes up
(most of us)
empty and scared
(some of us)
Don't go to the library
and take down a book,
Rumi tells us, in
translation, always
In translation: Give
praise that there are books.
One of a thousand ways to
kiss the ground, to leave it
with leaves.

To Salah al-Hamdani, November, 2008

Sam Hamill

How many nights have I awakened, shocked,
my friend, at having dreamt of you again
as a young man learning to write poetry
in Abu Ghraib?

How many times have I invoked your name,
spoken of your exile, since that bright afternoon
five years ago when we met and embraced
on a stage in Piacenza, Italy?
I did not know your tongue, nor you mine,
but in our poetry we claimed fraternity,
solidarity in this alien world. Time
has not been kind to your beloved Baghdad.

Al-Mutanabbi Street where you drank coffee
and searched the bookstalls long ago
has been bombed and bombed again.
The national library is no more.

You can bomb a bookstore or ban
a book, but it will not die. You cannot kill
a poem like you can a man.
Al-Mutanabbi Street will rise again.

America will soon be led by a saner man.
The war in Iraq, for Americans, will end.
But for you and I and millions more,
exile doesn't end with the end of a war.

Five years ago we vowed to meet
one day on al-Mutanabbi Street,
and I hope that day will come.
But now it must be growing cold

and gray in Paris. In Buenos Aires,
summer is coming on, the great
acacias a canopy
over Palermo's narrow streets.

Sometimes I hear in the night
the clatter of hooves—horses
hitched to wagons, everything recycled—
and I am reminded: we too recycled,

we, too, are "known to horses,
to the wilderness and the night ..."
But by no sword
will our brief song or enduring love survive.

This poem was printed as a broadside by Ian Boyden for the Al-Mutanabbi Street Broadside Project.

Thirty Days after Thirty Years

Salah al-Hamdani

Should I not name things
like a hand extended to one who's drowning,
like the unfolding of the seasons?
Have I not said
a thing always finishes at the expense of what's beginning?

A flush of dust wends its way with an odor of childhood
while its procession carries off my uncertainty,
slowly
gliding on the mainspring of the day.

I want to come close to you,
to bring you in words, what the exiled leave undone.

The dawn rises on Baghdad
and it consumes me.

My mother, like the light,
needs no obscurity,
just a little silence
when her son, the exile, returns,
settles on her branch
in the company of a star tattooed by the fog.

For he returns home
like a refugee passing through,
a fugitive looking to share
a smile,
a piece of bread,
a corner of a bed,
and the witnessing of the drowned twilight.

Baghdad, March 25, 2004

Translated from the French by Sonia Alland.

Excerpt from **Blue**

Gail Sher

RARE BEAUTY IS BEGUN, he thinks, seeing into the room the limitation of my seeing where the dead person lingers.

It is myself, I muse, looking at the grass, seeing its kindness suddenly.

Food is offered, though a throat could disappear.

Every given moment that you perceive is the same thing, you say and I'm thinking, *It's the bardo. It just arises and you see.*

The flesh of the bird was broken that day.

Which wouldn't hold its feathers, as the flesh was *keen.* (Old ones said *provoked.*)

I see you on the edge, a fissure or cleft where a breach has been made and I think, *Am I the breach?*

The gestation of wrongness is not carried by wings nor the deep drop of cliff overhanging the swollen stream.

Rubbing the bird, stroking its hair so that it is soothed.

The old ones receive until they realize *I'm dead now.*

The hair is not an image of sky, though it has sky qualities and has come from the sky.

I am half ghost. I eat all of their hair, always.

Someone belongs here, she thinks, having the memory of her mother's hands. A bouquet of birds contains her mother's feeling for color.

A half-burned page on al-Mutanabbi Street

Dunya Mikhail

Is   this   a   sign   then?
Floating   in   the   air,   this   single   page,
A   single   page   from   a   half-burned   book?
A half-burned   book   on   Mutanabbi   Street
Mutanabbi   Street   whose   tales   were   cut   short
    by   a   bomb?
A   bomb   that   scattered   all   those   pages?

As   if   searching   desperately   for   a   meaning?
This   very   page   from   "The Pigeon's Ruff"
Flew   up   and   floated   down
Between   the   scattered   bodies
To   cling   to   her   chest?
Aren't   these   the   same   lines
once   recited   to   her?
"As I come to you, I hurry
Like the full moon crossing the sky
And as I leave— if I leave—

I move slowly like the high stars

fixed in slowness."

Translated from the Arabic by Dunya Mikhail, Dima Hilal, and Beau Beausoleil.

My Days Lack Happiness and I Want You*

Irada al-Jabbouri

I clutch the thumb of his right hand, my hand a trembling bird afraid of getting lost. It's 1973 and I am eight years old. The streets are vast places, they could devour me … so many cars, people, a red double-decker bus. "Father, please can we sit upstairs." He smiles and walks on. I run to keep up and not lose hold of his hand. We cross to the bus stop … and take our places on the upper deck. I press my face to the window. I want to breathe in everything and hide it inside my chest.

I am happy, free; my father's proud of me, he takes me with him wherever he goes. Eventually, we get off the packed bus. He turns around "Hungry?" I shake my head. "Thirsty?" "Yes."

He buys me an ice-cold Crush. I sip slowly and flick my eyes side to side—people walk in all different directions. Where are they going, where have they come from? Ohhhh, Baghdad is so big—one can get lost in it. I shouldn't be afraid. I take hold of my father's hand again.

We weave our way through a mesh of alleyways. How does he not get lost? We walk between endless rows of bookshops … my father stops at one … asks for a title … the bookseller says the book will be there next week. "And what do you like reading?" he says … "Aren't you in school yet?" The question makes me mad, I turn my face away … and watch a pigeon, a twig in her beak, she disappears over the roof of one of the buildings … my father pulls me along my eyes search for the pigeon, I want to see her building her nest. We go onto a café full of men: I'm embarrassed, I'm the only girl there … no one notices me except a young boy, he looks at me with surprise and, possibly, disdain … I throw him a proud, challenging

---

* The title of this piece is from a song by the Iraqi singer, Hussein Ni'ma. The lyrics are from a poem by Zuhair al-Dijaili—I received them on my mobile phone as I was writing the last words of this piece. I felt it was a sign—reflecting how nostalgic I feel for my Baghdad … for al-Mutanabbi Street, where I haven't been since December of 2004 except for one moment in April 2007 when I went to bid a belated farewell to those souls buried with the books … and to the footsteps of an eight-year-old girl clutching her father's hand.

look...then I ignore him. My father sits with his friend. I'm not interested in their conversation. I scan the place ignoring the boy staring at me. I get tired of looking around and I drop my eyes to the bubbles in the *nargila* (water pipe) ... I forget the looks of the angry boy and lose myself in the *nargila*'s chuckle and click of my father's worry beads.

Twice a week we leave Mustansiriya University Students' Club at lunchtime, behind us the clatter of cutlery and teacups, the voice of Um Kalthum* and the busy chatter and laughter of girls and boys, an escape from the military communiqués—"the number of human casualties."† On the way to the British Council in the Waziriya area, we stop at the print shop ... we pretend to drink tea on the pavement of the next door, while we wait for our photocopies of forbidden books ... in the British Council garden we swap books and talk—Iraqis from Baghdad and the provinces, Arabs, foreigners. We borrow books, films, music tapes from the Council's library.

On autumn days and spring days, I continue my walk from there. To reach him. From Waziriya to Bab Al Mu'adham, to Sahat Al Medan, and hurrying through Souk al Haraj (the flea market). It's hard for a women to look at anything thoroughly and at her own pace in a place full of men ... and so, my images are sketchy, but I still hope that one day, the picture of the place and the people and the things will be complete and full—that day may or may not come ...

To al-Rasheed Street with its pillars and cafés, watching the passers-by. It's an open, unfinished text, not possible to complete. It says and does not say, like Hikmet, the king's barber, who switches roles all day—now barber, now client, as he sits or stands in front of the mirror—for decades—watching those who go by.

I enter the bookshop, leave my case and books on the table and I dive into the bookshelves. I'm confused when he asks, "Are you looking for something specific?" Always the same question.

I surface and shake my head no. I'm about to ask the question I always want to ask: "Did you get the book my father ordered from you ... years ago?" I look at the sliver hair and think, "If only he hadn't been forced to wear the khaki uniform, they would have been the same age now, and I wouldn't be wearing black." ... I stifle my desire to say what I've been thinking and to ask him if he is indeed that same person!

I wander between the bookshop storefronts. I browse. The street is full of books, men and a few women ... I recognize my lecturers at university and young men I've seen here before—they come to this street

---

* Famous Egyptian singer of the 1940s, '50s, and '60s.

† A reference to the Iran-Iraq war of 1980–1988.

in their military uniforms—either going to join their units or returning from them. I approach the front of the Shabandar Café, but I don't dare enter. I busy my eyes looking at the gate of the Kushla—the former head-quarters of the Ottoman government—my ears pick up the voices of the café's customers and the chuckling of the *nargilas*, the click-click of the worry beads.

In the library of the Iraqi Museum in the Alawy area … the mornings anointed with quiet and the aroma of tea—the librarians make tea and I have never tasted better, despite it's poor quality … I begin my weekly journey to it … through al Salhiya, al Shawaka, with its alleys and market—the scent of fresh bread from a market bakery stops me in my tracks … the warmth of the two flat loaves I carry on top of my case creeps up my arms … I arrive at the Shuhada' Bridge … and stop there … I nibble warm bread and watch the seagulls search for food under the bridge …when no one else is there I throw a bit of bread to them, they gather and crowd all around me … then the bread is finished and they abandon me … I leave the bridge and make my way to a special place known to only one other person. He promised not to tell anyone else about it. He called it "Irada's Pier," rather than its proper name al Nawab Pier (the Nawab family was robbed of its wealth by the English in India) … from the Nawab house, I walk down the steps to the river and sit on my rock—I see everything from al Ahrar Bridge, to Shuhada' Bridge to July 14th Bridge … my soul embraces all I can see, and what I couldn't see until I arrived here at my spot: al Mustansiriya School … al Asifiya mosque … the Kushla … Beit al Hikma.*

I embrace my Baghdad.

The damp of the river creeps up my body … I leave and walk slowly across Shuhada' Bridge. Al-Mutanabbi Street. I see faces I know: writers, journalists, artists, professors, students … many men, few women.

Photocopies of new and old books flood the street, and it's become common to see writers displaying their personal libraries on the pave-ment—for sale … some stand at a distance from their books in embarrass-ment; others sell to book dealers in the street.†

I look through some books on the pavement … one reminds me of one I had many years ago. I flick through it … and see my signature and

---

* The Mustansiriya School was a medieval center of learning whose vast library was destroyed when the Mongols invaded Baghdad in the thirteenth century. Dar al Hikma, the House of Wisdom, is a center for translation, research, and publication.

† In 1990, after the invasion of Kuwait, the most comprehensive sanctions in history were imposed on Iraq and the result was a massive impoverishment of the population and dete-rioration of its health and education system. Many intellectuals and academics were forced to sell all their books in order to feed their families. The sanctions were enforced until 2003.

the date I bought the book . . . 1986 . . . I buy it back and try to remember who borrowed it from me, but I can't. Someone taps me on the shoulder.

It's my Tunisian journalist friend. We eat *kubba* (a stuffed lamb and wheat meatball) from Abu Ali's standing up. She looks over at the Shabandar Café and I offer to take her there to drink tea. We go in—I pretend to have the confidence of someone who goes there everyday. They are only slightly disturbed by us. It's not Friday and it's not crowded . . . we sit in the first available place . . . the waiter runs over to us and tries to seat us in a corner—out of the way. "Thank you, we're fine here." I order a *nargila* and we smoke it and leaf through the books we've bought, its bubbling laughter mixing with our stifled giggles.

The employee at the Dhilal Transport Company confirms the departure time of the coach to Amman.* I cross over and stand in the spacious courtyard of the Iraq Museum, closed since 1991. I walk across the Ahrar Bridge. I enjoy the shade on this hot August day in 1997. I cross Nahr Street, almost empty of women who were the backbone of its life and economy . . . most of the jewellery, clothes and shoe shops have shut their doors, only small sewing workshops left. I look in at the courtyard of the Mustansiriya School and I want to enter, but the guard says they're doing repairs . . . I gaze at the jewellery shops, full of items dear to their owners, sold for the price of a pair school shoes or a bag of flour. I shut my eyes. I cross to al-Mutanabbi Street and turn to see the statue of Rasafi.† It's as if he's looking in the opposite direction to the one that the sculptor forced on him!!!!

Years ago, he stopped asking me if I was looking for a specific book . . . as soon I walk in, his face shines with the sweet, loving smile, with which he always welcomes me and bids me goodbye. We exchange smiles without a word. I used to wander into his bookshop without thinking or planning to. I never bought a book from him . . . I thought that one day I would remind him of that little girl with her father, an image that was with me, every time I came to al-Mutanabbi Street. I hold on to this image and so suppress my desire to reveal it.

I walk around. My eyes wander over the books and magazines . . . I pretend to leaf intently through a book to avoid looking at people I don't want to say goodbye to . . . I hear Naim al Shatri's (a well-known book auctioneer) loud booming laugh. I smile—tomorrow he'll be calling in the book auction. I see Said Abdel Hadi with all his refinement near the Adnan Bookshop, carrying books, and I imagine what kind of books they are and who will now buy them from him.

---

* The major road transport company used by people wanting to leave Iraq via Jordan during the years of the sanctions, 1991–2003.

† A famous twentieth-century Iraqi poet.

I leave al-Mutanabbi Street with letters friends have given me to take by hand to people in Jordan or to send by post to those outside Jordan … to ensure that they arrive and don't come under the inquisitive gaze of the censor.

I cross Shuhada' Bridge … and gaze at the Tigris. She's indifferent to the steps, and the looks of the people crossing her breast from Rasafa to the Karkh and vice versa (the two banks of the river) … and she's indifferent to those suspended between on the bridges … and indifferent to my meditation from the spot that used to belong to the people who were robbed of their wealth in India by the English.

Al-Mutanabbi Street was the last place in Baghdad I went before I left, and the first when I returned. The whole time I was away, my dream was to be in al-Mutanabbi Street with my daughter, Dima. I would give her my right hand and we would walk together … we would live our small moments of joy before leaving it and going to the other bank of the river from a small quay near the Tujar Coffee Shop or down the river to Qasr Sha'shou'.*

My mother warns me—"stay away from anywhere crowded, or close to a police station." I worry, so I don't take my daughter with me, but like all other sons and daughters of parents, I don't consider my mother's heart. My soul leaps ahead to al-Mutanabbi Street on that cold December day in 2004 … I get there with my husband, and feel the earth spin under my feet … I almost pass out—I have missed it so much … missed my life … missed myself … It's crowded, as it usually is on Fridays; established and new writers, journalists, artists, academics, politicians … people I know well, some only slightly, some not at all. Faces of people who had been with us "here" on our journeys through war, losses, sanctions, poverty, hunger, fear, and faces of others, who had been deprived of the blessings of "here," although they have had those of "there."†

I see people from "here" and from "there," all together in al-Mutanabbi Street: the Communist, nationalist, Islamist and even the Ba'athi— the loyal and the opportunist, the deep and the superficial, the intellectual and the businessman, the victim and the torturer. My husband stops to talk to his colleagues and I move away towards the bookshop. I look for his silver hair and his shining smile. But he's not in his usual place. Instead a young man stands watching nervously as people walk in and out of the shop. I don't go in.

---

* Sha'shou' Place, a big house on the banks of the Tigris, which belonged to an old Jewish Baghdadi family, the Sha'shou's. It was where Feisal I, the first king of Iraq, lived when he first came to Iraq from Hijaz in Saudi Arabia in 1920.

† After 2003, many Iraqis who had lived in exile for many years returned to Iraq. Some remained and some returned to their places of exile.

My friend Nahla waves at me from a distance. She's told my friends that I am back in Baghdad and they'll come to meet me in al-Mutanabbi Street. We approach the Shabandar Café. The noise and clouds of *narghila* smoke float out of the door like a flock of sheep fleeing a wolf—it makes you hesitate before daring to plunge in search of the face you want to see. No one's arrived yet. Our talk races ahead of our steps, which hurtle towards the pavements, full of the books we used to exchange in secret, and which we'd heard of but never seen. We laugh, remembering how when we despaired of a book, sent by a friend outside Iraq, ever reaching us, we'd come here to look for it. We called the censor "the well-read thief," because he knew the value of the books and confiscated them for himself. We laugh, my friends and I, remembering everything we'd been through. But then we stop, and our words falter when we get past the past we've lived and shared with each other and arrive at the here and now ... A while ago we didn't even use certain words—liberation, occupation, terrorism, resistance, democracy, pluralism, sectarianism, citizenship, martyrs, murderers, promised prosperity ... and, and, and ... now we utter them, but cautiously. This is the beginning of a new waiting, not to reclaim our dreamt-of image of the country, but to re-find each other and what joined us together for so many years. Al-Mutanabbi Street was our witness and in the blink of an eye, it was gone, in the gap between our dream and its loss.

Remnants

Dilara Cirit

Under Middle Eastern stars,
Fire ravages yellowed texts,
Chars centuries of thought
Bound in ancient leather.

As smoke twists to the sky,
Crumbling ideas wither to ash.
A bookseller blinks back tears,
Hands clasped in quiet prayer.

Burnt pages of poetry, history,
Philosophy litter empty streets.
Memories seep through earth
To revive the city's heart.

Ashes

Niamh macFhionnlaoich

The sin burst in metal shards
Tearing through centuries
Of words and walls
On al-Mutanabbi Street.
White flames spewed
From smoking wreckage
Scattered over the pavement.
Fire darted over pages,
Turned knowledge
Into kindling to feed
The hungry storm burning
Through book stalls.
Silence fell as scorched words
Fluttered amid pale ash.

The Color She Wears

Erica Goss

I will never know
the names of the men
who loaded a car
with death and split
Mutanabbi Street open,
or the names of the men
who read poems
just before their bodies
deconstructed; yet
every man's name
was first a word
that appeared
in his mother's mind,
shaping her mouth
before she spoke,
lips pressed against
his damp, just-birthed
face.
They say
the poets kept
coming, for days
they waded through
remnants of photographs,
paper, bones, glass
fragments, books
curled in damp fingers.
Someone must have finally
shooed them away,
started sweeping—
some man's mother
robed in black,
the color she wears
every day.

No Man's Land

Daisy Zamora

To the poets I love

We are a minefield of clarity,
and whoever crosses the barbed wire comes back to life.
But who's interested in crawling through undergrowth?
Who dares sail a tempest?
Who wants to come face to face with purity?

That's why we're fenced off in this no-man's-land,
under permanent crossfire.

Translated from the Spanish by George Evans.

On al-Mutanabbi Street

George Evans

The books blew up and words
swirled aloft among teacups and ears
exploding black and deaf
against red.
Mythology also transforms the living—
disembodied, disgraced by this god, that,
rivalry, greed, unrequited or jealous love,
so obliterated nothing can save them—
they live, but the gods win.
Vessel destroyed, essence
retained to some
purpose.

In war: no myth but purpose,
bone that will not survive,
its kiss more final
than final.

On Mutanabbi Street the words whirled
up from their books
in funnels and ash cones,
chevrons longer than rivers
streaking the sky, nets
the size of oceans,
screeching hoards peppered with warning.

Some spoke like Socrates, some desert song,
some gibberish, unruly, absurd, religious, melodious,
uncountable numbers trailing clouds in their wake,
drowning the world with noise until nothing
else could be heard and none
would shut up.

The books blew up and people,
cafés and stores, but the words remained,
hovering, circled, waiting

The Friend

Steve Dickison

that the bird with the enormous velvet nerve-body
articulated legs more like an insect than I knew
greedy mouth wanted to feed out of my mouth
apparently they are always hungry
"what they are screaming is *ada ada* the word for pain"
the verb was the same as in spanish *ayudar*
echoe'd "are you there?" or in arabic *wadada*

"tears become pears for mothers to feed their children"

19iii08   **for McN**

The River Turned Black with Ink

Maysoon Pachachi

February of 2004 and I was back in Baghdad for the first time in thirty-five years. I planted my elbows on Abu Nabil's table to steady my video camera; he was showing me the painting he'd bought from the looters—blue vase and feathery white flowers. "We're patient, we know this chaos will stop sometime . . . it's enough now." The hole-in-wall shop was crammed with battered and etched silver ewers, copper bowls, old photographs from the time of the monarchy, and antique jewellery, like the ring I had on my finger; a line from the Persian poet, Saadi was carved into the oval carnelian stone—roughly translated, "who knows what lies in store for us when we die, we only know that we have this one life, so let us care for it and live it well." Dr. Lama'an had given the ring to my uncle and when she died, he gave it to me and I had worn it every single day since then. In the 1930s, she'd become one of the very first women doctors in Iraq, a role model for many. I had known her all my life.

Abu Nabil put the painting down. "Come with me." We walked through the Souk al Sarai market to his storeroom . . . I drank it all in—Baghdad had changed beyond recognition and I felt lost, but here, in the heart of the old city there was a sense of continuity despite all the violent ruptures of history—and finally I knew where I was.

I followed Abu Nabil, filming all the way; the man re-stringing *sibhas* (worry beads) at his small stall, the row of men sitting on wooden benches drinking tea, talking, smoking waterpipes in the half-light of a crumbling colonnade, a jumble of timepieces piled behind a dusty, streaked shop window.

Stacked among the cornices, old wooden cabinets and mirrors in Abu Nabil's storeroom were forty-six thick, carved doors. There was a glint of amusement and also pride in his eyes. "Look at these doors, they were all looted from the Kushla . . . the old headquarters of the Ottoman administration, near here. We managed to buy them back from the thieves, and when things settle down, we'll return them to the Kushla. Maybe, in the end, we can save a few things."

I walked out of the souk and towards al-Mutanabbi Street and the Shabandar Café, past a wall where someone had sprayed "Yes to liberation, no to occupation."

The streets were full of rubbish and broken glass and there was something unsure and careful in the eyes of the people I passed, but it was Friday and the place was teeming—they had taken possession of their area again; this was their patch—and had been for thousands of years.

Every inch of the Shabandar Café was occupied; older and middle-aged men crowded together on the pale green benches, sipping tea, telling worry beads and arguing about literature, politics, and history. As a woman, I was an anomaly in all this male hubbub, but I stood my ground behind my camera lens and filmed—and no one gave me more than a cursory, uninterested glance. Off in quiet corners, some of the men managed to read, and write their notes, and some leafed thorough books they'd just bought in al-Mutanabbi Street.

I wove my way through the crowds, thronged around the bookstalls—hungry, avid. For so many Iraqis, books have always been like the food of life. If you can't get them, you starve, and al-Mutanabbi Street is where you came for nourishment.

I ambled down Nahr Street towards the river. A young boy struggled with a heavy red patterned carpet, and finally managed to hang it on the railings outside the Mustansiriya, the medieval school where Avicenna had taught and practiced medicine. It was now a museum. Mustafa said he was sixteen, but looked twelve. "I've left school, I mean I passed the entry exam for high school, but I was really bad in English, so they said 'School isn't for you.' And I stopped going. I'm not smart like my brothers—I just don't really understand stuff." He seemed pretty bright to me. Maybe he was just dyslexic. He'd fallen through the net; the years of war and sanctions had all but destroyed the educational system in Iraq.

I entered the Mustansiriya School and for the only time I was in Baghdad on that trip in 2004, I shed tears. I had first visited this place with my aunt when I was ten years old. The grace of its huge courtyard had somehow overwhelmed me. As I'd stood there trying to take in what I was feeling—being alive in this space—the guard had shuffled over to us. "This place contained the knowledge of the world, you know, but on that black day when the Mongols invaded, they sacked the library, set fire to the city, dragged people out of their beds and killed them, looted the shops; rice, grain, gold—everything. They threw all the books in the river and the river turned black with ink." I imagined all the horrible things he'd seen, and it was only later that I discovered this had happened some seven hundred years before. We Iraqis seem to live with a very present sense of our history and the image of that destruction is embedded deep in our consciousness.

So, it was the first thing we all thought of when in March of 2007, almost three years after my first return visit to Baghdad, the Iraqi women I was making a film about and I watched the report of the al-Mutanabbi Street bombing on TV in Syria. Somehow, I had known it would come to this. The project I was filming was full of harrowing, upsetting stories, but I had managed to control myself—I had to be a witness and it was not me who should cry, if crying were to be done. But now, yet again, I was weeping.

A couple of days after the bombing, Baghdad's artists, writers, booksellers, readers, and café regulars came to participate in a wake for al-Mutanabbi Street. I tried to remind myself that the opening lines of classical Arab poetry are often a lament over ruins. Once the lament is over, however, the poem gets on with the rest of its work. And sometimes it seems like the rhythm of Iraqi history is one of destruction, lament and repair … destruction, lament and repair …

II. KNOWLEDGE IS LIGHT

Matter and Spirit on al-Mutanabbi Street

Summer Brenner

Troughs in sand.

Footpaths beaten to the hut of the beloved,
the quarry, the healer, the judge.

Going and coming: the great human activity.

Path, road, highway, street. Point to point.
Congregation, collaboration, community.

The Sumerian city of Ur (in SW Iraq) built the world's earliest roads of
stone (4000 BCE). Stone, timber, brick. Ancient roads, ancient walls: one
to make welcome, the other to deny it.

In Sumer the oldest recorded laws in the Code of Ur-Nammu (2112–2095
BCE) with these injunctions: *The orphan was not delivered up to the rich man;
the widow was not delivered up to the mighty man; the man of one shekel was not
delivered up to the man of one mina.*

In Sumer the world's first known epic poems, impressed in cuneiform
on clay tablets. From *Inanna, Queen of Heaven and Earth* (circa 2000 BCE),
we read:

> *My Lady weeps bitterly for her young husband.*
> *Inanna weeps bitterly for her young husband.*
> *Woe for her husband! Woe for her young love!*
> *Woe for her house! Woe for her city!*

Civilization: roads (marketplace), rules for behavior (order), year-
around agriculture (secure food supply), and poetry to reflect upon the
frailties and failings of man and gods (selfhood).

Sumer falls to the Akkadians, the Akkadians to Amorites and
Babylonians. The legacy of conquest and conquered.

The Abassid Empire advances road technology. It tars surfaces with
sticky viscous bitumen gathered from the local oil fields, then heated
and distilled. Early Baghdad is reputed to have the finest roads on earth.

Both cradle and crossroads, primed with traders, travelers, readers, scholars, raconteurs, wise men, and fools.
Congregation, collaboration, community.

A cart parks in the shade of a wall on al-Mutanabbi Street, named for a poet. Beside the wall, a man holds an urn of mint-flavored hot water and a few clay cups. Nearby another man stands with a cluster of Medjool dates and basket of honeyed sweets, baked by a wife. Seated beneath them on a small carpet, spread over the hardened bitumen, is a seller of scrolls.

In the cool morning and indigo twilight of the desert, between prayer and commerce, men gather. Booksellers and cafés proliferate on al-Mutanabbi Street. Readers browse. Scholars debate. Travelers enthrall. Poets sing.

In 2006, UNESCO and the World Monuments Fund place the entire country of Iraq on its list of Most Endangered Sites.

In March 2007, a bomb explodes on al-Mutanabbi Street. Fragments scatter beneath the black stinking sky. Humans and sirens cry.

First, losses are measured in lives, meaning deaths.

Next, damage to property is tallied in number of shops smashed, number of livelihoods ruined.

It is harder to quantify the simple urgent need to find a book or engage in conversation or exchange ideas on al-Mutanabbi Street. The intricate vibrant fabric of congregation, collaboration, community: a thousand years to build, a few seconds to destroy.

Hardest to assess are centuries of spirits embedded in stone, tar, leather, wood, paper, and ink.

The spirits of al-Mutanabbi Street hover in the debris, then rise above the city, and enter the electronic networks powered in the heavens. They speed around the world so others, we the living spirits, might be touched.

"Al-Mutanabbi Street! Al-Mutanabbi Street!" we utter in amazement as they embrace us.

Untitled

Jen Hofer

less then more then less again then — — then again — none —— not
one — the absence of — necessary — silence — —

> I challenge anyone . . . to say what has happened, what's
> happening now, and what will happen in the future.
> —Mohammed Hayawi, Iraqi bookseller murdered
> in the bombing of Mutanabbi Street

> How do you experience something you're not experiencing?
> —Scott Pound, "Circulars"

crashing upon the shore nothing is (nothing)
is too coordinated (complex) complex of
designed to prevent congregation overly
to shush demurely resolutely unnoticed
we will continue until there is no need

necessarily alone participatory transit
the self looks out from (the self) and is
known public (a red line in outline) built
too late as what was being before is not known
exactly so as—so as through a participatory
process to console (beauty crabapples nicely
not largely)   we had made plans but so what

to be being   is birdsong
in the blue blue of having been

having is wrinkled, pocked against the marked canvas (the marketed
        power)
folds in the former floor shush refusal (what is not heard) all terrain
        excess
convoy rebuttal obeys no drafted cartography in a rising wind or bounty
(not acknowledged) plainly a case of terrifically bad luck (clearcut)
        fledgling
those glints aren't birds they're answers that never asked like the green
        green

grass grinning thirstily sweet grown thinner with no effort if it can be
    said
that lack is not effort or exceptions obey brittle memoranda escalating
in the realm of the predictable register sight (preparation for
    preparation) measured
actions—sights—thousands and thousands the familiar smell the
    unrecognizable view
(thousands and thousands)   someone made this bed, now lie in it

at some not prescribed point all of us
having been and not being and not being birds
also not sudden nonetheless breathless airborne
or never the more breathing in the grounded precision
of activity which (grounded) bears no resemblance to bombing
which bears no resemblance to freedom which is a conglomerate (word)
and bears no resemblance and resemblance endures beyond
    understanding
which (wordless) is many migratory words—scarcely—(resourceful)
    and which like
archeology bears no end of exploration

the threads of not listening wrap diligently
the having changed by the being changed
or spool in looks unwelcome easily explained
if not so easily avoided outrage
falls livid on the man-made prepared surface
which otherwise would be inaccessible, very quiet

mostly we export products and feelings
products being trends, bents or belligerence
or being unable to accept the being otherwise
engaged and so less likely to appreciate that many
birds happen in filaments or slices against a gradual
forming an alternate daybreak tilted and mercurial
but who's counting faltering faulting in grid-like
formation canisters at the ready or gridlock
on purpose so as to be hemmed in

mostly a demise in manners as designated patterns
organically lift toward an outer limit not defined in
sights peripherally trained fields empty tirades empty

as there is no stated location
we are everywhere or we are nowhere
as there is no stated location

that obsessive thought   (sky)
(sparrow) (winding streets) (a plan)
like a crow like a door (not a call to arms)
a cement block not unlike servitude
in a long pink dress tethered there are ways
not to forget   aids   colors   places   homes
withers every night on the vine
and every day reconstitutes (at attention)
constituent parts in vehicles striking out
in the absence of color a tangible
color a loud noise
a loud unpleasant noise

if a wall is a river
a bit of interference
flowing past the checkpoint
makes the image accurate
made by the maker of rivers
if a wall can be beautiful
why is it not made beautiful

Untitled

Rijin Sahakian

The first semester of my senior year in high school, I was enrolled in an honors English course, "Literature Around the World." It was 1996, five years after the first Gulf War had ended. During the course of the class, we studied literature from Europe, Asia, Latin America, and Africa. When it came time to cover the literature of the Middle East, the class was told that because of strict Islamic guidelines, nothing had been published in the Middle East since the advent of Islam. Our teacher related an anecdote that involved a friend of hers who went to Saudi Arabia and found no books; this presumably served as evidence of the complete absence of literature in the whole of the Middle East. As our Middle East curriculum, we were given short pre-Islamic fables to read.

At the time, I was not all familiar with the literature of the Middle East, but I was aware that reading and writing was not a banned activity there. My father, an Iraqi, had a library lined with books in Arabic and read voraciously. Apart from this, it was simply an incredible statement from a teacher in a very liberal Northern California high school. There may be no greater erasure of history than the absence of a written form of knowledge, and in effect, what our teacher was saying is that there was absolutely nothing to know of the Middle East in centuries.

I didn't say anything in class that day, though. I was slightly shocked. After all, she was my teacher and what if somehow she was right? I lived in a small university town, and that weekend I rode my bike to the campus's library. A quick library search at the ground floor's banks of computers brought up hundreds of books by Middle Eastern scholars, writers, and poets. I looked at the green rows of results that filled the screen as I scrolled down and clicked forward through the pages of results. I was relieved. Relieved and disappointed. I had always liked this particular teacher. She'd been handicapped as a result of an accident, but retained an almost manic energy. She was always a little scattered, which generally added to her humor. She'd throw her hands in the air and talk to herself while rushing into the classroom. It was fun and exotic to see an adult, a teacher, this way: a glimpse into what we'd discover later. We would all turn into adults and possibly never be prepared for it. More than this, she'd always simply been an encouraging educator, facilitating debate, assigning independent projects, and taking genuine interest in our work.

If it was that simple to find the literature in question, why didn't my teacher, entrusted with instructing an honors English course, take the time to find it before coming to such an inconceivable conclusion, presented to the class as fact? I never discovered what her reasons were, but perhaps more important than her reasons is the idea that her conclusion was conceivable, both to her and the rest of the class.

It was while looking through rows of modern Arabic poetry that I found something that amplified the importance of knowing that this literature existed. Flipping through an anthology in search of something I could present to the class, I came across the work of renowned Iraqi poet Badr Shakir al-Sayyab. I read his poem "Rain Song" and wept. For the words, for its tragic timelessness, for the recognition I saw in his work that would not have existed in that classroom.

Rain Song

Badr Shakir al-Sayyab

Your eyes are two palm tree forests in early light,
Or two balconies from which the moonlight recedes
When they smile, your eyes, the vines put forth their leaves,
And lights dance ... like moons in a river
Rippled by the blade of an oar at break of day;
As if stars were throbbing in the depths of them ...

And they drown in a mist of sorrow translucent
Like the sea stroked by the hand of nightfall;
The warmth of winter is in it, the shudder of autumn,
And death and birth, darkness and light;
A sobbing flares up to tremble in my soul
And a savage elation embracing the sky,
Frenzy of a child frightened by the moon.

It is as if archways of mist drank the clouds
And drop by drop dissolved in the rain ...
As if children snickered in the vineyard bowers,
The song of the rain
Rippled the silence of birds in the trees ...
Drop, drop, the rain ...
Drip ...
Drop ... the rain ...

Evening yawned, from low clouds
Heavy tears are streaming still.
It is as if a child before sleep were rambling on
About his mother (a year ago he went to wake her, did not find her,
Then was told, for he kept on asking,
"After tomorrow, she'll come back again ...")
That she must come back again,
Yet his playmates whisper that she is there
In the hillside, sleeping her death for ever,
Eating the earth around her, drinking the rain;
As if a forlorn fisherman gathering nets
Cursed the waters and fate
And scattered a song at moonset,
Drip, drop, the rain ...

Drip, drop, the rain …

Do you know what sorrow the rain can inspire?
Do you know how gutters weep when it pours down?
Do you know how lost a solitary person feels in the rain?
Endless, like spilt blood, like hungry people, like love,
Like children, like the dead, endless the rain.
Your two eyes take me wandering with the rain,
Lightning's from across the Gulf sweep the shores of Iraq
With stars and shells,
As if a dawn were about to break from them,
But night pulls over them a coverlet of blood.
I cry out to the Gulf: "O Gulf,
Giver of pearls, shells and death!"
And the echo replies,
As if lamenting:
"O Gulf,
Giver of shells and death …"

I can almost hear Iraq husbanding the thunder,
Storing lightning in the mountains and plains,
So that if the seal were broken by men
The winds would leave in the valley not a trace of Thamūd.
I can almost hear the palm trees drinking the rain,
Hear the villages moaning and emigrants
With oar and sail fighting the Gulf
Winds of storm and thunder, singing
"Rain …
Rain …
Drip, drop, the rain …"

And there is hunger in Iraq,
The harvest time scatters the grain in it,
That crows and locusts may gobble their fill,
Granaries and stones grind on and on,
Mills turn in the fields, with them men turning …
Drip, drop, the rain …
Drip …
Drop …

When came the night for leaving, how many tears we shed,
We made the rain a pretext, not wishing to be blamed
Drip, drop, the rain ...
Drip, drop, the rain ...
Since we had been children, the sky
Would be clouded in wintertime,

And down would pour the rain,
And every year when earth turned green the hunger struck us.
Not a year has passed without hunger in Iraq.
Rain ...
Drip, drop, the rain ...
Drip, drop ...

In every drop of rain
A red or yellow color buds from the seeds of flowers,
Every tear wept by the hungry and naked people,
And every spilt drop of slaves' blood,
Is a smile aimed at a new dawn,
A nipple turning rosy in an infant's lips,
In the young world of tomorrow, bringer of life.
Drip, drop, the rain ...

Drip ...
Drop ... the rain ...
Iraq will blossom one day

I cry out to the Gulf: "O Gulf,
Giver of pearls, shells and death!"
The echo replies
As if lamenting:
"O Gulf,
Giver of shells and death."
And across the sands from among its lavish gifts
The Gulf scatters fuming froth and shells
And the skeletons of miserable drowned emigrants
Who drank death forever
From the depths of the Gulf, from the ground of its silence,
And in Iraq a thousand serpents drink the nectar
From a flower the Euphrates has nourished with dew.
I hear the echo
Ringing in the Gulf:

"Rain…
Drip, drop, the rain…
Drip, drop."
In every drop of rain
A red or yellow color buds from the seeds of flowers.
Every tear wept by the hungry and naked people
And every spilt drop of slaves' blood
Is a smile aimed at a new dawn,
A nipple turning rosy in an infant's lips
In the young world of tomorrow, bringer of life.

And still the rain pours down.

Translated from the Arabic by Lena Jayyusi and Christopher Middleton.

The Poet

Jane Hirshfield

She is working now, in a room
not unlike this one,
the one where I write, or you read.
Her table is covered with paper.
The light of the lamp would be
tempered by a shade, where the bulb's
single harshness might dissolve,
but it is not, she has taken it off.
Her poems? I will never know them,
though they are the ones I most need.
Even the alphabet she writes in
I cannot decipher. Her chair—
Let us imagine whether it is leather
or canvas, vinyl or wicker. Let her
have a chair, her shadeless lamp,
the table. Let one or two she loves
be in the next room. Let the door
be closed, the sleeping ones healthy.
Let her have time, and silence,
enough paper to make mistakes and go on.

"Close to God"

Jack Marshall

"Close to God" is easy to say;
to harness like a draft horse
is harder. This, too, is easy to say.
Give it a rest, wavering,
as in childhood, day and night,
as wavering now you wake.

Nothing has passed except the look
of the recent dead, fresh
in the distance. In their place
is the rubble you trample.
Nothing has passed but their warm,
woeful eyes, the pupils idle.

Today is the day long ago,
when looking close at a loved one
as if from a great distance, you saw them
one day, far away.

A Book in the Hand

Susan Moon

Here in Berkeley, standing at the corner of Haste and Telegraph, I think of al-Mutanabbi Street. The big bookstore windows are boarded up now at the old Cody's Books, though a florist still has her stand in front. Bookstores are dying all over town, not because they are being bombed by religious fundamentalists but because fewer and fewer people are buying printed books in bookstores anymore. Berkeley was once famous for its many bookstores, and people used to come from far and wide to buy books here. Now, even the big chains like Borders and Barnes and Noble, the big guys who put the little guys out of business, are being destroyed by the Internet.

As a matter of fact, Cody's actually *was* bombed by a religious fundamentalist in 1989, when someone threw a firebomb through the store window where Salman Rushdie's *The Satanic Verses* was displayed. A month before, Iranian clerics had issued a *fatwa* (religious ruling) against the book for its blasphemy. Cody's kept the book on display in spite of the attack, carrying on the tradition of bookstores as sanctuaries for the protection of human rights and freedom of speech.

The boarded-up windows at Cody's give me a glimpse of al-Mutanabbi Street. But what if Moe's Books down the block and Shakespeare & Co. across the street were boarded up, too? Or, worse than boarded up, were piles of rubble with burned books trapped under the twisted rebar?

Yesterday a friend showed me his Kindle, an electronic book made by Amazon.com that operates on cell phone technology. You can purchase and download your choices from thousands of titles; every book is $10. You read the book on a virtual page on the screen, and you click a button to turn the page. You can choose the font and the point size. My friend, a man in his seventies, is overjoyed. He says he's reading more than ever before.

But I love books for their bodies as well as their minds. When I was fifteen, my parents took my siblings and me to Europe. We walked along the Seine, and I was amazed by the bookstalls. The smell of old books mixed with the smell of the river, I felt the softness of old book-covers, touched their dustiness, heard the sound of footsteps on stone.

I love books for the sharing of them, too. One of my earliest memories is of my grandmother reading aloud to me from Robert Louis Stevenson's *A Child's Garden of Verses*. She opened the big blue book on her lap, I curled up beside her on the sofa, and together we bent our heads over its giant wingspread and looked at the picture of a little girl on a swing with her skirt flying out behind her. This was back in the days when al-Mutanabbi Street, in Baghdad, was full of writers and readers talking about books and ideas in cafés and bookstores, before Baghdad had heard of Saddam Hussein, before the UN sanctions on Iraq, before the U.S. invasion. I imagine sweet mint tea, poured in a long thin stream from the teapot into the cup.

Now I have the pleasure of reading to my own small granddaughter—and we point and laugh together at the dogs driving sports cars and wearing silly hats. These days it must be hard for grandmothers in Baghdad to find a cozy corner to read aloud to their grandchildren.

Like most Americans, I am ignorant about Iraqi culture. I had never heard of al-Mutanabbi Street before it was firebombed in 2007. I had not known that it was named after a great Arabic poet, al-Mutanabbi; I had not known it was the intellectual center of Bagdad for centuries. But now I'm sad about it. It's like learning about someone's amazing life at the memorial service, and you wish you'd known what a great person she was before she died instead of after.

I'm sitting in the Nomad in Oakland, drinking a cup of green tea, and the café is full of people working on their laptops, as I am doing. They are not talking to each other, but perhaps they are talking to someone I can't see, over the Internet. This café is a green business free of plastic, and it fosters community; on weekends local musicians and poets perform here.

Recently, two hooded robbers came into this café in a "takeover robbery" and held up the café and its customers at gunpoint. Still, I'm not afraid to go to a public café and talk to my friends about what I'm reading and thinking. As a matter of fact, I can hear two people at the next table talking critically about the war in Afghanistan. They might be doing that on al-Mutanabbi Street.

Here in the United States, a lot of the book talk happens out in space, without vocalization, as bodiless people discuss bodiless books. Long gone is the parched smell I loved of the orange-covered Penguin paperbacks. People in Baghdad talk about books on the Internet, too—if they are lucky enough to have computers and Internet access. There are even a number of people blogging from Iraq. So, even as we lose neighborhood bookstores, we gain the ability to talk to people all over the world and find out what's happening in their neighborhoods. And how strange that a person in Baghdad can look at photos on the Internet of the inside and outside of Moe's Books in Berkeley, one of our old-time bookstores that is still alive. And that I can look at photos of a bookseller on al-Mutanabbi Street, with his books spread out for sale on the hood of an old car. I hope his bookstall gets rebuilt.

I have the copy of A Child's Garden of Verses that my grandmother read to me, and I'm taking good care of it so that I can read it to my granddaughter when she visits me. My house is full of books with bodies. While I'm grateful that I can discuss invisible ideas with invisible people out there in space, I relish the weight of a book in the hand and the face-to-face meetings that may take place over its pages.

I hope the bookseller's wife has a quiet spot to snuggle with her grandchild and read aloud a book she loved as a child.

Revolutionary Letter #77
Awkward Song on the Eve of War

Diane di Prima

The center of my heart is Arab song.
It is woven around my heartstrings
I cannot uproot it.
It is the song of the Beloved as Other
The Other as God, it is all about Light
and we never stop singing it.

The root of my brain
(the actual stem and medulla)
is the Tree of Life.
It is the story we have all been telling
The story of the journey and return
It is all about Light
and we never stop telling it.

I cannot uproot this Tree from the back of my head
I cannot tear this song out of my heart
I cannot allow the two to war in my cells.

This is a prose poem and it is didactic

It remembers the perfumes of Lebanon, lapis of Persia
The mountains, ziggurats, ladders of ascent
The hut in the field we entered as Her body.

The fabric of our seeing is dark & light
Ahriman / Ahura the two lobes
of the brain. Or yin and yang.
The paintings of Turkestan echo in caves
of North China. The Manichee's eyes are carved
in Bone Oracles.

I cannot cut the light from my eyes
or the woven shadow from the curves of my brain.

The dance of the I *Ching* is the dance of the star tide
Mathematics of the Zend Avesta
Geometries of Ife
There is only one sun and it is just rising

The golden ikon of the Black Virgin
stands at the stone gateway of Tashkent.
The flowering valleys of Shambhala
haunt our dreaming.
What skeletons stalk there?

Do you see?

If even the plants send out warnings to each other
If even the brine shrimp mourn each other's passing ...

My eyes stare from ten thousand Arab faces
A deer sniffs at the stiffening corpse of her yearling.

There is only one sun and it is rising
It is much too strong in the desert of our minds.

Shield us from the desert of greed
The desert of hate
Shield us from the desert of chauvinism
Le désert désespéré
Desperate desert of no song, no image
Shield us from the desert of no return

That Arab song burst out of mountain cave
That fine-worked silver glisten in the sun

> Loving, yes, loving, woman, and
> digging on each other
> thousands of years,
> digging the differences ...

Let the gold-clad men and women
dark skins gleaming
dance at the stone gates:
      Shiprock, New Grange, Tashkent
Let the goddess walk again on the African plains
      The Orisha brighten the air

There is only one sun and it is rising.
May the peaches of Samarkand bloom in the Okanagan

Reprise:
There is nothing we have been that we will be
None of the myths suffices.

Let us read each other's maps at the foot of the Tree
Where the stream of Song moves out in all directions.

Al-Mutanabbi Street

Evelyn So

One December morning, in 2007, about twenty-eight Saratoga High School poetry students visited Montalvo Arts Center and took part in a regional initiative, IRAQ: REFRAME. As students met and spoke with Iraqi-born refugee artist Wafaa Bilal and Michael Rakowitz, an American artist of Iraqi and Jewish heritage, I was reminded that these student poets were too young to remember the first Gulf War, part of my coming of age experience. This was the Bay Area, in the post–September II era, and I had just joined Judith Sutton, veteran English teacher and founder and director of Saratoga's intensive three-year creative writing program, and my colleague Erica Goss in teaching poetry to sophomores, juniors, and seniors. At the same time that I was learning how to teach poetry to high school students, I, too, was a poetry student, working toward an MFA in creative writing. As Wafaa and Michael shared stories about their experiences with the project and their artistic practices, I wondered how young adults accustomed to Saratoga, a small town community in Silicon Valley would respond to the al-Mutanabbi project.

Located in the Saratoga hills, Montalvo occupies a Mediterranean-style villa on 175 acres that Senator James D. Phelan bequeathed to the people of California to establish a non-profit "dedicated to engaging people in contemporary concerns through the arts," per Montalvo's web site. After learning of the first al-Mutanabbi Street Memorial Reading and accompanying exhibit of broadsides by letterpress printers from Iraqi poet Sinan Antoon, then in residence at Montalvo, Rijin Sahakian, arts programs manager and IRAQ: REFRAME curator, met with Kathy Walkup, coordinator for the call to letterpress printers, and Saratoga Library staff. In that meeting, the idea arose that a youth perspective on the Al-Mutanabbi Street Project would be best served through creative writing. Rijin then contacted Judith and invited Saratoga's poetry students to participate.

Over the winter and spring months, every student worked on poems in response to the al-Mutanabbi project, eventually sharing them publicly through readings and exhibits at the Saratoga Library as part of the IRAQ: REFRAME Program, at Rijin's invitation. As students encountered Iraqi culture and people through poetry, art, and hands-on educational programs, the project also helped some students form connections between the abstract and the concrete. Steven McLellan e-mailed me five months after his involvement, saying, "The project affected me most by the way it showed that the Iraqi people were more than just other guys that we could kill; they were people with a culture and a way of living that is more similar to ours than I thought." Aaron Garg e-mailed me, "We got to experience [at Montalvo] at least a tiny bit what it was like to eat Iraqi food, to live there cramped in that tiny house ... [and] suffer through the bloodshed of war. It allowed us to think about them as people, not as our enemies." Based on these comments and my observations of other students engaged with the project, I feel the al-Mutanabbi project probably increased most students' awareness of the bombing and also that our response affects what one "sees" and shares with others. Steven wrote about the Montalvo experience as being "really diverse and gave me the understanding of a more cultural Iraq than one that I see get blown up everyday. I really enjoyed writing about how I felt because it felt easier to explain what I meant writing it than in trying to explain."

So that students might better "see" al-Mutanabbi Street, Beau Beausoleil visited the school in March 2008 and screened a documentary by Emad Ali, A Candle for the Shabandar Cafe, filmed before and after the bombing. As they heard and saw Iraqis react in shock and grief, students began to learn the stories of Iraqis personally affected by the bombing, such as the café owner who lost his son and four grandchildren in the attack, and the filmmaker who lost his wife and father in a mortar attack before the bombing on al-Mutanabbi Street, and who was shot twice in a kidnapping attempt near the end of filming the documentary. After the film ended, students wore serious expressions, frowned, and fought tears, listening intently and asking questions.

For Aaron, the most affecting part of the al-Mutanabbi project was watching Emad's film. He emailed me, "Watching [the Iraqis'] ... candlelight vigil sent a powerful message of hope for the future, and I couldn't help empathizing with them." Adeeti Aggarwal also shared her experience, emailing me that seeing Emad's film and visiting Montalvo led "me to feel emotions for the Iraqis similar to what I felt during 9/11, and that is why I compared the two events in my poem ... I can truly say that I was angry when I heard about al-Mutanabbi Street, and how much the people lost: not just members of their family but an intellectual [haven]." At first, Adeeti's comparison of both attacks surprised me, but when I reread her poem, which uses two different perspectives—an American perspective and an Iraqi perspective—I was impressed with the powerful connection to the Iraqi people that she had experienced.

Something else Aaron shared reminded me of my learning experience while students participated in the project. He'd learned that in Iraqi culture, "reading books was so valuable … [the people] would die for it"; that those who had bombed al-Mutanabbi Street had failed to rob Iraqis of "the precious gem of knowledge"; that this could not be destroyed "unless their spirit was broken." However, he added, "their spirit has proven to be rock solid." Over the months, I found my own awareness and appreciation of literature and culture widening in response to my experience at Montalvo, the students' engagement with al-Mutanabbi Street, and a seminar I took on Middle Eastern literature, especially with respect to the importance of a sense of "home."

In their poems, many students memorialized the bombing, protested the destruction, and eulogized Iraqis who were killed. They sought to evoke a sense of emotional urgency. Some offered commentary on larger issues such as the war in Iraq, hopes for peace and friendship between the American and Iraqi people, the power of words, censorship, and continuity of culture and civilization. For example, Connie Shang's "Kindred" expresses fellowship between American and Iraqi people through their shared emotional experiences—anger at injustice, grief over suffering, worry about the safety of loved ones, measured hope for the future: "we pen / Letters, hope soldiers— / Her father and mine— / Will read them soon …" Daniel Lee's "LOST" attests to al-Mutanabbi Street's historic importance as a place to exchange ideas and its enduring significance as a powerful symbol of free speech:

> Book, my paper friend …
> Wipe those tears away!
> This exploding street dies,
> But still we read your pages
> Because you whisper …

In commemorating the memory of what was lost in the attack—the open sharing of ideas, books, and lives—this poem envisions a future in which a new generation of Iraqi people regains the hope and intellectual freedom that al-Mutanabbi Street represents. Steven's "ANALOGY" was inspired by the atrocities of destroying books and writers during the Qin Dynasty from 213 to 206 BC, in China, and on al-Mutanabbi Street in Iraq. This poem comments not only on the deaths of Iraqis during the bombing of al-Mutanabbi Street, but the larger implications of this attack on language and thought: "Weep at the hungry flames, pray / Someone will stop the madness … / While pages float along the street."

In teaching poetry at Saratoga, I have been struck with how the project affected some of my students, and how I have been affected by their participation. I was excited that these young adults would participate in this cross-cultural project. However, perhaps in part because I already felt passionate about intellectual freedom and education through my work as a poet, writer, and librarian, I did not anticipate finding myself, over time, profoundly affected by their participation. One reason student participation moved me so deeply is the project's position that personal experience matters; that words, poetry, and broadsides offer ways to engage personally as well as with a larger community; that, to quote Beau, anywhere someone sits down to read or takes up a pen to write, al-Mutanabbi Street starts.

The experience of hearing students read their poetry at Saratoga Library during a special program in partnership with Montalvo Arts Center and the al-Mutanabbi Street Coalition, and later rereading their poems on display at the library was powerful. I found a ritualized gesture from their reading especially affecting. In silence, before presenting their poems, students ceremoniously opened black binders and placed crimson ribbons down the center, draping the excess, holding a place for readers and, metaphorically, for listeners, writers, and anyone else who shares the story of al-Mutanabbi Street. It's now October 2008, and I've just learned that a letterpress printer will publish their poems. I'm reminded of something Beau once told them. "Never underestimate the power of your writing—your own words."

Ethics of Care: The Retreat of al-Mutanabbi

Nahrain al-Mousawi

Derrida Foucault Levinas.

Number one says I'm too old to chase,
So he prefers I hold court
Within this war
Without war.
But, why should I care?
Number two says who cares if bombs drip and drop in
And advises me to get high on higher education
And vomit it in my sleep
Because even care
Is a war-like relation.
Number three is convinced of nothing
Except that
My brain scan would render only images of
Cat litter and Chernobyl,
And carelessly adds that
The ethics of care consists of nothing but this:

"Cook, read, write, translate, weep, and eat.
Rinse and repeat."

Who cares if I care?
I tell them to fuck off …
In my dreams.

Derrida Foucault Levinas.
They are no ordinary trio.
In fact, they don't get along.
They point their twig fingers at me,
One by one,
In the court I keep
And lead a charge of defeat:
"Defeat, Defeat, Defeat!"

One accuses me in Baghdad:

"Does the live news feed you with vital dreams?
Does it wait for digestion just once?
Will you forever gorge on its turbid streams?"

Two reduces me in Rutba:

"It repeatedly abducts my cousin,
Twice removed."

Three loses me in Mosul:

"A just war?
It trains its gun-sights on my uncle's paunch
Thrice, and
Leavens him on his doorstep
Like a delicious dish
Of hot, steaming intestines."

They shamelessly drip and drop in,
One at a time,
And leave me
Shamed.

And here we all return to Baghdad,
On al-Mutanabbi Street.
Once again,
Wide awake
In my dreams,
They follow me on
My mother's shattered street.
With a bag of books on each braceleted arm,
She's now
As real to me as
Derrida Foucault Levinas.
On al-Mutanabbi.

How in unison do they
Surround with sound,
A single, nearly perfect triangle,

Shake their sunken jowls at me,
Repulsed chanting ghosts, and breathe:

"Cook, read, write, translate, weep, and eat.
Rinse and repeat."

I can't seem to lose them.
We all traffic in the same memories,
In what we all teach.
I pass the stalls,
I finger the spines,
I am thrilled not to see their names.
I see Jahiz, Faulkner, and Darwish,
And then pick up Sidney Sheldon
And throw it at the corners
Where I think their sunken voices meet,
At all they teach.

They all make me shudder.
But most of all number three.
Wide awake
In my dreams,
I retreat and chant back at him,
"Cook, read, write, translate, weep, and eat.
Rinse and repeat.
I care I care.
About the absurd.
About just wars and war
Waged against war.
About all you and I teach."

I reach the desperate traffic of Al-Rashid.
I no longer care
If they follow me.
I am as wasted and hysterical as what I see.
I turn to the trio and I mouth,
As senseless, grotesque, and careless
As the scene:
"Shi'i Rebel Leaders are sexy—
Even with their third-world teeth."

A Secret Question

Ko Un

Tell me, cricket, what do you think you're doing
night after night, slicing through the dark?
Why don't you slice through people's sleep too,
shedding scarlet blood?
Ah, nowadays people don't shed blood.
All they want is an easy life.
Yet there's not an inch of ground,
not a single hill, not soaked in blood. Sad.
Cricket, old cricket,
drunk on icy dew, cricket friend:
every last drop of this country's dew,
each single one of our children's tears
is all blood, nothing but blood
but blood before and behind sleep asleep;
is deep sleep all there is?
Is there nothing but sleep so numb it would never notice
if you cut out its stupid liver or gall-bladder?
Cricket, old cricket, go on!
Slice through the dark, slice through sleep,
and jolt minds awake like autumn frost,
like an early, biting frost.

Translated from the Korean by Brother Anthony of Taizé, Professor Young-moo Kim, and Gary Gach.

This poem was printed as a broadside by Jennifer Patchett for the Al-Mutanabbi Street Broadside Project.

The Road to al-Mutanabbi Street

Joe Lamb

Here in Puerto Varas, Chile, the way to al-Mutanabbi Street begins where the Costa Nera turns East toward the Sacred Heart Monastery. A black dog, with feet the color of butterscotch, accompanies the man walking down the gravel road. Looking for something to herd, the dog rushes up the road, and back to the man, up the road, and back, his plumed tail waving like a flag in the shape of a question mark.

Gesturing as if making a point in an argument, the man also appears to be herding some unseen creature. He is, in fact, deep in conversation with the ghost of the President of the United States. The man's furrowed brow and wild gestures indicate that this invisible companion causes him pain. He has not, in the strict sense, chosen to share his time with this particular ghost. He would prefer to be discussing the way ideas move across the face of space and time with the spirit of Yeshua, or Charles Darwin, or Giordano Bruno, or Shams al-Tabriz. The walking man with the black dog considers his own time vanishingly small; he spends some of it ushering the President of the United States down the road toward al-Mutanabbi Street because he considers it a holy mission that his President's ghost bear witness to the book market in the moments immediately after the blast. He feels it important to the collective soul of humanity that his President smell the burnt hair in the cloud of smoke, that his President read what is written in the clouds of ashes as they settle onto empty tables.

Imaginary conversations with his President are part of a spiritual exercise the walking man calls "loving your enemy." You may think it strange that this man uses words like "holy" and "sacred" and "collective soul" and that he engages in spiritual practices, because the man is a devout agnostic, one who questions the existence of gods and believes that countries are ephemeral when compared to volcanoes, or a rivers, or a human beings. The exercise is all the stranger because he doesn't consider his President his personal enemy; he has no personal enemies. But he considers his President an enemy of the pursuit of truth—he fears that the world is in danger, and that salvation, if there is salvation, lies in the pursuit of truth.

Because he feels a twinge of empathy for his President, he thinks his practice may be succeeding. It's the kind of empathy you feel for a beauty pageant queen in the homecoming parade who drinks too much bourbon and falls off the float. When he talks to the imaginary President, the walking man's stomach twists and his throat tightens; he feels an overwhelming sense of urgency, as if he were watching a horse trapped in a burning barn, or a raccoon stranded on the median of a freeway during rush hour.

Few think of agnostics as spiritual seekers. Like the President, many people succumb to the temptation to codify their fears by dividing the world into black and white; believer and atheist; friend and enemy; into "for us, or against us"; into crusader and *mujahid*, into Shia or Sunni, into Protestant or Catholic, into martyr and collateral damage. The walking man asks a question for his President over and over: does dividing the indivisible into kingdoms of good and evil create spiritual apartheid, does it create the evil it crusades against?

While herding his President's ghost along the spine of the Andes on the long pilgrimage to al-Mutanabbi Street, the agnostic seeker prays for strength from a holy trinity of humility, radical mercy, and evolving truth; he prays that his President find the humility, the radical mercy, and the strength to allow truth to evolve. He tells his President that his spiritual odyssey must pass by 200 N.W. 5th Street, Oklahoma City, Oklahoma, United States, that he must taste the ashes made of books and flesh that settled on Oklahoma City after a man who was Christian, and American, and white, parked a truck filled with explosives under a daycare center in the Murrah Building, and then taste the ashes that settled on al-Mutanabbi Street to see if they taste the same.

Advising the President that the crimes of humanity are committed by humanity, the walking man stops on a bridge and notices a swastika spray-painted on the cement. He looks over the railing into a stream far below for his reflection, and for the reflection of his President; he hopes to tell his reflections that the best place to fish for the devil is in the mirror. In a small pool, next to a fallen tree, he notices that two of the shadows are actually salmon waiting for rain to swell the stream. In the distance the volcano Calbuco gathers the clouds around her like a saint adjusting her shawl.

Untitled

Katrina Rodabaugh

Books exploding,

or paper & words been set to flame in halves & thirds &

scattered. Severed letters from letters so the ink had lost its meaning.

But for many the letters are not just letters that can be set

to flame & severed to lose their meaning.

Instead, each letter is a tiny cell

that is alive with us. Instead, inside each exploded word

there was a name.

My name, maybe. Or yours.

This poem was printed as a broadside by Katrina Rodabaugh for the Al-Mutanabbi Street Broadside Project.

For I Am a Stranger

Badr Shakir al-Sayyab

For I am a stranger
Beloved Iraq
Far distant, and I here in my longing
For it, for her ... I cry out: Iraq
And from my cry a lament returns
An echo bursts forth
I feel I have crossed the expanse
To a world of decay that responds not
To my cry
If I shake the branches
Only decay will drop from them
Stones
Stones—no fruit
Even the springs
Are stones, even the fresh breeze
Stones moistened with blood
My cry a stone, my mouth a rock
My legs a wind straying in the wastes

Translated from the Arabic by Mounah A. Khouri and Hamid Algar.

This poem was printed as a broadside by Deborah Cowder for the Al-Mutanabbi Street
Broadside Project.

Untitled

Mohammed Hayawi,* by way of Anthony Shadid,
by way of Laurie Szujewska

I CHALLENGE ANYONE TO SAY WHAT HAPPENED, IS HAPPENING NOW, AND WILL HAPPEN IN THE FUTURE.

---

* Iraqi bookseller, killed by the al-Mutanabbi Street car bomb, March 5, 2007.

This statement was translated from the Arabic by Anthony Shadid and printed as a broadside by Laurie Szujewska for the Al-Mutanabbi Street Broadside Project.

Excerpt from **Five Hymns to Pain**

Nazik al-Malaika

It gives our nights sorrow and pain;
it fills our eyes with sleeplessness

We found it on our way,
one rainy morning
and gave it, out of love,
a stroke of pity and a little corner
in our throbbing heart

∾

It never left or vanished from our way,
stalking us to the corners of the world.
If only we gave it no drop to drink,
that sad morning!

It gives our night sorrow and pain;
it fills our eyes with sleeplessness

∾

How do we forget pain,
how do we forget pain?
Who will light for us
the night of its memory?

We shall eat it, we shall drink it,
we shall pursue it with songs,
and if we sleep, its shape
will be the last thing we see.

∾

And in the morning, its face
will be the first thing we discern,
and we shall bear it with us
wherever our desires and wounds take us.

We shall allow it to raise walls
between our longing and the moon.
our anguish and the cooling stream,
our eyes and our sight.

Translated from the Arabic by Husain Haddawy.

Al-Mutanabbi Street

Raya Asee

I couldn't be bothered to get out of bed—not because I'm lazy. I just didn't feel like going to work. I'm bored of going out and I'm afraid that every time I do, I'll hear that we've lost someone else. I'm beginning to hate hearing the news from my colleagues, from drivers and guards ... someone was killed, another lost his hand in an explosion ... news of nothing but death and destruction.

I missed the car that would take me into work that day—I told them I'd be coming in late. I decided to have a cup of coffee and chat with my mother. I took my first sip from the huge mug my brother gave me because he knows how much I like coffee. My mother started talking about how beautiful the weather was and that made me melancholic. For me, good weather is an invitation to walk around Baghdad's neighbour-hoods talking with my friends—to stroll down Abu Nawas Street by the Tigris, or al-Mutanabbi or al-Rasheed Street.

I drank my coffee in a hurry and smoked a cigarette that I didn't enjoy because all I was exhaling was pain and frustration.

I walked to work, thinking I'd fulfil some of my dream ... A few hours after I got in, a colleague ran into my office: "They've assassinated al-Mutanabbi."

What did he mean? The poet al-Mutanabbi had died centuries ago—who was he now? He said there had been an explosion on al-Mutanabbi Street. I screamed. "Has Hulago (the Mongol leader who sacked the city in 1258) come back? Will the river turn the colour of ink again—like it did when they threw all our books and all the treasures of our history in the water!?"

Two days later I went with my friends to al-Mutanabbi Street to mourn another monument's collapse while we sit impotent with our hands tied, voices silenced, and our will defeated by the weapons of war. They are changing our days into a painful illusion and an agony is eating away at our insides.

I crossed al Shuhada Bridge, looking at the sad Tigris, who started wearing her mourning clothes years ago when Abu Nawas Street was taken over by armed militias—this street that was named after a famous poet known for his love of life. And the river also mourns the ancient Mustansiriya school, which has been abandoned by its researchers, its visitors and all the lovers of Baghdad.

I walk through al-Mutanabbi Street looking for Abu Hossam and his bookshop, looking for the Shabandar Cafe and all its clients, looking for Adnan and all his customers—he was always proud that he had all the latest publications. Ash. Everywhere.

Alas, al-Mutanabbi, you and your sword.

You were proud of your sword, and of your nights and now they are breaking your mighty pen and quills—they are cutting out our tongues with a sharp sword and our nights are pitch black.

I search for the face of the one I'm missing. Muqqdad al-Naqash walks by and says they've assassinated history and knowledge, this time, not just people. He says "here comes Hulago again to erase the history of a people and the story of a civilization." I stand in the ruins of the Shabandar, the only remaining literary café in Baghdad. I am dazzled by the ash and blackness. Where did all the poets, writers, journalists, retired people, liberals, Communists and even Ba'athists go? Where are all the old photographs of Baghdad in the '20s and '40s that used to line the walls?

During sanctions, this street was our survival. Researchers, poets, writers, intellectuals of all kinds, had to sell their only treasures, their books, on the pavements here, to feed their children. When the statue fell, we rushed here to see if we could replace flimsy photocopies of books that we'd been forced to make with proper bound volumes. I watch people's feet and I remembered how my own feet grew year after year as I walked down this street. What an illusion to think that my son would also be able to grow up here. We stand mourning the ashes of the books, the destruction of the street and the bodies of our sons, which we can't even find. We didn't kiss them goodbye—they are not buried in the ground, but between the ashes of our books and our dreams—dreams that one day our country will be well again.

An excerpt from this essay was printed as a broadside by Celeste Smeland for the Al-Mutanabbi Street Broadside Project.

Attention

Saadi Youssef

Those who come by passing,
I will remember them,
and those who come heavy & overbearing,
I will forget.

This is why
when air gushes between mountains
we describe the wind
and forget the rocks.

Amman, July 8, 1993

Translated from the Arabic by Khaled Mattawa.

This poem was printed as a broadside by Suzanne Vilmain for the Al-Mutanabbi Street Broadside Project.

Destinies

Gazar Hantoosh

The retired man
The brown crane-like boy
The woman with the blue shawl
And the poet with the diamond heart
Are waiting for the red bus
That will take them.
The retired man to:
Café "Hasan Ajmi"*
The brown crane-like boy
To the boy scout center
The woman in the blue shawl:
To al-Mansoor†
And the poet with the diamond heart
To Hell

Translated from the Arabic by Saadi Simawe.

---

*   A traditional café in Baghdad.
†   An upscale quarter in Baghdad.

This poem was printed as a broadside by Felicia Rice for the Al-Mutanabbi Street Broadside Project.

A Book of Remedies

Mark Abley

In Montreal, where I make my home, al-Mutanabbi Street surely is not this: a road that slithers along the mountain's southern slope past a reservoir, a football stadium, and a hospital that took its name from an English queen. But just off Pine Avenue stands the medical building of McGill University and if you pass through its doors and climb to the third floor, you find a library devoted to the history of medicine. Thousands of leather-bound diseases and diagnoses hide its walls. Instinctively, you shrink your voice to a whisper. In an inner sanctum of this library, I've pored over an illuminated manuscript known as *A Book of Simple Remedies*.

That's an English translation of its title, *Kitab al-adwiya al-mufrada*. The author, Ahmad Ibn Muhammad al-Ghafiqi, worked in Cordoba during the glory years of Arab civilization in Spain. A botanist with a vast acquaintance of Iberian plants, he was also a pharmacist adept at herbal medicine. His manuscript is a herbal encyclopedia. Al-Ghafiqi understood the virtuous powers of nutmeg, of juniper, of jasmine. "In our country," he observed, "hunters put rosemary in the interior of venison to prevent its rapid putrefaction."

And today? If I turn to a medical website, I read that "Dried marigold has been used for many years to treat a variety of skin problems. Research has in fact identified several essential oils in the marigold compound that help relieve inflammation as well as fight bacterial and viral infections." Nearly nine centuries ago, al-Ghafiqi was using marigolds to treat scrofula. He prescribed a medicine made from the flower to help sterile women and impotent men—and to induce abortions.

He lived in the twelfth century, by our system of reckoning, in the midst of a proud Arabic-speaking culture that was reasonably tolerant of minorities. Already it had introduced papermaking to Europe. It was starting to exert an acute influence on Western medicine and mathematics, physics and astronomy. It had also salvaged knowledge from Europe's past, knowledge that otherwise would have been lost—some

Greco-Roman texts survive only in Arabic translation. Cordoba was one of the intellectual centers of this culture. Few cities anywhere had more inhabitants, more aspirations.

One of them was Baghdad. The caliphate who ruled Baghdad from the eighth century onwards had designed and built what they called a House of Wisdom—a complex that included a public library, a translation bureau and an astronomical observatory. In such an atmosphere, arts and sciences flourished alike. According to the Harvard scholar Andras Riedlmayer, by al-Ghafiqi's time, Baghdad had become "a crucible of learning and the production and transmission of knowledge, the center of a literary world that extended from Samarkand to Cordoba." Did al-Mutanabbi Street already exist, curling down towards the Tigris? If so, it may have been on this street, or somewhere near it, that during the century after al-Ghafiqi's death, an artist whose name is lost to history copied the text of the herbal and decorated it with hundreds of colored drawings. The manuscript I saw in Montreal was created in Baghdad.

That anonymous illustrator knew what he was up to. His poppies, cyclamens, eggplants, and other vegetation as well as a few animals stretch and twine beside al-Ghafiqi's remedies with astonishing vividness. The artist was working on thick Oriental paper of a finely woven texture. There are other manuscripts of *Kitab al-adwiya al-mufrada*, and the Montreal book is not complete. Even so, it ranks among the finest editions of al-Ghafiqi: a volume that was meant to last.

And so it did. It escaped the demolition of Baghdad in 1258, when a Mongol army flooded the city's canals and massacred hundreds of thousands of its citizens. I wonder what kind of passion drove the invaders to ransack hospitals, mosques and libraries, the House of Wisdom included. I wonder what pleasure they took in destruction. To claim, as some did, that the Tigris ran black with ink from February until August must have been a wild exaggeration. But it suggests the felt extent of the loss.

What happened to the herbal with its practical remedies, its elegant calligraphy, its lucid drawings? How did it resist a death by fire or water? Before Baghdad turned to dust, the manuscript had probably traveled East into Persia. An oval seal shows that it was being kept there in what we call the seventeenth century. Eventually, it was offered for private sale in Tehran and bought by Sir William Osler, the Regius Professor of Medicine at Oxford University. Osler was an avid collector of medical books and an admirer of Islam. Some years after his death in 1919, most of his library was shipped across the Atlantic to McGill, the university where he had studied and first taught.

Thanks to Osler, the herbal is safe now. Or so we imagine. It spends its nights and days in a climate-controlled vault. It endures in posterity's cool grip. To see the book, you have to provide identification, win a librarian's approval, fill out a form, slip on a pair of white gloves, and step into a private room. Tapping a pencil, the only writing instrument you are permitted, you wait until the manuscript is brought to you. It would not have enjoyed such privilege, such security, in the Baghdad of 1258, or 2003, or March 2007. In a climate of terror, books are dangerous.

The price of privilege is that al-Ghafiqi's remedies and the artist's drawings exist outside the Arab realm that gave them birth and meaning. The book has become merely a precious object; it is divorced from danger. I look through its catalogue of treatments, and without an interpreter I am lost.

As are we all. What ails the Arab realm, and ours, has no simple remedy. No flower on this planet can defuse a car bomb or disarm an invading horde. Against the malignancies of history, I can offer nothing but the image of a book, a work of healing, a book that has survived.

On the Booksellers' Street of Baghdad

Majid Naficy

I saw al-Mutanabbi returning from Persia
He had heard the sound of the Tigris, by the Kor River
Calling him back to Baghdad.
On his way, he had given his sword
To the Qarmati rebels in Gonaveh
Because he knew that from then on
He would have no friend but the pen. He had told himself,
"I, al-Mutanabbi, poet, prophet and swordsman
Moved into the desert from Kufa
With the bedouins of the Qarmati revolt
Looking for the secret of brotherhood.
I went to Aleppo with Prince Sayf of Hamdan
To stand against the Frank crusaders
And traveled to Persia with King Azod of Daylaman
To spread the seed of Arabic poetry.
Now I want to return to Iraq
Only to look from the bridge of Baghdad
At the fishermen in their nutshell boats
Who are gently rowing on the Tigris River.
I want to see the gnostic Mandaeans in their white towels
Making ablution in the shallow waters
While looking at the North star,
And from the diners on Abu-Nuwas St.
I want to buy lentil soup and Mazgoof fish
Barbecued on pomegranate sticks. How happy it is to walk around
Near the reeds by the river
And watch the kisses of a young couple
From behind a palm tree
How happy it is to sit by the old harpist
And listen to the story of the Tigris River
Rushing from Mountains to the Persian Gulf,
How happy it is going to the Turkish bath
Before muezzin calls to prayer
And surrender one's body to the caressing fingers,
Cotton washcloth and bubbling soap and when taking dry towels
Ask the receptionist for a glass of ice water
Then in a happy mood
Going to the House of Wisdom

And seeing the dazzles of joy
In the eyes of the youth."
al-Mutanabbi told himself,
"I am becoming a child again
Enchanted with playing words."
Looking down from the bridge of Baghdad
Al-Mutanabbi saw nothing but blood
Running constantly in the Tigris River.
Fishermen were hunting the dead
Farmers planting human bones
Mothers giving birth to headless babies
Behind bushes and sand domes
The beheaded running in the shallow waters
And the water-sellers shouted in the alleys:
"Fresh blood! fresh blood!"
On the booksellers' Row, a red fog
Had covered the sky and the earth
Muhammad, the binder, was looking in the ruins
For the cut-off head of his brother
Father of Hussein, the hummus-pedlar,
Was talking to one of his son's shoes
Shatri, the book-seller, was shedding tears
Running behind the half-burnt leaves of poetry
In the alleys on the east-side of the Tigris River
He was humming one of al-Mutanabbi's couplets,
"Even the blind can see the letters, and the deaf hear the sound
of my poetry."
Al-Mutanabbi stood
His robe clung to his skin
And his headdress was wet with blood.
He asked himself,
"People or Books?
Books or people?"
Should he put down the pen
And take the sword again?
The Tigris did not answer
It was running fast
Like an arrow shot from a bow.

March 19, 2007

Crossroads

Lewis Buzbee

For centuries, the booksellers had been carrying their wares from house to house and town to town. It had been a successful enterprise; no matter where they traveled, readers purchased their medical tracts, spiritual guidebooks, ribald romance, almanacs. But the booksellers had grown weary of the six-foot shelves strapped to their backs, the gaudy red flags waving high above their heads.

There was simply too much to carry any longer; the number and kind of books was staggering—poetry, mathematics, astronomy, atlases of fabled lands. The more readers in the world, the more books. How could they carry entire libraries?

So they stopped at a place where two roads crossed, and set down their books, unfurled an age-worn rug, and opened shop. The readers would come to them now.

Readers tramped East and West, North and South on these roads, each reader on a unique voyage. And because the voyage is long and exhausting, the readers stopped at the booksellers and purchased those volumes that offered entertainment and information and solace, books that eased the shock and numb of travel.

The booksellers soon discovered that these readers, intent on their voyages, also required paper and pen, and some required scribes as well. So the booksellers began to write missives for the readers—letters of longing and hope, news of fortune and disaster, complaints, love letters, contracts, requests for aid. They wrote for those who could not.

The crossroads served the booksellers well. Books were copied, written, sold; missives composed and inscribed. Over the years, more rugs were added, and then tables to display the books more easily. Soon, the tables became counters, across which money was exchanged for nothing more than books. And from these counters, walls rose, and soon, the booksellers could lock up their stock at night, sleeping in rooms above the shop. The rug had become a building, and inside it was everything that the readers wanted, needed, dreamed of—all in the shape of books.

The readers who traveled East to West and West to East, they brought new books from far away, and those they purchased from the booksellers at the crossroads, these books traveled to far away corners of the world. And the readers who traveled North to South and South to North, they bought and sold books, too. The world—so the booksellers imagined—was now a web of books.

Other merchants saw the booksellers' success in the streams of readers that tramped by every day. These merchants unfurled rugs and added tables and counters, and new buildings grew up, and soon there was a market at the crossroads—food, clothing, any supplies the voyagers might require. And around the market, a town grew up, and around the town, a city. And the booksellers knew that they had helped create the market and the town and the city. For in order to build such things, one has to imagine them first, and books, from all over the world, sold and traded freely, stirred grand imaginings in the people who settled the crossroads.

While the bookstore was no longer the distinguishing feature of the crossroads, it was yet central to it.

In the market, as the centuries crawled by, the booksellers saw the flags of the city's rulers flown from the top of the city's magnificent buildings. But as the centuries sped by, those flags changed, it seemed, with each new gust of wind. The temples of the city changed, too, and the fashions worn there, and modes of transport, and even the food and drink of the city, all changed around the booksellers. But the booksellers stayed on, as required by both the conquerors and the conquered; both faces of conflict need fresh words to discover what comes after victory and what comes after defeat. So the booksellers stayed, indulging in their simple and unremarkable art, while the city changed around them, time and time again.

How many thousands of years? How many catastrophes? How many tides swept through the city? And still the booksellers remained, insisted upon by the readers.

Then came one awful day, the most horrible of all days in the market. The explosion ripped apart the market, turned it inside out, brought chaos out of quiet, and because the booksellers were at the heart of the market, they were the most harmed. Many were lost that day, and the sky rained pages and the ashes of pages. Fragments of words fell quietly to earth. It seemed, for a moment, as if even language had lost all meaning, words now nothing but wreckage. The market had a black hole in it, where the booksellers had been; the city had a black hole; the world had a black hole.

But the booksellers had been at this crossroads for too many years, years beyond counting, and there were now too many of them for the bombs to destroy them all. They salvaged what scorched books they could, and began the laborious, tedious, and essential task of creating and gathering more books and still more books. Soon the booksellers had enough books to begin again, not many more, mind you, than they had had when they first settled the crossroads.

They diligently swept the soot and blood from the street where the bookstore had been, and without much ceremony, they unfurled another rug, another age-worn rug, and set out what books there were, and sold them, as they always had.

The readers came that first day, and every day after, and they bought the books, and at night, in a city torn by eternal war, they read the books—one reader for each book—and the readers came to believe that their reading might be the only way to heal the black hole in the world's heart.

Untitled

Ibn al-Utri

Who invaded you, Baghdad?

Weren't you once as dear to me as my eye?
Wasn't there a time when people lived
within you, when being neighbors was
            a blessing?

                        Then
            the crow came

and   divided them.

                        How much
                        grief can you endure?

From a poem by Ibn al-Utri on the destruction of Baghdad in the early ninth century. Recited by bookseller Naim al-Satri on September 14, 2007, as a curfew was lifted on al-Mutanabbi Street in Baghdad, six months after a car bombing that devastated the historic book market. The arrangement of these lines is taken from a broadside printed by Bonnie Bernstein at Woods Creek Press as part of the Al-Mutanabbi Street Broadside Project.

Thanks also to Damien Cave of the New York Times.

Remembering al-Mutanabbi

Thomas Christensen

Some day we'll stop making the goddam funeral pyres and jumping into the middle of them. We pick up a few more people that remember, every generation. —*Fahrenheit 451*

As the fifteenth century was drawing to a close, William Caxton, England's first printer, traveled to the Flemish city of Bruges. Today the city, with its late medieval architecture and meandering cobbled streets, seems a museum piece, but then it was a lively trading center where Italians, Germans, Spaniards, and others met and exchanged goods—and ideas. Arts and culture flourished, and new technology was everywhere. Visitors were assured of eating well thanks to the invention of drift nets, which resulted in an abundance of seafood. Followers of Jan van Eyck and Hans Memling were filling the city with paintings in a medium new to Northern Europe, oils. And the printing press with movable type—the machine on which Johannes Gutenberg had printed his forty-two-line Bible a couple of decades before—was changing the intellectual life of the city. (Printing on movable metal type was well established in Korea, and information about it could have traveled through the vast Mongol empire to West Asia, and from there to Europe.)

There in Bruges, at a table overlooking a foggy canal, over a meal of mussels and beer, Caxton would discuss the new printed texts with scholars and artists who were arriving from all across Europe. Among those joining him would have been Colard Mansion, a Flemish scribe who printed the first book using copper engravings, as well as the first books in English and French. Also at the table would have been Anthony Woodville, the second Earl Rivers, an English Francophile and translator. Woodville had recently completed a translation of a French text called *Les Dits Moraulx des Philosophes*. The book was a compendium of the wisdom of ancient philosophers. Would Caxton have a look at it?

The English printer set about editing and proofreading the translation. In Bruges, working with Mansion, he mastered the art of printing, and when he returned to England he established a press there, and made *Dictes and Sayings of the Philosophers* the first dated book printed in England.

And so, the seed of free speech that was planted by followers of Muhammad found fruit at the very inception of bookmaking in England—for the French version of *Dictes and Sayings of the Philosophers* was itself a translation from Latin. It, in turn, was a translation of an Arabic text, *Muhtar al hikamwamahasin al kalim*, written in the eleventh century by Abul Wafa Mubasshir ibn Fatik, an Egyptian emir.

The Islamic world was then and remains today one of the great centers of book production. Arabic calligraphy lends itself to textual decoration, and demand for glorious Qur'ans spurred book arts to unprecedented heights. But another factor was equally important in the flourishing of Islamic bookmaking—its tradition of freedom of speech.

Omar, the second caliph, whose caliphate began just two years after the death of Muhammad himself in the seventh century, declared that the weak must be allowed to "express themselves freely and without fear." Subsequent caliphs expanded on Omar's notion, and established a system of *madrasahs*, or educational centers, in part to encourage such expression. This system became the explicit model for the concept of academic freedom in European universities.

But freedom of expression is never an easy sell—shifting shape like a djinn. It all too readily assumes the attitude of "You are free to express your agreement with my beliefs." In the mid-seventh century, Omar's successor, the third caliph, Othman, established an authoritative Quran through the simple expedient of burning competing editions. In the eleventh century, while Abul Wafa Mubasshir ibn Fatik was writing the text that would journey through Latin and French to become the first dated book printed in England, Turkish forces were busy demolishing the Royal Library of the Samanid dynasty in Persia (which contained one of the earliest Qurans and other rare books). Two centuries later, the waters of the Tigris were said to flow black for six months from the ink of books when the Mongols destroyed the House of Wisdom in Baghdad. And in an echo of that event Iraq's national library was burnt following the U.S. invasion in 2003.

In Europe, Jewish and Islamic literature was being destroyed in Spain even as Caxton was publishing *Dictes and Sayings of the Philosophers*. Later, the nineteenth-century Romantic poet Heinrich Heine would reflect on the Spanish auto-da-fe, saying: "Where they burn books, they will also, in the end, burn humans." That observation is recorded on a memorial at the concentration camp at Dachau so that we will not forget the Nazi book burnings of the 1930s and 1940s (20,000 books were burnt in a single public spectacle in 1933), nor the Holocaust that followed. Such memorials are important, for tyranny hates memory.

And so al-Mutanabbi Street starts here—it starts wherever books are made, exchanged, and shared. It starts when we remember the bomb that destroyed part of Baghdad's historic booksellers row, killing more than thirty people and injuring many more. The intent of the bomber was to prevent the free discussion that books attract. And, to a degree, he was successful. But so long as we do not forget to remember, he will not, in the end, prevail.

Al-Mutanabbi Street is named for Abou-t-Tayyib Ahmad ibn al-Husayn al-Mutanabbi (915–965), one of the great poets of the Arabic language. But al-Mutanabbi is also renowned for an extraordinary feat of memory—he is said to have memorized the contents of a thirty-folio book in a single reading. Tyrants and bigots like emperor Qin Shihuang of China's Qin dynasty who burnt most of the country's ancient literature (and buried many of its scholars alive), or the priest Diego de Landa who destroyed the entire written literature of the Maya people with the exception of four codices, seek to erase cultural memory in order to bask in the eternal sunshine of the cleansed cultural mind. For them, books are a target, because they represent and enable remembering.

Consider the case of Afghanistan's Taliban, who tried hard to enforce forgetting throughout that unfortunate country. In an effort to erase all trace of the region's pre-Muslim past, they blasted into bits the monumental Buddhas of Bamiyan, and they smashed artworks and destroyed books wherever they could find them. They destroyed the National Museum in Kabul and smashed most of its artworks.

But even as they did their worst the museum's staff found a way to hide many prize items, and over the years of Taliban rule they refused to divulge their hiding place despite intense persecution. Years after the museum had been destroyed, when the Taliban had been driven from power, those artworks were brought forth from their hiding place. The museum itself was rebuilt. The art objects went on a world tour to demonstrate that Afghanistan's cultural heritage had survived.

Today, in bold Arabic script on a banner above the museum's entrance, a new motto is written: "A nation stays alive when its culture stays alive." Through his act of remembering, al-Mutanabbi helped to keep his culture alive. By remembering the poet, al-Mutanabbi Street did the same. And by remembering al-Mutanabbi Street, we keep alive the seeds of freedom.

On Ashurbanipal's Library

Amy Gerstler

You cannot unsing these songs

You cannot unsay these prayers

the rainsoaked
firebaked
windriven
record
of us

…Sometimes a scribe had no choice but to write "BREAK" on a new
copy of his clay tablet where the brittle original he was copying from
had simply crumbled away.

CONTENTS OF THE LIBRARY INCLUDE:
　　　—remedies for nosebleeds, using crushed seeds and cedar resin
　　　—queries to the sun god about peace treaties and giving a
princess in marriage

Say: Knowledge is light.
Say: Knowledge is better than wealth.
Say: One of the world's oldest known libraries, discovered in Northern
Iraq, was located near what is today the city of Mosul.

　　　—and instructions for the wearing of a necklace of protective
stones

clay letters
in clay envelopes
they cracked open
like almonds
to get at the message—

　　　—and a sick man's prayer to be spared death
　　　—and a celebratory blessing for the writer's city (including
requests for abundant beer!)
　　　—and recipes for making glass and perfume

"Take and read out from the lapis lazuli tablet
how Gilgamesh went through every hardship."

      —and instructions for a ritual to prevent bad dreams
      —and laments to be repeated by priests, accompanied by kettle
drum

25,000 or 28,000 clay tablets (depending on what source you consult)
comprising the world's first catalogued library, unearthed in present day
Mosul, were then kidnapped to Britain.

      —An incantation to cure epilepsy,
plus a description of rites
to be performed
such as hanging a mouse
and thorn bush sprigs
over the patient's
doorway.

"Writing is the mother of eloquence, the father of artists."
–Babylonian proverb from the Library of Ashurbanipal

      —and lists of birth omens
      —and catalogs of celestial phenomena
      —and reports on animal sacrifice and the reading
of sheep's entrails for divination

Protective inscription
inside King Ashurbanipal's library:
"May all the gods curse anyone
who breaks, defaces, or removes
this tablet with a curse that cannot
be relieved, terrible and merciless
as long as he lives, may they
let his name, his seed be carried
off from the land, and may they
put his flesh in a dog's mouth."

—and a "tablet of destinies"
—and lists of temples
—and a desperate letter beginning "Half My Kingdom to the Man Who Cures My Child!"
—and an elegy for a woman who

(REST DESTROYED)

III. GATHERING THE SILENCES

In the Valley of Love

Genny Lim

For Farid ud-Din Attar

Give me a thousand hearts
That I may sacrifice one for each moment
Open the door to each heart that
The Light of love may enter
Burn away the senses
For the truth of pleasure lies
In the truth of loss
Love itself is the flame
From which the self is wrought

This poem was printed as a broadside by Amanda Matzenbach for the Al-Mutanabbi Street Broadside Project.

Night in Hamdan

Saadi Youssef

We in Hamdan say:
Sleep when the date palms sleep.
When the stars rise over Hamdan
the lights of the huts are put out,
the mosque and the old house.
It is the long sleep
under the whispers of faded palm fronds:
the long death.
This is Hamdan …
              tuberculosis and date palms.
In Hamdan we hear only what we say,
our night, the date palms, esparto grass,
and the old river
where lemon leaves on the water drift.
They are green like water
like your eyes, I say.
You, in whose eyes I behold spring,
how can a friend forget you?
I will meet you
when the setting of the stars covers Hamdan
when night bears down on the city.

....

....

Together we will roam the depths of Baghdad
when the setting of the stars covers Hamdan.

Basra, 1955

Translated from the Arabic by Khaled Mattawa.

This poem was printed as a broadside by Lisa Beth Robinson for the Al-Mutanabbi Street Broadside Project.

Burning

Judith Lyn Sutton

Mute, I escaped to books beaming from our refuge
Under the sun—a place bursting with color alight
To console us every Friday free from responsibility
And help us forget destruction aflame in our land.
Nearby, friends reveled in the scent of pages turning
As did I, cocooned, though edged by streets where
Bombs ruled. Still, on this loved lane, peace reigned;
But that bright morning, dark agents blew it to pieces.
I, wounded, lit candles for comrades buried in ash.

Luis and Celso on al-Mutanabbi Street

Josh Kun

Here in Tijuana, al-Mutanabbi Street starts where the bodies go missing, where there are no records of the stolen ones. It starts on the bedroom nightstand of the Chief of Police, where his copy of the book *Transnational Crime and Public Security*—bedtime reading for a city under siege—is riddled with bullet holes.

Here in Tijuana, al-Mutanabbi Street can be the finger that arrived in the mail bubble-wrapped in a sealed envelope with no return address, next to the gas bill and the grocery store coupons. By then, Luis had already been gone for two months of his thirty-four years. His severed finger—they didn't even put it on ice, they just let the blood dry, the skin purple, the smell swell—was proof that he was alive, that he existed, that the rest of his body was somewhere, still warm, still beating. The finger meant they wanted more money. If he was still alive enough to lose a finger, then there was still money to be made. They took him from right in front of his house, in front of his wife, his three young children inside, in plain view in the middle of the day on his quiet street in Playas de Tijuana, a tranquil coastal neighborhood known for its remove from the chaos of downtown where the only big news of late was the opening of a Starbucks. They asked for directions and Luis walked over to the car to help out. They pulled him inside. They were not wearing masks. In the logic of kidnapping, the mask is a chance for survival; if the kidnappers cannot be identified, they might consider releasing their hostage. No mask and the release is nearly impossible. Luis must have known that, too; he knew his fate as soon as he hit the backseat. He was never coming home.

My in-laws were active in raising money. There was a breakfast, the whole family brought checks, whatever you could afford. Every dollar counted. They wanted $2 million. We gave them $100,000. We don't know when they killed Luis, if he was even alive when the money was being gathered. We do know that they drove out of town to dump his body alongside the highway to Tecate. He was picked up and brought to the city morgue as a John Doe and only weeks later did a family friend who works in forensics recognize his face in a photo search.

The memorial was wrenching. There were people everywhere. The men stood on the steps by the entrance, looking like guards or escorts, trying to look tough and proud and strong but their faces gave them away—they were outside because they couldn't bear to go in. Especially Luis's father. I had met him just a few months ago. It was my father-in-law Rogelio's birthday and we took over the concrete backyard of one of his niece's homes in Playas. There were family photos on the folding tables and balloons tied to chairs. A man with perfectly gelled hair was singing boleros and pop ballads into a portable P.A. system, a stout woman with the face of sweating stone was chopping meat and pressing corn into tortillas, and all of the nieces and aunts and grandmothers took their turn on the piñata. Candy fell. The little ones scurried. I couldn't keep my eyes off Luis's father. He's tall and thick with the muscles of hard work. He had his jeans up high, belted tight; he had his cotton long sleeve Oxford unbuttoned midway down his chest full of furry gray ringlets of hair. He kept his big arms crossed, his face unmoving, stern, serious. He crushed my hand when he shook it. His fingers were like hardened sausages, their skin rough, I imagined, from building things and fixing motors. He looked like El Indio Fernández, the guy in classic Mexican films who protects the village, who stays alive as the sun sets. One thing he wasn't though was a man who cried. So when I saw him on the stairs of the memorial hall, it rocked me to the core. The shirt was still unbuttoned, the jeans still high, but his son was dead and now his face was red and pickled; his eyes were pools of salt. It was as if his body never expected to know what it was now knowing, as if his muscles and strength had never fathomed that something as intangible and immaterial as sadness or grief or loss could break them down.

Upstairs in the chapel, deep silence was sporadically punctured by spasms of grief, anguished cries quickly muffled by the sweaters and shawls of comforting shoulders. In his prayers for Luis, the priest told us not to grieve him but to use his loss as an inspiration to keep living our lives to the fullest—plenamente, plenamente—to leave the service focused squarely on the here and now. He prayed for the family, for Luis's kids, for his poor, poor wife. And then he prayed for the city. He begged God to have mercy on Tijuana, to take its streets back into His loving arms. I put my arm around my sister-in-law and asked what she was feeling. "Sadness," she said. "And a lot of anger."

Anger is the right word. Luis was thirty-four. He had just opened a little store to sell glass for windows. Sure, he liked a new car now and again and sure, he liked to pick up the check and be all macho and valiente once in a while and sure, he liked to take his wife to Saverios and not read the prices on the wine list. But he was solidly working class gone middle class TJ and he was not a criminal or a drug dealer or a money launderer or a CEO or a corporate scion or a politician. He was taken just so he could be used to get some money for someone who had even less. He was taken because he could be taken. He was taken because he could die and it didn't matter to his killers, because his life like their lives didn't matter. This is no city, no country, no world, no time, no era to get precious and high and mighty about the precious value of human life. Our blood—all of our blood—runs cheap. We mean nothing to anyone. We are as good as we are worth—to factories, to smugglers, to bosses, to marketing companies, to kidnappers. Discardable. Dumpable. Interchangeable.

At the end of the memorial, I met an old friend of my father-in-law, El Manitas—little hands (his were anything but). "I hear you write about Tijuana up there," he said. "Did you see the letter in the paper today," he asked me. I hadn't. "It's about the kidnappings, all this horrible mess. You need to read it. Then you need to write about it. It's important for people in the United States to learn about what's happening here. It's the only way things will change."

The letter was written by Aiko Enríquez Nishikawa. Her brother Celso had suffered a fate similar to Luis. Like Luis, Celso came from a hard-working family that came to Tijuana to pursue the opportunities the city promised to offer—first during the industrialization boom of the '60s and '70s and then during the global boom of the '90s. He was a father and a husband. He was clean. He was taken, money was given, phone calls were made, threats were issued, proof of life stopped so the family stopped giving money. The kidnappers surrounded the house with cars and opened fire, ready and willing to kill anyone they could for more money, for more fear. As the father of a dead narco-junior once said, "I gave my son everything—the best home, the best car, the best family name. I now realize that I could never give him what he wanted most—power."

Aiko's family called the city police, then the federal police, then the military police. Nobody came to help.

Celso was surely dead and they had endured all that they could. So they packed up their house and like so many, left the city to live across the line in Chula Vista.

This is how she ended the letter:

> This letter represents the pain, the anguish and the anger that we feel. It's a desperate cry for an answer, an explanation, a hope, a demand of our rights, the ones we never had while living this hell that we don't

wish on anybody. More so when we couldn't get help from the people who are paid to protect and serve, combat and take care of, guard the safety of citizens. But unfortunately they are the ones who protect and help the criminals get what they want.

When are you going to take action? When are you going to clean the municipal, state and federal institutions in a real and forceful way? When will there be real laws that punish kidnappers and the bad behavior of corrupt agencies, with sentences that serve as en example so that this doesn't keep happening?

What will happen to our country with its good people? When will we stop living so cowardly and start fighting for a better future for the sons and daughters of Mexico?

I love Mexico and Tijuana, it's the place were I was born, my country. But it's impossible to live here.

Goodbye Tijuana.

For those who leave, Tijuana has become a painful blur of al-Mutanabbi Streets, a nearby but faraway place of embattled memory they've been forced to escape from. For those who stay, there are al-Mutanabbi Streets around every corner watched over by military tanks, places that keep taking their hits while they wait for a different kind of life to return.

Lullaby

Dana Teen Lomax

Al-Mutanabbi Street starts here in San Quentin
in the cell of the rote
in the fear of the written
in the blood red states
of affairs a heart or hand transgresses
and is locked away
numbered homes and names, pages in an unread book
the narrative we've all been told:
  God raises the knife to Isaac
  creates the floods
  sends Eve out on her belly
the prison in the story as we live
hiding what's unknown
or worse, claiming to know it
but sleep tight my love although in the
O of our doubt.

I Recall al-Sayyab

Mahmoud Darwish

I recall al-Sayyab, screaming at the Gulf in vain:
"Iraq, Iraq, nothing but Iraq..."
and only echo replies.
I recall al-Sayyab: In this Sumerian space
a female overcame nebula's sterility
and bequeathed us land and exile together.
I recall al-Sayyab... Poetry is born in Iraq,
be an Iraqi to become a poet, my friend!
I recall al-Sayyab, he didn't find life
as he imagined between the Tigris and the Euphrates,
but didn't think like Gilgamesh of immortality herbs,
and didn't think of the judgment day that follows...
I recall al-Sayyab, taking from Hammurabi
the tablets to cover his loins,
then walking toward his tomb, a Sufi.
I recall al-Sayyab, when I am stricken with fever
and I hallucinate: My brothers were preparing dinner
for Hulagu's army, they were only servants... my brothers!
I recall al-Sayyab, we didn't dream of what
bees don't deserve of sustenance. And we didn't dream
of more than two handshakes that greet our absence.
I recall al-Sayyab. Dead blacksmiths rise
from the graves and forge our chains.
I recall al-Sayyab. Poetry is the twins, experience
and exile. And we didn't dream of more than
a life like life, and that we die in our own style
"Iraq,
Iraq,
Nothing but Iraq..."

Translated from the Arabic by Fady Joudah.

Country of Large Rivers

Etel Adnan

Yes, a country with two large rivers tumbling down
from mythic mountains
the water rises and runs from under cold skies
down to territories still owned by the gods
the sun, in its full anger, asserts its authority
by drinking the waters and starving the land

lone palm trees mark ancient boundaries which
vanquished all invading armies

the Gulf's ebbing tides regularly uncover tablets on
which is written the world's beginning

This is Iraq as you all know
take a deep breath
those of you who brought destruction to it shall
answer to the Last Judgment
if not God's, then mankind's
we're used to the alternating of water and fire

so we will come back with brighter flowers
spring after spring

and on a single page we will repeat
forty and one times
al-Mutanabbi Street's name.

The Murderer

Bushra al-Bustani

A man is left lying on the roadside.
No one dares approach him.
His face is turned towards the sky.
On his chest a flower.
From a distance, his wife weeps, and repeats:
"The American killed him because he said:
Iraq is my home."

***

A boy lies on the roadside.
No one dares approach him.
A red thread spurts from his chest.
His arms lie sleeping on his books and school bag.
From a distance his mother weeps and repeats:
"The American aimed at the Iraqi flag on his arm."

***

A girl is left on the roadside.
No one dares approach her.
A branch of roses braids her hair.
Her dress is white as her young heart.
From a distance, her lover weeps and repeats:
"The American shot her for she loved freedom."

***

The poet is left lying on the roadside.
No one dares approach him.
His pen is warm and his heart bleeds a green stream.
From a distance, the woman poet weeps, and repeats:
"The American killed him because he said to me:
'I love you.'"

***

The Professor lies on the roadside.
No one dares approach her.
Her lecture planted questions in students' eyes and persistence in their souls.
The American killed her because she said to him:
"You won't replace our bread with your McDonald's,
Nor our knowledge with your post-modernism."

***

The journalist lies on the roadside.
No one approaches her.
Her blood soaks through the columns.
In her bag is her last essay on intimacy.
From a distance, another journalist weeps as he repeats:
"The American killed her because she exposed the truth of their new democracy."

***

The doctor is left on the roadside.
No one dares approach her.
Her blue shirt bleeds.
From a distance, the patients weep and repeat:
"The American killed her because she loved us
and sang us the song of recovery."

***

The artist is left on the roadside.
No one dares approach him.
The sketches for his paintings are unfinished.
His fingers bleed motley colors.
From a distance, an artist weeps as she repeats:
"The American killed him because he drew the Tigris and Euphrates
flowing together with a forest between them."

Translated from the Arabic by Wafaa Abdulaali.

GHAZAL: Dar al-Harb

Marilyn Hacker

I might wish, like any citizen to celebrate my country
but millions have reason to fear and hate my country.

I might wish to write, like Virginia: as a woman, I have none,
but women and men are crushed beneath its weight: my country.

As English is my only mother tongue,
it's in English I must excoriate my country.

The good ideas of Marx or Benjamin Franklin
don't excuse the gulags, or vindicate my country.

Who trained the interrogators, bought the bulldozers?
—the paper trails all indicate my country.

It used to be enough to cross an ocean
and view, as a bemused expatriate, my country.

The June blue sky, the river's inviting meanders:
then a letter, a headline make me contemplate my country.

Is my only choice the stupid lies of empire
or the sophistry of apartheid: my country?

Walter Benjamin died in despair of a visa
permitting him to integrate my country.

Exiles, at least, have clarity of purpose:
can say my town, my mother and my fate, my country.

There used to be a face that looked like home,
my interlocutor or my mate, my country.

Plan your resistance, friends, I'll join you in the street,
but watch your backs: don't underestimate my country.

Where will justice and peace get the forged passports
it seems they'll need to infiltrate my country?

Eggplant and peppers, shallots, garlic and cumin:
let them be, married on my plate, my country.

A Home on al-Mutanabbi Street

Richard Harrison

I am a word. I am a word in Arabic, in English, and in Farsi. I am a word in Kurdish and German and Hebrew and French. I am a word in the mouths of prophets and hawkers. I will get you tea. I will bring you joy and to tears. I am a word in a book. I lie open to the sun that reads me over the shoulder of someone looking to buy. I am the imagination of the enemy come home to its enemy's understanding because the leap from enemy to friend is as swift and sure as the journey from paper to eye. I am loved. I am reviled. I am feared. I am myself and I am you. When the book opens, you can hear me sigh in pleasure at the touch of your mind. When the bombs go off, I am scattered from all that I have known, and the wind and ashes take me. You might think I disappear, but I do not. The fires die down, my place in the house, on the street, in the rebuilt cafés remains. I am memory and the stuff of memory. I survive the past because I am always the present. I survive death because I am the future. I survive hatred because I am love. Build me a home, and I will return and be heard. And when you see me filling the page again, you will know I never abandoned you.

This poem was printed as a broadside by Trisia Eddy for the Al-Mutanabbi Street Broadside Project.

Proof of Kindness

Fady Joudah

Taxi driver drives through Main his plates are legitimate
A father and son in the shadow of snipers

To pray surrounded by guards to pray to the guards or
To the invisible god in the guards or the one surrounding the guards

Among the rubble I send them
Caterpillars that eat their mothers and taxed pronouns

Does your house have a gardener, how long around the wall?
Our age is a checkpoint

We grieve like palm trees by the river
Dance like palm trees by the river
We reach the pigeon coop check on the pigeons the pigeons fly

We find a stray puppy, son calls to the puppy in his enemy's tongue
Taxi exits Broadway

Son poses like a kid in the shadow of snipers

Hearing of Alia Muhammed Baker's Stroke

Philip Metres

How a Basra librarian
could haul the books each night,
load by load, into her car,

the war ticking like a clock
about to wake. Her small house
swimming in them. How, the British

now crossing the limits
of Basra, the neighbors struck
a chain to pass the bags of books

over the wall, into a restaurant,
until she could bring them all,
like sandbags, into her home,

some thirty thousand of them,
before the library, and her brain,
could finally flood into flame.

Prayer for the Living

Hayan Charara

Go to the mother,
to the father, to the house
where no trees grow,

to the bedroom, the door
closed, to her fear
and to his fear,

and their shame, their
longing, and to their bodies,
their bodies young,

their bodies separate,
their bodies together.
How far must you

go back? Her womb.
Her child body
and his child body.

Go to their first hairs.
To their flesh,
their chests, arms, faces,

their buttocks and stomachs.
There, a wrinkle. There,
color, nipples, and bellybuttons.

Go to the eyes,
see what she sees
and what he sees.

To the fingertips,
which want what
the eyes have made

their own.
Go to want, to love,
to what wants

more than love.
Go to sins.
What are your sins?

Go to where the mother
is not mother,
the father is not father,

and kiss her lips,
and kiss his mouth.
Do not be ashamed

or afraid.
The past is a strange land.
Go because

you can. Go
because you can
come back.

Interpenetrate

Annie Finch

Like the bleached fibers and their haunted ink,
interpenetrate each others' solitudes,

not penetrating, not dissolving; stay
rolled with the single patterns of the days,

linking through pages to burn with speaking lace
and thread to bodies, evenly alive.

The Contract

Kazim Ali

When sleep screamed your name into the angry silence
     you hardly stirred.

You turned back instead to the round-edged mountain—
     round because once it lay knee deep in water—

and swam down to the basilica nestled in the trenches
     of the ocean floor.

I am here to quote you decades of shame's rosary
     and turn in your hands the length of silence,

the other lifetimes you didn't speak. Your silent decade
     sent you an urgent request—you did not respond.

When the blue sent your name cannoning to the surface,
     you let it go and descended further instead into

the sediments of city. There at a mosaic uncovered beneath
     the cruciform floor you contracted yourself to me;

promised yourself a lifetime in which to decide to speak,
     and then praying your breath would last you

to the surface, swam madly up to the watery sun.

Curves in the Dark

Deema K. Shehabi

There will be no creeks left
in the hills below Diablo mountain.
No blowsy almond orchards
or rust-purple grass before green;
No-one will come to us and ask:
Do you recall the struggle
of moon-veined blossoms
and the carnage of squirrels
in this thinned-out valley?
No gray-haired woman will be left
to tell a flood of warm-eyed children:
Weave those acorns back through the leaves
so they can be found by animals starved by winter.
And you thought the Iraqi moon
high above palms
would fall over our fragments,
and this live oak you placed in California earth
would give us refuge
against shadowed rustling,
but this moon is neighbor to everyone,
barefooted blade of silver
searching for a flawed heart to swell.
I touch the chill in my forehead
and wonder what it would be like to lose all my hair:
Jasmine with your knife of scent:
I hope my child never has to kneel
over my grave and weep
beneath a sleepless flesh of sky.
And you thought these weight-filled branches
would braid themselves
against the roof and root this house to earth,
but how often have we tugged
at curves in the dark
to remake our scars and slay our death?

Here the truck sounds are unhealed,
like all our comings and goings,
but what of making a home, you ask?
while across the street the bulldozer
flattens the torso of the last almond tree.
Tomorrow they will flatten Fallujah,
the newswoman says swiftly—no sign
of carnage in her eyes,
and through the stomach
of the house, my child is asking:
how many moons did we leave behind?

The Booksellers of Pansodan

Kenneth Wong

In Rangoon, Burma, the city of my childhood, al-Mutanabbi Street began on Pansodan Street. Every morning, like a nomadic settlement, a tent city sprang up around Sule Pagoda. Hastily assembled from bamboo poles and tarpaulin sheets, the cluster of bookstalls resembled a Tatar outpost along the ancient Silk Road. Some of the booksellers brought along their household gods. They had pictures of Burmese and Indian deities hanging on their inside walls (which were often the outside walls of some office buildings). After making each sale, the devout merchant, usually a sarong-clad Burmese with a satchel slung over his shoulder, would make a token offering by fanning his makeshift shrine with the bills from the buyer.

The book district couldn't be contained on Pansodan alone, so it spilled into the nearby streets, commingling with noodle stalls, sidewalk teashops, and imitation Ray-Ban and Rolex booths. Burma, like many developing third-world nations, was blessed with a thriving black market that supplied its citizens with what the government couldn't, or wouldn't. During the two decades I lived in Rangoon, I never once set foot in Sar Pe Baik Ban, or the Hall of Literature, as the government-run bookstore was called. But I went to Pansodan nearly every weekend.

The black market was also an exercise in free market, clearly at odds with the regime's quasi-Socialist model. Unlike the State-controlled commodities market, the book district wouldn't tolerate price fixing, not for Dickens, not for Kipling, not even for Shakespeare. Their works, along with those of revered Burmese writers, were bought and sold strictly based on the classic principles of supply and demand. One year, for some unknown reason, the Ministry of Education decided to put *Wuthering Heights* on the high school syllabus. Suddenly, Brontë began flying off the shelf (or off the pavement, to be precise). Then, when the Ministry withdrew Brontë's gothic epic from the reading list, an influx of *Wuthering Heights* got dumped on the booksellers. These were hard times for Heathcliff and Catherine. They found themselves at the bottom of the pile.

Its ponderous pace and flowery prose notwithstanding, Brontë's epic was a welcomed relief for the schoolchildren of Burma. Their exposure to literature consisted largely of Burmese essays and poems about pastoral life, handpicked by the Ministry. Through a series of Buddhist parables, the curriculum taught self-sacrifice and obedience. History lessons promoted nationalism and socialism (not Marx's but a version concocted by the General Ne Win, the Burmese military chief at the time).

One good piece of writing that appeared on the list was a long poem by Ananda Turiya, a twelfth-century courtier and minister. Unjustly accused of treason and condemned to die, he composed a long poem expressing his forgiveness for the King in his final hours. It made me wonder if the minister's swan song was deliberately chosen to discourage the would-be dissidents and to promote tolerance of the government's failings.

In monsoon, when the streets were flooded, the bookselling herd relocated, migrating to the dry spots beneath the colonnades and porticos of the buildings nearby. Thus, the stalwart colonial architectures that housed the Burmese bureaucrats and civil servants also gave shelter to those peddling Orwell, O. Henry, and Somerset Maugham. Alongside these canonized classics, one could also find copies of Ian Fleming, Robert Ludlum, and Sidney Sheldon. Also in the mix were titles by Mya Than Tint, a well-known Burmese writer. Sometimes, his autobiographical masterpiece *Dar Taung Ko Kyaw Ywe Mee Pinle Ko Phyat Mi* (I'll Cross the Mountain of Swords and the Sea of Fire) and his translations of *War and Peace* and *Gone with the Wind* could be found next to one another.

In the heart of this open market, where civil servants browsing for books during their lunch break and the housewives on their way to the market must negotiate the tight corners, where both were subjected to whiffs of fresh papayas, fish broth, and exposed sewers, literary hierarchy couldn't possibly exist. On Pansodan, pulp and poetry shared space on the same sidewalk. It was, for better or worse, a democratic literary setup, where Steinbeck, Stephen King, and Danielle Steele competed on equal terms, where Burmese literary idols like Mya Than Tint rubbed shoulders with fashion magazines featuring pop idols on the cover. Here, one would rarely find propaganda, such as political pamphlets and newspapers published by the government. The booksellers didn't stock what they couldn't sell.

My love affair with Pansodan came about as a result of my occasional dalliances with the book rental places. Since most Burmese couldn't afford to buy books, nearly every neighborhood was dotted with rental places, operating out of apartments and garages. On my street, an enterprising Chinese family set up shop in their living room, converting it into a mini-library. They rented Burmese books and magazines on one side; on the other, they sold dried prunes, potato chips, and salted peanuts. (Eventually, they expanded the business to include cassette tapes. I have no doubt that, if they're still in business today, they'd be renting DVDs.)

One day, I stepped inside.

"Can I help you?" asked the pudgy proprietor in an undershirt, fanning himself furiously with a two-month-old magazine.

"I'd like to open a rental account under the name Ko Min," I said.

He took a sip of tea as he inspected the eleven-year-old boy standing before him.

"I know Ko Min," he said. "I went to school with him. You're not him."

"He's my uncle," I said. "He asked me to open an account here."

It was my ploy to avoid the required cash deposit to establish an account. It worked. I told my uncle what I did after the fact. He was happy to lend me his identify, provided he got to peruse the magazines I rented. So an agreement was struck.

My staple diet included Burmese detective novels (I later found out my favorite ones were modeled on Conan Doyle's Sherlock Holmes stories), escapist romances, and translations of Chinese martial art epics. Of these, the last captured my boyish imagination. Featuring righteous swordsmen, mysterious assassins, and femme fatales, the swashbuckling sagas were my bedside companions in my teenage years. In scope and plot construction, they rivaled Wagnerian operas, often requiring a series of ten to fifteen books to unravel. Each time I finished one installment, I rushed to the rental shop for the sequel.

"I'm returning Book Three of *The Legend of the Condor Heroes*," I told the owner. "Can I get the next one?"

"Someone borrowed it last night," he said. "Come back in three days."

At the end of Book Three, the hero had been severely wounded, left with a poisoned dart in his chest. I just needed to take a peek at the beginning pages of Book Four to find out what happened next. I wasn't about to spend three sleepless nights wondering.

The Sule Pagoda spire stood like a stake in Rangoon's throbbing heart, always encircled by frantic traffic. Temporarily forsaking their Buddhist upbringing, drivers spat out profanities as they zoomed past distracted pedestrians; the latter responded in kind as they swiftly jumped off the oncoming cars' path. I joined the mass on foot, elbowing my way towards the bookstalls.

"What are you looking for, kid?" asked one bookseller, who sold both Burmese and English materials.

"The fourth book in the Condor Heroes series," I announced. "Do you have it?"

"Here," he showed me a copy, "right off the latest batch from the printer."

Free of finger grease, the stiff copy felt like a solid weapon, like the condor hero's dagger. I opened it to the first page.

"Kid, are you going to buy it or read it?" asked the owner. Apparently, I wasn't the first one to attempt to catch up with the hero without paying the required premium.

By then, I had become distracted by something else, a paperback copy of *Casino Royale*. The silhouette of a willowy woman on the cover beckoned.

"Can you read English?" the bookseller asked.

"I can read if it's not too difficult," I told him.

"This is not a simplified Reader Digest book-of-the-month version, you know," he warned me. "It's the original."

"I have an English-Burmese dictionary at home," I replied.

Little did I know that the dictionary wouldn't be of much help in deciphering the British Intelligence lingoes and Cold War references that were an integral part of Fleming's storytelling.

"How much is it?" I asked.

"Seventy-five kyats," he said.

He didn't expect me to pay this price. He knew we'd haggle over Bond, just like my mother did over a pound of shrimp or a fishtail whenever she went to the market.

"How about twenty-five?" I made a counter offer.

"Look, this is a very good copy," he argued. "The spine is unbroken, no smudges on the pages, no stain on the cover. Make it fifty."

"I brought only forty with me," I said, pretending to walk away.

"All right, all right, forty it is," he relented.

Then, leaping over the Condor Heroes, he walked over to a corner to pay homage to his guardian. He waved my crumpled bills, what was supposed to be my entire month's allowance, before the framed picture of a smiling brown man in an orange robe and a larger-than-life Afro hairdo. That was Sai Baba, an Indian guru who, despite having never gone to Burma, managed to cultivate a healthy following among the local population. The bookseller admitted *Casino Royale* was his zay-oo-bauk, the first sale. May Sai Baba bless him with many more! He could certainly use the guru's help; he still had unsold copies of *The Spy Who Loved Me* and *Diamonds Are Forever* in his stack.

In the following weeks, I'd come back to the same stall to pick up *Murder on the Orient Express*. Through the first bookseller, I was introduced to another, who dealt almost exclusively in espionage and mystery novels. I added *The Honorable Schoolboy* and *The Bourne Identity* to my little growing English library.

In my teenage years, I was a regular on Pansodan. My classmates saved their allowances to buy a pair of Ray-Ban or Nike (or Taiwanese and Singaporean knockoffs that would pass for the same). I had stacks of John le Carré and Agatha Christie novels to show for my dwindling pocket money.

Years later, after immigrating to California, I spent many weekends on Berkeley's Telegraph and Shattuck Avenues, trying to relive the cherished hours on Pansodan. But it was not quite the same. The last time I paid for my purchase, the clerk at Moe's Books didn't say a prayer to a patron saint on premise.

Last week, a friend of mine in Rangoon decided to ship me some books.

"What should I get you?" she asked.

"I'd like some Burmese history books if you can manage it," I said. "I've been doing research on the Konbaung Dynasty (the last dynasty of Burma)."

"I don't know where I can find them," she said. "They're pretty hard to come by."

"Try the government bookshop," I suggested in jest.

As it turned out, her father, a retired Burmese gentleman with a love for books, knew exactly where to locate them. He found an entire set devoted to my research topic. He didn't find it at Sar Pe Baik Ban. He found it amidst the bookstalls of Rangoon. It wouldn't be an exaggeration to say that, without Pansodan, or Burma's al-Mutanabbi Street, Burmese history could face extinction.

The paperbacks in Rangoon had been seasoned in Asia's scorching heat and punishing rain. They were coated with the anxious sweat of the Burmese intelligentsia, a breed that had been slowly dying out during the last four and a half oppressive decades under successive military regimes. Orwell's masterpieces now quietly collecting dust on Rangoon's pavements had actually seen 1984 come to life. For the booksellers of Burma and Iraq, a blessing is long overdue.

The Proper Purgation

Elmaz Abinader

Peace to a grove of figs.
Peace to this darkness.
Peace to a shell that hid its blood in wet sleep.
Peace to this ruin
—from "Thank You Imru Ul-Qais" by Saadi Youssef,
translated by Khaled Mattawa

Muscles and vessels barbed
twists names mix wire with
home, home wraps around
heart, heart grows a shell in hopes that
we do not learn again what
is happening and what is happening to
whom trying to mark one, two to
declare our innocence and our
absence our silence it's the only way to
live some think you see writhing
hurts so much, the tearing so
insistent and monsoons flood in
drown the lobes that move each
action to emotion and if we could only
control eyes and ears and elements that
rake the skin with wire,
the boils swelling inside
the underarm between the toes lining
the mouth holding the unspeakable until
nothing until the silence leaks until
the temporal levees crash the walls until
the certain magnitude unravels the
ventricles arteries aorta bypass
grief bypass horror bypass saying
it's unspeakable because it is not
the proper purgation rhythm, "harmony" and
song and we are just in time bypass
the humidity of history and its recognizable
scars we inflict repeatedly transplantation in-
operable these words are not enough are
not coming as quickly as tragedies do

our language is not our language instead
invented by the murder of the heart, of
hearts ruptured by magnitude coming
too fast and the words hold fire hanging
in wait and what we want to say is not
that this is our world smothered by every
moment a massacre seen as bodies and not
brothers seen as battlefields and not
homes seen as acts of god and not the god-
less I reach for the syllables to put together
the artistic ornament that moves us to act
three to where we say peace peace peace to
this ruin makes it easier to breathe
and live on.

In the Country of the Dead

Habib Tengour

> **TIRESIAS:** Why then, o unfortunate one,
> thus abandon the sunlight and come to see
> the dead in this place without tenderness
> —*The Odyssey*, Book XI

All these dead

who among us will question them

will it still require a massacre
and tears
for the road beneath the earth to be traced for us

unless this wind that rips into us hasn't
made us lose our reason

to the point that we don't care about the meeting

All these dead
what names should be called in the circle

hands extended for a prayer of parting
but reluctantly

we don't wail the way we used to

so many people die each day that our hearts
refuse to register grief

is this a metamorphosis

Shadows 3

All these dead
whom we never see
was it part of their destiny to die

women children youths old men and soldiers
many are like poor Alpenor
not even able to keep their balance

the newspapers sometimes grant them a column
despite the censors

we say that they are numerous so we forget them

Shadows 4

All these dead
their legs entwined
no one can specify their number
they become cumbersome

the city wears a blindfold

"every soul tastes death" in fragments
and sadly rejoins the senseless flight of shadows

such silence around the pit
that vertigo at the moment the guide steps back

Shadows 5

All these dead
some of them manage to speak
to surprise a groan wrenched out of us
despite death which lurks
in confusion

I crossed the city looking for a bar
where my friends hang out

to imagine in silence

what would be worth dying for

Shadows 6

All these dead
grimacing in their sudden death they stink
we dare no longer mention them during the nightwatch
the burial rites are barely carried out
we prefer silence to the litany grief
has hardened so in our hearts

what messenger will go to being the news
to those whom exile has eroded

back there

the song which weaves itself in the blood calms the soul

All these dead
when the south wind blows
I hear their death-rattle in the night I get up turn on
lamps in the living-room
a niche of light to give the lost one bearings
then go back to bed
this act every night the south wind blows

the shivering soul
those few steps from the bedroom to the living-room

the dogs of the city bark in their turn

Shadows 8

All these dead
like the parched bird above the skull
waiting for some deliverance
from what image will the hero be reborn
the one who'll give his own blood for the victim to drink
to renew the dialogue with the deceased
rediscover a word's intonation
then say what needs to be said to each one
alone withdrawn waiting for a sign

vain phantasmagoria of the dead and the living

All these dead
with no memorial to recall them to us
in a comforting image
to give some sense to that which has none
and thus permit us to go to the limit of our suffering
without a grimace even if the pain persists
how long can we hold on like this
as for me, I grieve in solitude
facing the strain of the effort

they say the entry to the kingdom the next door

Shadows 10

All these dead
who slowly slip out of our lives
what have we offered them in all this time
words too unraveled to give birth to the poem
words held back by regret or that fear
suspended before our eyes
since the dawn of time as the old saying goes
words whose usage becomes obscure to us
we ask ourselves sometimes about the celebration
their splendor fails to illuminate our strange desire for memory

Translated from the French by Marilyn Hacker.

Adolescence of Burnt Hands

Khaled Mattawa

Suddenly I found my sorrow among
strange trees, on dusty squares.
I thought yes,
yes,

I knew it had come.
I had seen it on men's faces.
But too early, too soon.
I said,

"Sorrow of the distant mother,
Ghosts of schoolyard friends,
Father broken backbone
I am too young to live without anger."

Then everywhere I went
It was the valley of God's absence,
the forest of the cold bosom,
the deserts where children raised children.

And I cradled my flame.

This poem was printed as a broadside by Greg Shattenberg for the Al-Mutanabbi Street Broadside Project.

From **Tales of a Severed Head**

Rachida Madani

III

She moves upstream against the current
her veins open
she moves in torrents.
From metamorphosis to metamorphosis
from poem to poem she moves forward
and every poem is a skiff
headed for the other shore.
Give me your hand, my rose
the stream is still there to be crossed
all its depths of sludge
who knows how many more shipwrecks
before dawn?
Give me your hand
I'll sing gently
sweetly for you in the dark
and my voice a wave in the night
will carry to the other shore
the frail butterflies of your dream.

IV

She sings for her child
as if a song could
       preserve her laugh
so that laughter would be the final song
after the blackest night.
As if she could put all her tears
          outdoors
and come back to hang her laundry out to dry.
She sings as if all men
         were behind her
and all women in their places,
as if fear were not that river
which crosses the city's length and width
as if fear were not the song's
        one refrain.

V

But beware of songs
in which the sea is absent
for what music my rose
if the storm does not shake you?
I sing so that marble will shatter
so that all crystal and palaces shatter
where I was once a dutiful slave
or royal concubine,
thus my death will be the last song
after all those deaths.
And sing for me
when I tumble down
on the other shore.

VI

Each poem is a skiff
headed for the other shore.
Here, the wind shakes its yellow head
                of a pagan mourner
and men fall from the branches
like rotten fruit.
Here houses bend from all
                their windows
and crash into the street.
Here, the poets die in prison.
Here, a black car waits for him.
Here, he was taken elsewhere
where his fingers were cut off
where they blindfolded him
and fired into his mouth.
Here, just over there
they could not bury him.

I will rescue you from the cities
as I plucked you out of the desert
my rose dressed in winds and rains,
the two of us in the skiff
and my mad rebel slave's blood howling
howling till we reach the other shore.

VII

The two of us in the skiff
and the ocean around us blue with spite
drowned women float up towards us
hanging from seaweed;
Their eyes are not hollower
their hands are not emptier
than the heart of a city …
No less mortal is the lighthouse
which guides us.
I will die of loving you too much, my rose
I will die from being simply a mother
but let that death happen
on the other shore.

Translated from the French by Marilyn Hacker.

Untitled

Amina Said

I live here in the basement of the Gare de Lyon
he says you'll find me when you come back
and suddenly beneath the ash of neon lights
day was done before daybreak

your eyes stopped me he says
with a flame dying out in his own pupils
and dusk drowned itself suddenly
in the empty glass of his bottle

you speak several languages like me
he says you travel a lot
torture of the motionless traveler
and dawn died suddenly before dawn

I was born in Jerusalem … he smiles
I was born in Morocco, Salah, yes, homeless
you'll find me here when you come back
and night was over before nightfall

thirty-two years I've been living in Paris
he says far from my mother's prayers
darkness of failed departures
sun and sand churn in her memory

you come from somewhere else too he says
and the stones moan with absence
the earth stops turning
once yes once I also had a country

one can see in your eyes that you love life
he says … only a solitary smile
as a talisman for the soul
there are seven doors left to pass through

the seven doors passed through and the thousand and one trials
perhaps we will be delivered
(if that makes any sense)
from the south of madness   the madness of the south

I borrowed the sun's wings
to fly toward that spot between two shores

I built towers of sand
where that shadow lived which served as my body

body ripened by a sun of extreme summer
I was in the wind's thoughts
intonations of light
composed my landscape

I was ten years old in the color of day
I scowled with the stones
where scorpions sheltered
on the island, women went masked
perhaps out of modesty

sky in my head I would make myself invisible
to see better knocked at windowpanes
where the day gathered
in an ordinary hymn
I looked for meaning in form—
somewhere out there the world had to exist

I was twenty years old impatient
to shore up at new continents
I left my father's house
gave my avian liberty up to the light
entered the space of darkness

I tried to open invisible doors
claimed to read the very stuff of silence
like a mother tongue
made a beginning of the past
and a double absence of the present

body more alive than dead
I refused to let night separate me
from day or day from night
watcher of dreams whom a dream invented
what was I looking for when I opened my eyes
on the colors of the world
which the sun never lets out of its sight

from words' second memory
real feeling is born
I inhabit that music
which I can't be the only one to hear

shadow which follows or precedes its shadow
on the border between dream and real
I stay on my own margins
in space and time

how to know if in this nowhere
place where a voice sets itself free
I came of my own free will
or if it was imposed on me

Translated from the French by Marilyn Hacker.

What Every Driver Must Know

Alise Alousi

No one to witness and adjust
No one to drive the car
—From "To Elsie," William Carlos Williams

If it was good enough for Baltimore, it
was good enough for Baghdad.
—Rajiv Chandrasekran, *Imperial Life in the Emerald
City*, on the completion of a new traffic code for
Iraq, modeled after the State of Maryland's

More phantom hands in this dying city
now leaving blue booklets
tucked under our windshields.
Traffic instructions so worthless
King Hammurabi won't even lift a finger
to breathe meaning into these laws.

light reflective clothing should be worn
when walking during darkness or
cloudy weather, hold the steering wheel
with both hands, for every hour driven,
rest for five, learn to yield to wait

We drive old Toyotas, clothesline holding
the doors closed, "Seven Eyes" muted turquoise
dangling from the rearview to protect us from evil
eyes, as if anyone could find someone
left to envy here.

The courtesy at a four-way stop,
white-gloved traffic police
with ten confiscated cars and pockets full of dinars.
Checkpoints, IED's, decisions to make
every time we venture out in a car,
speed or stop, flee or comply.

The potential to bleed, we all have it—
to explode in a market, soccer game
among friends, in lines waiting
for a job or news of the missing.
We carry our dead the way ants do,
dragging corpses with intensity and care.
There are many to bury
before the sun goes down.

While you speed to reach beyond the barricades,
cool greenness of safety enlightened
occupiers. Dusk the most dangerous time
to drive, except here. Suburban GMC's, Hum-
vees, obey the speed limit set
35 miles per hour.

the driver must be seated, focus on the task
at hand, keep from staring at any one object
for too long, avert your eyes from the sun

From our arak-soaked dreams some valium
cloudy mornings, we speak of leaving.
Measure the miles with pebbles, dropped teeth,
bones, burnt clothing, scarves.
Leave you to embed your limbs in our cars
streets, homes, when we have all
gone, shoulders pushing through doorways, exit
map in hand.

Roadside shells of cars line the highways
burnt then whitewashed by the sun
brought to life by the wind only,
passing vehicles.

The trees will greet you then,
the ones that grow here and
no place else on earth.
Remember the taste for me
of the fruit, sweet then bitter
and the small petals falling
white in the yards.

Explosion

Sita Carboni

How do we say goodbye?
March 5, 2007
Al-Mutanabbi Street.

Singed pages flutter open
butterfly wings try to escape
words that we choke on
Allah, America.

Separated poems search for one another
scaling limbs of bodies in debris.
Sticky stanza's drag titles and couplets
over blood leaving lines of broken thought.

Najah calls for his son,
does not hear the Quran's tears.
He witnesses black tea with sugar seep
from the Shahbandar Cafe,
a pulse silenced.

Literature and the literary become elemental
fire, blood, dust, tears.
There is nothing left for Moean,
an extremity to be buried,
a torn piece of clothing,
a single letter   y   y   y.

When does a story end and the world begin?
How can we say goodbye?

Letter to My Childhood Friend, the Baghdad Car Bomber

Fran Bourassa

You never said but I know you believed them too
That He could see all, He could hear all.
We already knew then there was nowhere to hide
in their blessed prison

You, a hero with your toy sword and I, a virgin princess,
given up for sacrifice
as They bound our grubby hands
together in prayer after prayer after prayer
stealing from us the green of our thoughts
the song of your own voice
And my small truths forced to a whisper
confessions through the lattice window
We thought noone could escape from

Even the big yellow sun
coming up from over our side of the mountain
could be drawn in, turn against us
Trapped in the web
of the stained glass windows

The rays shattering to the floor
marking our innocent faces
red as blood
and sometimes a broken piece of cold blue
would slice across a lip
a purple bruise would bloom over an eye

But you, my cellmate, you my commiserator, my old friend.
They must have held you down much longer
To never have found your way out
never found a way to steal back your own words
—one at a time until you had a long line
long enough to set you down to freedom

They must have knelt you down so long
That you could only dance
the crippled dance of the faithful
hobbling to al-Mutanabbi Street
past the booksellers, bookbinders, stationers,
past the people and poets sipping sweet tea in the Shabandar café
you with a trunk full of dynamite
a head full of Their curses you believe are your own original verse
Your faith so hard and sharp—it is a blade
Cutting the tongue out of the words

And after, you watch from a tower
The spines of books broken open
Arms letting go of pages
Flying through the air like white birds
Like souls

And you the one now who
marks the innocent faces
red as blood
A broken piece of cold blue
slices across a lip
A purple bruise blooms over an eye

Chrysalis

Jabez W. Churchill

The envelope that holds us
keeps us from spilling
formless into the night,
the empty labyrinth
of narrow streets,
New York, Madrid, Fallujah,
How many places more!
after the rubble has been swept away,
voiceless into the eternity
between 2:00 and 4:00 a.m.,
where only disembodied reign,
is thin.
The envelope,
the skin around our eyes,
the mask that hides the ecstasy and pain,
is growing thin.
Too thin
to hold back tears.
But we
who tested every corner unto breaking
must wait until it ruptures
unprovoked
that we
in form as yet unknown
may fly into the dawn.

Al-Mutanabbi Street: Foot Notes after the Fire

Daniela Bouneva Elza

when words come down   from the sky
you know   lost

the mindless haze   outlines
shadows   silhouettes
mourning   page   after page   limb

after limb   body after   body   bending
straightening   meandering
gathering   (broken spines of thought

ॐ

scattered script   once carefully strung
in the prayer beads   of narrative   or verse

apart at the seams—   word   flesh
bone—   this page Arabic   this English
this French.   piles   under foot

what *would*   this tome of   history   say
if we put it together?   will it tell
what color the sky is   when we weep?

ॐ

we catch them   in mid air   torture
words   into making sense
(in our seamless world   so far away

the light   dies   slowly
thinning itself out   until   the horizon is
a flutter   a line   (the edge of
someone else's   grief

when words come down   from the sky
do not think   it is god   speaking

Poppies Are Not   (Enough)

Daniela Bouneva Elza

I drink a blood sunset   down Cardinal Avenue.
my shoes soaked poppies   my mind quiet as

a book   with a bomb   in its mouth.

was it at the bus stop   the fruit leather that hung like
a general's ribbon   from the hands of a homeless child

that reminded me of the red truth dripping down our throats?

she wishes upon a bone moon. the same moon
that climbs in my eye. our gazes meet   up there:

an "almost"   neutral   territory.

her smile   a coca-cola   scar.

Psalms and Ashes

Linda Norton

"Near the old Jewish quarter of Baghdad, at Al Rasheed Street, there is a meandering alley named after the Iraqi poet Al Mutanabbi. The poet's street branches away from Al Rasheed and heads down through a tissue of dilapidated buildings with thin columns that hold up warped balconies. Bookstores of every description occupy the street-level spaces, selling technical manuals, ornate copies of the Quran and a nice selection of pirated software." —*Salon*

I first heard about al-Mutanabbi Street when this ancient neighborhood of booksellers, archivists, poets, and scholars was bombed in 2007 in the civil war triggered by the U.S. occupation of Iraq. People of many faiths and tribes worked side by side there, as in the World Trade Center, where the attacks on September 11 killed blacks and whites, Europeans and Americans, Muslims, Jews, and Hindus, the very rich and the poor who shined their shoes and delivered their sandwiches, coffee, Chinese food. I have worked in bookstores, libraries, and publishing houses since I was sixteen years old, and I could picture the scene—the faces. And ash: the distillation, the perfection of destruction, a kind of snow.

Identity papers, erotica, letters, invoices, calendars, and potboilers. Arabic translations of the Torah and the Gospels and the Psalms of David, books Muslims consider holy, as they were revealed by God prior to the revelation of the Quran. Who knows these things, the way all books flow from one source and seem to have been written by one author, as Emerson said? The poets know. The booksellers on al-Mutanabbi Street, a mixed neighborhood of readers, writers, and talkers, knew this too, which made it possible to laugh and argue together, to drink tea and smoke in an ancient café, in safety and comfortable squalor.

"There was always much paper about the dead and the debris of this attack was no exception." Hemingway was writing about an attack in Italy in World War I. All comes to dust in war, but first there is fire, blood, and gore.

In al-Mutanabbi Street, there were books in Hebrew, French, English, everything. Where there are readers or musicians, nationalism gives way to cosmopolitan couplings: an Iraqi Christian specialized in translations of the Torah and American literature. Hemingway, Faulkner. And Sidney Sheldon! Even *Tom Sawyer* was available in an Arabic translation.

In the spring of 2003—at the beginning of the occupation—an Iraqi bookseller, a scholar of the Psalms of David with an interest in American literature, recognized a U.S. Marine walking down al-Mutanabbi Street: a regular Huck. He smiled at the American. "Salaam, Huck," said the bookseller, giving the boy some candy and papers, stamps, and envelopes so he could write to his mother back in America. Her name was Sarah. "Salaam, Sarah," said the bookseller, writing it in Arabic on a scrap of paper for the Marine.

Those were the good old days.

...

Huck signed up after 9/11. Hated all Arabs. Would go anywhere and kill anyone to avenge the deaths of secretaries who jumped from the World Trade Center on 9/11.

His mother gave him a Gideon's Bible, small enough to carry everywhere. The New Testament, Psalms, and Proverbs. That's where he kept the slip of paper with his mother's name in Arabic, to hold his place at John 3:16.

"Moab is my washpot." Some things in Psalms were funny. And then there were the other parts, written thousands of years ago to be sung to the music of a harp. Written for a U.S. Marine from Missouri: "My soul follows close behind You. Your right hand upholds me. But those who seek my life to destroy it, shall go into the lower parts of the earth. They shall fall by the sword; they shall be a portion for jackals."

...

Never seen a jackal before I came here. They look just like you think they would look. Prowling around ruins.

Huck shouts at the jackal—"You fucker!"—to scare it away from the corpse in a pile of books. He wasn't al-Qaeda or anything. Wore a cross around his neck. Sold envelopes and candy, but mostly sat reading newspapers, drinking tea and smoking all day. Sometimes gave candy to kids who couldn't pay.

Huck flicks a candy wrapper off the dead man's face.

...

"There was always much paper about the dead."

My friend stood on his roof in Brooklyn that day and watched paper drift across the river. Awful confetti. Cancelled checks, payroll stubs, a piece of a diploma. Envelopes with wings. Recipes and tickets, a corner of a birthday card. Blueprints, mysteries, romances. Baby pictures, or pieces of pictures. Why do people put pink headbands on baby girls who don't even have any hair yet?

A love poem. Profit and loss statements. Divorce papers. The name "Maureen" and the word "milk" written in perfect penmanship on the bottom half of a Post-It.

He had heard that an old orthodox Jew stuck in World Trade Center Two recited the 23rd Psalm on a cell phone while talking to his wife as he waited to die. When he could not continue, she finished it for him: "You prepareth a table before me in the presence of my enemies. You anoint my head with oil. My cup runneth over."

...

The café on al-Mutanabbi Street used to be crowded with men. Then suspicion set in, and the café was nearly empty, and started to close early. It was dangerous to linger with a book. Marines used to walk the streets, smiling. No more.

Mamoud was dusting that day. He had meant to do some dusting for years. Why not now? So he was distracted, sneezing, when he noticed the package left next to the stack of pirated Microsoft Word software. Packages could be bombs. But this one was not. He saw the spine of a book sticking out of the padded envelope. A treatise about the great translator, physician, and ethicist Hunayn. Legend had it that Hunayn had refused to misuse his medical knowledge to make a poison the Caliph could use against his enemies. "First do no harm." Mamoud stopped his dusting to read a bit.

A car, too, could be a bomb. When he heard the explosion, Mamoud held a book over his face like a shield; the book and his face fused in the fire. "Why do you stand afar off, O Lord? Why do You hide in times of trouble?"

The awful quiet after the explosion. Like the ritualized pause in the Psalms: "Selah." The eerie silence as a snow of ash settles over everything. All that we hold dear—books, faces, the archives of a mind, a voice, a heart—interpretations, understanding, memory and psalms—reduced to ash.

Black and Red

Fred Norman

Al-Mutanabbi Street.
What was there is gone, and yet
not quite gone, for it is here today,
a dead place yesterday, now reborn.

The spoken and the written word
are man's most frightening enemies.
To protect himself, he kills.
He rapes, he maims, he bombs

until the only words that he can hear
are his, and there are no words to read.

And so it is with books,
those compilations of words doomed
to destruction merely because their author
might have sowed ideas of forbidden fruit.

Man burns these books,
words disappear in smoke, ideas die, fire
consumes each sentence, charred paragraphs
rise to darken the sun, that source of energy

without which ink becomes ice, the human
brain freezes to the quick, evolution slows.

Those who read and understand
are shivering if alive, rotting if dead, dead
if without hope, if silent under kicks and bricks
of libraries once womb to ideas born in freedom

now tomb to ideas lost,
ideas that frightened empty brains with thoughts
of rebirth in the sun, of knowing night and horses
and the desert, of caressing parchment with the pen,

ideas that once invited Baghdadi men to sit side
by side as brothers without fear of sect or sin.

Never clear, brown with life
disguised as mud, the Tigris now flows black and red
polluting fertile crescent and oasis, swamp and land
reclaimed from sand, exchanging coffin for the cradle

whence long ago we learned
to read, whence long ago we changed from animal
and wild to man and civilized by law, to citizens
ruled by law and ruling governments above the law.

Black and red, the colors of the anarchist, violence
and death, but also hope, the colors of the phoenix.

Nazik al-Malaika

Fred Norman

When you died in June
so soon after al-Mutanabbi Street
had died, was it out of grief
for burning books and blind
Baghdadi men or did a thief
steal moonlight from the Tigris?

Where is the Baghdad Street
named after you, oh Malaika Street,
where women freely sit with men
to write in rhythm and in rhyme
or write in free verse freely time
to sing the happiness of night?

Would there be a Shabandar Cafe
not just for men but women, too,
and would the poets talk of sword
and lance and politics and manly
things, or would there be a word
for peace and children's laughter?

Had you not left Iraq for Egyptian
soil, you would have lived and died
alone, but I cry that you left a home,
though now destroyed, each bomb
like cholera, sad death of your youth,
left a home destroyed as is Iraq.

Come home, Nazik al-Malaika,
rebuild Iraq through verse, teach
al-Mutanabbi Street's cruel destroyer
to play the oud, to love both night
and day, both sun and moonlight,
peace, to love a woman's world.

Come home, Nazik al-Malaika,
cross the Tigris one more time.

Al-Mutanabbi

Bonnie Nish

I wear the dead
upon my shoulders,
feel them push down
until my feet
imprint the earth with memory.
Their words,
your words, stretched across my palms,
close as bombs worn
to darken the sky's sunset,
newspaper smeared across the horizon.

In the market place
a dark-haired boy
wears the dead,
they watch him
one blood shot eye at a time.
Glass shards that
in an instant,
cut their throats,
slowly rip his feet
as he picks through
what is left of his present,
future, past.

We are the dead
worn,
we hunger
for the pages
dropped behind,
the history bitter sweet,
the mistakes.
Anesthetized,
we move along the edge
keeping track, tasting
nothingness.
Never count out the dead
they watch.

random

Bonnie Nish

it is so random,
like a baby fallen from a carriage
in the middle of the night
or a nuclear waste disaster
turning fetus into seaweed.

the silence of its poetry
mouthed by fallen angels
as intense as young men
wearing time bombs strapped
to waist belts on busy Iraqi market days

or the cry of a one legged man
with seagull eyes,
racing across a continent
the spokes of bad fortune
leaving tread marks in his side.

we watch it angle, shift,
as patient as old birds
slightly out of sync,
there is no point in taking flight.
it is so random.

The Twisted

Janet Rodney

Breaking lives,
obsessive death.
The sun's whiteness
soft high cloud
being a film of high floating
white light its whiteness
sinews   pale   contour,
pain's arrows exploding
out of form into
                Gathering the Silences.

This poem was first printed as a broadside by Janet Rodney for the Al-Mutanabbi Street Broadside Project.

Tonight No Poetry Will Serve

Adrienne Rich

Saw you walking barefoot
taking a long look
at the new moon's eyelid

later spread
sleep-fallen, naked in your dark hair
asleep but not oblivious
of the unslept unsleeping
elsewhere

Tonight I think
no poetry
will serve

Syntax of rendition:

verb pilots the plane
adverb modifies action

verb force-feeds noun
submerges the subject
noun is choking
verb disgraced goes on doing

there are adjectives up for sale

now diagram the sentence

The Blues Sat Down on al-Mutanabbi Street

Cornelius Eady

The Blues don't read or write.
A book makes as much sense
As a penny in a sparrow's beak.
When a bomb finds a book
It doesn't bother with small talk,
All them fancy words; it wants
To scorch knowledge, spit ash, boil life down
To pulp.

The Blues don't read or write.
Happy-go-lucky, it disassembles the café table and chairs
Like a bad shake of dice. Your idea
About peace, listen to it sizzle now
Up and down the ruined block. Hear
The scared animal noise The Blues knew
Was hiding somewhere inside
Your even tone of voice. What were you
Thinking, The Blues wants to know,

Dark cloud over al-Mutanabbi Street,
Grey ash rising from the twin towers,
Numb god splitting open the belly
Of the Spanish train with its awful finger,

The Blues don't read or write.
It's an ignorant child, tipping over
What it likes to tip over, and baby,
It is smoke and gone by the time you decide
To rebuild the world from the shock of what's left.

March 9, 2007
Al-Mutanabbi Street, Baghdad

Julie Bruck

On a pile of bricks, someone had left a pink plastic
flower, a pair of glasses, and a book with crisp, white
pages. They glowed in the black debris of al-Mutanabbi Street.
This is his shoe, a man cried out, I bought it for him.
It was 9:06 a.m. The man was slim, with peppery hair
and square, gray-tinted glasses. He clutched a black chunk
of leather melted by the heat. I bought it for him.
He kissed the piece of leather, placed it gently
next to the flower, the eyeglasses and the book.
Come and see it, he yelled to five men carefully
digging through debris. It's his size.
This is your shoe, he yelled to the pale blue sky.
My son, I bought it for you. The six men, all relatives,
were hunting for a teenager's remains. The boy had been
shopping for notebooks on al-Mutanabbi Street, named
for a tenth century poet. They had been digging since
Wednesday, morning till night. The men stared blankly
at the shoe. No one had the heart to speak, so they kept
digging. Don't step so hard, the father said.
Don't harm him

Adapted from a Washington Post *report by Sudarsan Raghavan*

This poem was printed as a broadside by Carol Todero for the Al-Mutanabbi Street
Broadside Project.

The Secret Carpentry

Kwame Dawes

The art is in making monsters of our foes.
Further away, forgiveness is easier; a face
penitent with regret, stoic and resolved
mouthing the jargon of clean, precise,
well-reasoned bloodshed—a voice tutored
in the art of eliminating options, making
the logic of power seductive. Those are
the forgivable sins. After all, how are we
to doubt when we have not smelt the hint
of stale liquor on the breaths, caught
them in some cute hypocrisy, found
them out for lies they have told
or the cruel cut of their laughter
at some hapless fool? Power feeds
our hopelessness. To make monsters
of our foes, we rely on dogma
and the denouncement of nuance.
Still, a poet sits on an ancient
marble block staring at the pale
blue sky, scratching poems, soft
—in a notepad. He is counting
echoes while calculating the cost
of next month's rent in U.S. dollars.
He has learned the meter of elegies—
so many buried, their faces sallow
with dust. He still feels the terror
of concussions when he walks. For him
monsters carry the currency of dogma.
He has no taste for dogma, now.

He searches out, instead, the secret carpentry
of poems hoping that they will last
beyond the presidents, the envoys,
the ambassadors, the ayatollahs,
the advisors, the martyrs, the rabbis,
the shamans, the priests, the blooded freedom
fighters. The poet knows his own
monstrosity: the vanity of songs
in a world full of the dying. Night
falls across the earth's surface, a shadow
following light into the heart of dusk.

Baghdad, 2003

Blackouts

Ralph Angel

rolled through the city.
Whoever has an answer won't last.
Traffic muscles through. Whole families lazing on steps
eating grapes. "No I'm not," says the youngest
to her canary. You grew into your legs,
Tall One, didn't you." Then
no one. Loosed papers
flatten the fences. Bits of glass rest there
and burn. This part of nature
runs along ridges, sprouts
wings in the valleys and wanders
the world like a candle. A general steps
down from his pedestal. Everyone
hated that statue. She points
left and says "right." She could be
an orchid. All those seen from afar moving away
from the market. This part of nature
breaks down the butterfly, this part of man
into flutes. Flop
through your branches,
naked one. In room after room, your
strangers have raised you.

Moth

B.H. Fairchild

A moth devoured words.
                The Exeter Book

A larval tunneling between pages.
                Gorged on print,
wallowing in pulp, it falls into the long

sleep that later breaks and frays as wings
                sluggish as oars
begin to bludgeon the heavy air,

baffled by walls of dusk and lugging
                the soft body
toward a squall of light. Dun wings

flail, ribbed like gothic vaults and
                camouflaged with moons
large as owl eyes. Lurching through

the light's rain, it veers, collides,
                hugs the bulb
and falls away. And the singed antennae

recall in something like a mezzotint
                the larval dark passage,
the hunger, the gray dream of with, and, the.

Baghdad Callsby

Terese Svoboda

At the market where
Is that a melon? is
discerning, bloody

melon, like all else
still spurting,
that silence, while even

the big birds,
market-bound,
do not dive, in fear,

after the living begin
wailing, collecting
in the shade, before Help

has strapped on what
wings it has, the ringing
begins, every cell phone

flung from pockets
without torsos, from
fingers without purses,

their "Are you safe?"
stilled only when someone
parses the parts.

They Didn't Ask: What's After Death

Mahmoud Darwish

They didn't ask: What's after death? They were
memorizing the map of paradise more than
the book of earth, consumed with another question:
What will we do before this death? Near
our lives we live, and don't live. As if our lives
are desert lots disputed by the gods
of real estate, and we are dust's bygone neighbors.
Our lives are a burden to the historian's night: "Whenever
I hide them they come into my view out of absence ..."
Our lives are a burden to the artist: "I paint them,
then I become one of them, and fog veils me."
Our lives are a burden to the general: "How does blood
blow from a ghost?" And our lives
should be as we wish. We want to
live a little, not for anything ... other than to respect
resurrection after this death. And they quoted,
unintentionally, the philosopher's words: "Death
means nothing to us. We are and it isn't.
Death means nothing to us. It is and
we aren't."
Then they rearranged their dreams
in a different manner. And slept standing!

Translated from the Arabic by Fady Joudah.

The Airport of Language

Amir el-Chidiac

the sea shines
with martyred blood
coastlines pray & gasp

one bathing suit washes up
tangles up with garbage

garbage fills a space
a body once filled

schools transform into hospitals & shelters
wearing sheets of white

millions of wounds reopened
acned buildings fester

in the sun
an armless man   holds a gun

& fifteen years of civil war
a lingering pollen

that dances in the air
burning brightly in the eyes

& the people rub their eyes waking
from a dream—time can slip

& can become one again
mothers regurgitate numbers
children learn how to tell time
younger each year—counting rapid fire

in quick successions

born from frac-tions
children piece together
equations of sorrow

poets dig through vowels
starving for remnants

of a precious alphabet
stuck between their teeth

or a hunger bones remember
& bones throb in recognition

& poets rummage for metaphors
& the assaulted sky & the sky ...
& this is not romantic
& history is being written into the earth

& it is possible to hear
history being written

& the poets flee & the poets reach
the airport of language

& the poets take a vow
of silence

Rocks

Aram Saroyan

for John Densmore

The secret of poetry is to write
As if you are already dead
Which may be why a poet
Is naturally drawn to rocks

They are alive, of course
But at an infinitesimal rate
So that a single breath
Takes a year or more

In the same way a certain star
Sits in the heavens although
Science has determined
That was years ago

And what one is seeing
Has nothing to do with reality
But then so little does

This poem was printed as a broadside by Tina Brown for the Al-Mutanabbi Street Broadside Project.

April Stork

Saadi Youssef

He arrived like this ...
without drums or marching band.
He arrived tired and quiet.
The first decision: choosing a house.
The second: the straw that will make the nest.
The third: the nest ...
But the city
is still in ruins ...
It does not know why he came,
will not know what he will do,
will not notice him
when departure calls on him.

Batna, May 3, 1980

Translated from the Arabic by Khaled Mattawa.

Solos on the Oud (#3)

Saadi Youssef

Land where I no longer live,
distant land
where the sky weeps,
where the women weep,
where people only read the newspaper.

Country where I no longer live,
lonely country,
sand, date palms, and brook.
O wound and spike of wheat!
O anguish of long nights!

Country where I no longer live,
my outcast country,
from you I only gained a traveler's sails,
a banner ripped by daggers
and fugitive stars.

Algiers, August 16, 1965

Translated from the Arabic by Khaled Mattawa.

This poem was printed as a broadside by Toby Millman for the Al-Mutanabbi Street Broadside Project.

See Them Coming

Sholeh Wolpé

Here come the octopi of war
tentacles wielding guns, missiles,
holy books and colorful flags.

Don't fill your pens with their ink.
Write with your fingernails, scratch
light upon these darkened days.

This poem was printed as a broadside by Jamie Main for the Al-Mutanabbi Street Broadside Project.

Love Song

Sholeh Wolpé

Last night a blue jay flew into my house,
crashed against the skylight and died:
I want to write a love song.

Poppy seed cake on china plate,
tea like auburn gold, the New York Times
open on the table, black with news,
and the man I love still with me.

I want to write a love song…
but the newspaper says in Conakry
a man is sticking his Kalashnikov
into a woman. Now he's pulling the trigger.

Hummingbirds zip through the garden's
spring smorgasbord of blooms as my husband
slowly rocks in the hammock, his round glasses
on the tip of his nose, a spy novel on his stomach.

I flip a page and Bagdad is on fire;
ash inks the air, corpses
of books pile high in Mutanabbi street.

The child next door squeals with laughter.
My husband raises his head in our garden
where the bougainvillea has burst into pinks and reds,
the colors of Kabul's sidewalks after a suicide attack.

How hard is it to write a love song?
A little in-the-moment swim,
a bit of Bach—perhaps.

Until the Glaciers Melt

Sholeh Wolpé

Look how the foamy-mouthed sea
licks its own shores,
splashes and rolls
furious in its coming to reclaim
its fish circling death's tanks
in crowded cafés.

The sea comes, it comes
but does not arrive …

as we never arrive
no matter how intent
we are to liberate our kin
from hungry bearded serpent gods,
window-starved rooms,
from under voice-proof veils.

Our tongues lick time's spiny slates,
bleed saliva flavored with abstractions:
"injustice," "violations," "freedom,"
our eyelashes thrash in indignation,
and our eyes claim pain …

but like the sea, we keep coming
fiercely, and never arrive.

This poem was printed as a broadside by Michelle Brehmer for the Al-Mutanabbi Street Broadside Project.

Tonight

Nathalie Handal

water will reach
the rim of the glass but will not
allow itself to leave the glass

violence will erupt and horrors
will tie themselves to
every bare tree

tonight we will see
tattooed waistlines and Kalashnikovs
in the back trunks of cars

paralyzed memories and
revolutions behind
every house door

we will see red landscapes,
stones of light, light feathers swaying
in the nightscape

and wrinkles will multiply
on our faces tonight as each
dead rises from its grave

tonight exiles, immigrants, refugees
will be caught in songbirds,
cracked asphalt will recite old verses

tonight we will listen to the cracks of narratives
the screams of those strangled
by the night at night

we will listen to the longing
of purple evenings
under god's robe

tonight love will be difficult.

One (for al-Mutanabbi Street)

Beau Beausoleil

there are three words
at the wrist and the forehead

and these are the first words
of naming

there is a word in each word
a word responsible for the divine

and there are three words described of blood
these are the words offended by memory

This poem was printed as a broadside by Marie C. Dern for the Al-Mutanabbi Street Broadside Project.

The Timeless Legacy of al-Mutanabbi Street

Azar Nafisi

We are all gathered to talk about al-Mutanabbi Street. But why Iraq? And why al-Mutanabbi Street? What is it in al-Mutanabbi Street that makes it relevant today not just to the Iraqi people but to us, who live thousands of miles away from that world, many of us who have never been there—what is it? Not just why should we support projects such as this one, but what is it that makes it relevant to us? To us, who have still never set foot in Iraq? And why is it imperative to connect with Iraq, with Iraqis, through litera-ture and art instead of simply through what we learn from news outlets?

There are two traits that exist in every great work of art, in every great work of literature, in every great piece of music. The first is curiosity. By and large, news outlets and the popular media do not awaken our curios-ity, but in many instances either affirm what we already know, or excite our emotions which often, to borrow a phrase from Saul Bellow, create "an atrophy of feeling." When you read a great book, when you look at an amazing piece of sculpture, it makes you curious, makes you come out of yourself—and curiosity is very dangerous! Because who knows where it will take you? There is no guarantee that after you know the real Iraq, read its history, see what that country was once, and is now, that you will be the same person. And so, when I was asked to join the Al-Mutanabbi Street Project, I tried to reconnect to the Iraqi people through an alternative way of looking at them, through their culture, through their history, through the words and through the images that would redefine all the words and images that we have heard and seen about Iraq.

When I taught in Iran, I always started my literary criticism classes with what I believe is the best book on literary criticism, which is *Alice in Wonderland*. The whole idea, the concept behind *Alice*, is that out of millions of little girls, one little girl, Alice, wants to see the world differently. She's bored with just looking at the flower, without asking or discovering "how else can we look at the flower?" And that one little girl had the eyes to see not just an ordinary rabbit, but a rabbit that talked and wore a waistcoat and a watch. But she also had the courage to take the risk that every writer and reader, everyone involved in art, has to take: she runs after that white rabbit and jumps down that hole without knowing what she will encounter. When you read a great book, when you look at a great painting, *you don't know*. You have to give yourself to that book.

And that is why curiosity is so important. Vladimir Nabokov used to say to his students: "Curiosity is insubordination in its purest form." And I think that when we teach, we don't have to simply give our students great theories, we have to remind them that if they want to be insubordinate, they have to become curious, because if they are truly curious, they will not only pose the world as a question, they will pose themselves as a question. We must live in order to know. Curiosity goes against what we already know, and it wants us, it makes *us* want to know what we don't know.

Another important thing about curiosity is that it allows one to defy one's limitations. One of the best pieces I read about al-Mutanabbi Street was by Anthony Shadid of the *Washington Post*. In his article, "The Bookseller's Story, Ending Much Too Soon," he talks about the owner of the Renaissance Bookstore, Mohammed Hayawi. Shadid describes how in this bookstore, you would find all sorts of books on the dusty shelves. The Communist writers were lying side-by-side with fundamentalist clerics, with ancient Arab poets, and side-by-side with translations of Shakespeare. In this world—and this is also what happens when you go to a museum—you defy time: all of these books, all of these paintings and sculptures side by side, Italy, France, from the whole world, they defy the limitations of time and space. They defy all the limitations that we have to live with every day.

Your passport in the Renaissance Bookstore, or in a museum is not whether you are an American or a Persian or an Iraqi—your passport is your love and your passion for imaginative knowledge. It has become fashionable nowadays for us to try to fight prejudice with edicts and laws and apologies, as if rules and statements could make us clean and free of prejudice. But to be free of prejudice, you must go to a museum! Go to the library! Go to a bookstore! This republic of the imagination is a place that transcends and defies the limitations of nationality, race, gender, class, ethnicity and religion. And that is why al-Mutanabbi Street starts here. Because we *all*, in reality, have to live with limitations. But once you go into that world where Shakespeare is side-by-side with the Communist Manifesto, side-by-side with the Ayatollah Khomeni, side by side with al-Ghazali and al-Farabi, some of the greatest philosophers and writers of the Islamic world, then you know that al-Mutanabbi Street does start here, because it has no beginning, because it belongs to all of us.

But for the same reason, the greatest tragedies, the greatest atrocities, like slavery or the Holocaust, also belong to all of us. They make every single one of us ashamed. They implicate the most innocent, and standing up to them is also a victory for each one of us. An Iraqi bookseller said of this bombing, "Of course we were expecting al-Mutanabbi Street to be targeted one day, because anyone targeting al-Mutanabbi Street targets Iraq's civilization. He targets Iraq's history, he targets Iraq's heritage."

It is not just the physical destruction; already al-Mutanabbi Street has been renovated. Buildings are destroyed, and they are rebuilt. What is mainly targeted by violence is this spirit that al-Mutanabbi Street represents. Because it doesn't matter whether you are Saddam or Ayatollah Khomeni, or a demagogue in the United States of America. In order to impose your voice upon the voices of others, you have to destroy history. You have to rewrite history.

We don't remember Iraq. All of this chatter, and talk, and noise, all of it overlooks the real Iraq, which once was the cradle of civilization, whose history goes back over five thousand years. A country that was part of the great empires of Mesopotamia and Sumeria, a country that has created some of the most amazing philosophers and poets, it has been reduced to a stereotype. If we want to talk about the glorious days of Baghdad, when Islam stood for knowledge, because of its multiplicity of voices, this is the real Iraq. Even the name Iraq or Syria, Jordan or Saudi Arabia, these names all came out of the British and French Mandates of the 1920s. They didn't exist in this shape before that. Yet we take it all for granted, as if they always existed in this manner.

If you want to distort history, like all demagogues, if you want to turn the history of a country into an empty shell, the first thing you do is simplify the story. Even here in Washington, D.C., we forget that the first president of this country wanted to create a national university at the capitol, which would be representative of the Enlightenment. At the same time, he was also a slave owner. History is complex. We do not want to confront history, because it hurts, because it is risky; but we have to remember history, because if Iran and Iraq and Egypt were once the way they were, they could again be that way. Countries can become what their people imagine them to be. And that is the importance of imagination: it connects us to the past in a critical way, it defines and criticizes the present, and it predicts our future.

The second trait I wanted to highlight about great art and literature is empathy. The empathy that emanates from a work of fiction, a painting, or a work of music places us in the mind and the heart of those we have never met. And empathy makes us understand and celebrate not just the differences between us, but also our similarities. There is great power in imagination, in thinking and talking about the Other. You cannot be equal to one another if you do not talk about one another.

Nabokov used to say, "worship the details, the divine details." People don't become real to you until you can experience them, and you can't experience them unless you can experience them in detail, as individuals. Like the way Anthony Shadid talks about the owner of the Renaissance Bookstore: he was thirty-nine but he looked older. Shadid calls him, "a bald bear of a man." Hayawi's father, the patriarch, whose picture was in the bookstore with a Russian fur hat, had opened this bookstore in 1954, and so on. Shadid goes into these details until the bookseller becomes not just a nameless victim—one of more than thirty people killed in al-Mutanabbi Street—but a human being. And once you look a human being in the eye, it becomes difficult to accept their suffering.

The whole idea of the Al-Mutanabbi Street Project is to remind us that the artists and writers and people of Iraq are, in fact, people like you and me. Because the most important thing is the shock of recognition. It is like the question from Shakespeare's *Merchant of Venice*: "If you prick us, do we not bleed?" The point is, we all bleed. Mothers in New Orleans, or in Rwanda, or in Palestine, mothers in Kabul or in Baghdad, they all bleed when their children are killed. We all suffer, we all become jealous, we all love, we all hate; we all share the common state, our humanity, in its best and worst circumstances. And al-Mutanabbi Street is here to remind us of this common humanity. We must always remember that there should be more than bombs to connect us to one another. You can't just connect to Iraq because of the death and the destruction there. You have to connect to it in a different way.

A lot of people will ask, "But why are these books so important? Did the books save the booksellers of al-Mutanabbi Street from being bombed? Do books put bread on the tables of those mothers of children who are clamoring?" Why is it that in the worst times human beings turn to these works of imagination? Because obviously, art or literature can't save you from death and destruction. What is the miracle? I always remember that Primo Levi, when he came out of the concentration camp and was writing about it, said, "I write in order to rejoin the community of mankind." That is why we write and we read. The urge to connect is always there in the act of imagination. Because we are always half-human unless we can articulate ourselves, unless others articulate themselves to us, and see us. We need to be seen, and we need to be heard, and we need to be felt. So the main thing, why al-Mutanabbi Street is so important, despite the fact that Iraq is still bleeding, is that connection.

There is an essential subversion to art and literature. It protests not just the tyrannies of today but the tyranny of time. We have so little power in reality, but through literature we can protest the essence of death, the fact that life is fickle, that even if you are the richest and most privileged in your society, you're going to die. No one will save you. And this is why art, and its preservation of memory, which Nabokov used to call "conclusive evidence that we have lived," becomes important. That is what al-Mutanabbi Street reminds us of. That life is fickle, and the only way we can protest is by leaving behind evidence that we have lived. Art in this manner becomes the guardian of life.

I want to end with another moment from Anthony Shadid's article. He talks about when, in the year 1258, Baghdad was attacked by Mongols, it is said that the river Tigris became red one day and black the next day, and it was said that it became red with the blood of the victims that the invaders murdered, and it became black with the ink of the countless books from the libraries and universities. This image is symbolic of the connection between art, or imagination, and life. You cannot separate imagination from life. The moment you stop imagining, you will stop living. And that is why, I think, al-Mutanabbi Street starts here, and why each of us should learn to protect the imagination.

From a lecture given at the Corcoran Museum of Art on July 13, 2011, transcribed and adapted by A.E Munn.

The Sudden Cessation of Electricity

Dima Hilal

"Cairo writes, Beirut publishes, Baghdad reads."
—A famous saying in the Arab world

Beneath a stark sun
carpets line alleyways
miles of books strewn upon them
conversations flow
between coffee shop intellectuals
like endless hot tea from a kettle

A ceiling fan turns in slow motion
not dispelling the heat
simply moving
the suffocating air in lazy circles
several times a day
the fan settles into one spot to rest
the only way to note
the sudden cessation of electricity

Shari' al-Mutanabbi, al-Mutanabbi Street
home
to politics pressed between pamphlets
Qur'ans calling from storefronts
stationery waiting for a purpose and a pen
a cigarette vendor paces the street
a thoroughfare of ideas and arguments
ancient texts and software manuals

At 11:40, as the sun continues
to scale to its highest point in the sky
a car parks in the middle
of this bustling metropolis
while war-weary men inhale water pipes
the Hajji sits at the threshold of his bookstore
worrying beads between his fingers
a child chooses Pepsi over a Miranda

In this last breath
between second hands
Shari'al – Mutanabbi
al-Mutanabbi Street
lives

Market Forces Runon

Tony Kranz

Books and bones—
blown to bits—
fall from the sky,
a torrent of
gravity and chaos
churning a mixture
of broken bodies and
text blocks amid
the rubble
of explosions
triggered by insanity,
in the name of humanity,
filling the gutters of
al-Mutanabbi Street with
the remains of dog-eared
pages and people while
in our name,
America's flag
has been waved.

This poem was printed as a broadside by Tony Kranz for the Al-Mutanabbi Street Broadside Project.

Freedom to Walk

Jordan Elgrably

The freedom to walk, to move, to get up and go anywhere you desire, has always seemed a natural right and privilege to me. It is something that most of us take for granted—we're not concerned about roadblocks or checkpoints, random ID checks or *razzias* such as the cops in Europe routinely subjected non-European immigrants to when I lived there in the '80s and '90s. Nor do we, in America, worry about walking our city streets for fear of a bomb going off at a sidewalk café. Walking is freedom and a form of meditation with several variations—city, desert, mountains, beach.

My first taste for walking came when I was small child. I got up in the middle of the night, snuck past my mother's bedroom, and went for a stroll on the Hollywood Freeway. I was four years old. Some Good Samaritan, as family members called him, spotted me wandering along the freeway at three in the morning and took me to the nearest police station. Some think it an early indication of my nomadic genes, and it was the first of my youthful attempts to run away in order to see more of the world. The psychologically-prone might declare it an intuitive response to my parents' recent divorce—a way to release my anger and disappointment that I wouldn't have both my mother and father around to take care of me everyday. Walking as a form of protest?

Later, as a prepubescent kid, I discovered the mountain trails near Lake Arrowhead and the scraggly hills of Malibu and Topanga, where I went to summer camps, and one of my favorite wilderness walks was through the arid climes of Joshua Tree. At the time, I did not realize that other kids in countries rife with conflict and war—Lebanon, Palestine, Afghanistan, Iraq, Iran, South Africa to name but a few—were often unable to walk where they pleased, either from fear of being stopped by hostile forces or the very real possibility of stepping on a landmine or cluster bomblet.

One of the first books I came across while a freshman in college that inflamed my imagination was *Three Journeys: An Automythology*, by Paul Zweig, in which he describes driving and walking through North Africa's

Sahara, an other-worldly landscape of Berbers, Touareg nomads, mountains, plateaux and desert oases or *oueds*. "The landscape is becoming mountainous," Zweig wrote, "but mountains unlike any I ever saw: black carved slopes, like enormous reliefs chiseled and thrown down over a vast space. The harmony of colors and shapes is unearthly."

Zweig's narrative was a form of poetry and left me with the distinct sensation that there were still places in the world that remained virtually untouched. "Two hundred miles without a trace of life: no palm trees, no scrub, no people . . . in the Sahara, nature still possesses an archaic pre-human ugliness: rusty dunes, beds of dried blinding mud, rocky waste heaps strewn for miles."

It was also something of an introduction to Southern Morocco, the region of my paternal grandfather, who was a Berber Jew from the small town of Taroudant, which some called "the grandmother of Marrakech."

The Sahara would become a figment in my literary imagination, the primal place to walk, to be lost, to be away from the world, and later I often envisioned myself on a Saharan journey while living a writer's life in Paris. Paul Zweig's time there left an indelible imprint. "The Sahara drove itself against me physically and demanded a physical response. But, as it turned out, I had not come there to be 'in the world' at all. The enormous whispering I had listened to had been something else entirely. It had caused stabs of insomnia, dwarfing my uneventful 'literary' life . . . Instead, in the Sahara, sleeping in a tent, walking at night over a sea of rock, under a cream of stars, huger than anything I had ever known or imagined, the images which came to my mind were images of enclosure; as if I could not grasp this immensity and this simplicity, except as a way, not of being outside, 'in the world,' but of being inside something far different from the world. It was like being inside a soul."

My Moroccan family had moved to France before World War II, where my father was born. I went to live in Paris in my junior year of college, and soon began filing stories as a freelance journalist. After growing up the prosaic streets of Los Angeles and Washington, D.C., the city's historic monuments and buildings, cobblestone streets, bridges over the Seine, open-air markets, cafés, *bouquineries* and intimate quarters like the Marais, the Bastille and Pigalle were absolutely enchanting. On many occasions, both day and night, I would traverse the entire city on foot, and often during these walks, I ran into memorable characters.

One time in Montparnasse, I stumbled across the great playwright Eugene Ionesco as he quarreled with his wife in front of their apartment building; she demanded the octogenarian take a taxi, but the creator of "The Lesson" and "The Rhinoceros" insisted on walking to their destination. On another occasion, a little further to the south, I found myself facing the tall, gaunt figure of Samuel Beckett, the playwright from Ireland who had adopted France as his second homeland. The author of *Waiting for Godot* didn't slacken his pace, however, when we nearly ran into each other, but continued ahead, though I mumbled, "Bonjour, Monsieur." As he walked on, I remembered the famous stabbing incident, when a pimp had knifed Beckett almost fifty years earlier in those very streets. After he had healed and the police insisted on pressing charges, Beckett met his attacker briefly while in custody. When Beckett asked him why he did it, the man answered, "Je ne sais pas, Monsieur." Some believe it was this incident that fed Beckett's nihilist and absurdist imagination.

Later, living in the Andalusian town of Granada, up in the old Arab quarter, the Albaysin, I become an ardent lover of the Alhambra gardens. Each morning I would look out the window of my *cármen*—an old Moorish home facing the Alhambra across the hill, known as the Cármen Aben-Humaya—and prepare my thoughts for the day. After several hours writing and a simple lunch of bread, Manchego cheese, and Tempranillo or Rioja wine, I would stroll down the old Albaysin streets and across to the next hill, entering the Alhambra gardens through a secret back gate. I walked and lollygagged for hours each day in these lush Moorish gardens, with their Islamic calligraphy, ornate topiaries and bountiful fountains. Inside the palace, I especially enjoyed lingering beneath the *mudéjar* ceilings and studying the intricate geometric carvings.

Everywhere I walked, in Paris and Granada, I carried a book with me. I would often stop to read in a café, ordering an espresso and occasionally taking notes when inspired by thoughts of a character or a new story idea. Despite the fact that terrorist bombings had occurred many times in Paris and other major European cities, I never felt endangered. Like others around me, I presumed that the police would pursue the culprits as international criminals. We did not experience the same climate of fear that overtook America after 9/11; we did not lose our right to privacy under new Draconian surveillance laws like those enacted under the U.S. Patriot Act.

Thinking back on those years of personal and creative freedom, I offer a *baraka*, a blessing or prayer, for the Iraqis of Baghdad who have yet to discover their own freedom in a new era of sovereign democracy. These days, whenever my hectic schedule allows me to lollygag in a café in Los Angeles, I envision a time of peaceful coexistence in the Middle East—I imagine a region in which, like Europe, there will be open borders, so that nothing will stop us from traveling from Haifa to Damascus or Kirkuk. Call me a dreamer, but someday, too, the artists and intellectuals of Baghdad will once again be able to enjoy the cafés and bookshops of al-Mutanabbi Street without fear, and they will share with us the freedom to walk wherever their hearts desire.

Untitled

devorah major

on the day al-Mutanabbi street was bombed

did you notice
how quickly the open sky
folded in upon itself

the flaking burnt pages
like torn moth wings
flying up the fetid smoke
then drifting
down

the broken teacups
and coffee stained saucers
the splintered chairs
empty shoe
splattered blood

and
just before
that moment

did you hear the
euphony of the street
as men wrangled
and summoned
swore and cajoled
addressed
if not solved
defined
if not created
the problems
and the promise
of their country's
tomorrow

did you even know
of the dreams imploded
inside the molten iron across the narrow
book lined street
as debate turned
to barbed screeches
philosophy
into choked smoke
and a thousand
years of history
was buried in the rubble

or was there

nothing
except an inexorable
deadly silence

Words

Suzy Malcolm

Thinkers and writers and readers

Who found solace in those bookstalls

Knew the hope of turning pages

In a world of terror and walls

So when the browsers were bombed

With the Baghdad books

Torn and bloody in the dust

They broke the hearts of humankind

But not the poets' trust

That words blown like birds in the killing

Won't die in a smoking sky

That out of harm's reach

Freed fragments of speech

Will one day find reason and fly

This poem was printed by Scott Brown for the Al-Mutanabbi Street Broadside Project.

The Last Supper

Ibrahim Nasrallah

I am calling you—so come in your white dress
that brushes softly on the pavement, with that dream
in your eyes.
I call your horses, rivers, flying fish,
and the balconies that did not look down on us,
scattering their flowers.
I call upon friends who have defiled our poems
and the trails of jasmine inside us,
I call birds that have kept their weddings from us
and the wind that has knifed its horses.
I remember the streets,
the light taking shelter in a woman's bosom,
the roof overhead rising with a flock of pigeons.
I call the now deserted city
where I once hid among the crowd.
I call the beautiful one who hovers around these houses
and the one who died, my dear lady,
and the one who does not die.
I call your predatory birds,
wreaths, graves and departures.
There you are
and there they are
and here I am.
We are no longer birds in the sky
so let us eat our own wings.

Translated from the Arabic by Omnia Amin and Rick London.

The Celebration

Ibrahim Nasrallah

Flowers, songs, chants ...
A memory from antiquity ...
Saturday's dawning sun ...
An orphan is late ...
A widow comes by embracing another widow ...
A singer ...
Verses from the Qur'an ...
A flute on the outskirts of a neglected village ...
Ancient soldiers ...
Battles, defeated ages ...
Thirty wars announced by daylight ...
Another thirty still hidden in their sheaths ...
Little ones dressed up for a feast ...
Horses filled with the joy of their riders ...
A procession coming from far away ...
Ululations reaching the sky, a commotion ...
Men emerging from darkness ...
from yesterday's newspapers, from the inkwell.
All of them came,
took pictures,
cursed the end of life and memory,
and drank from the cup of a slain dream,
before their leader stepped forward
to cut the silk ribbon
and open the graveyard.

Translated from the Arabic by Omnia Amin and Rick London.

A Special Invitation

Ibrahim Nasrallah

My corpse hovered over a sea of silence.
My house was a cloud of dust,
the streets were a wild extinguishing dream
and the night was like the face of a friend divided
between silence and earning one's keep.
The trees opposed their own colors
and the wind opposed riding a song,
a bird in the air was a period
then a comma in conversation.
The sky was arid.
After being killed I washed by the river and the green along its banks
and when the mourners were late
I rushed to a wave in my mind and plucked a song.
I sang it for two whole nights until it waned
and broke like a mast.
When they were late
I turned onto every path to darkness,
like the soul breaking over the rims of flowers and wooden cups
and said: They will catch up with me on the way.
The road was lonesome and the moon ripped apart my body
although this was not the Age of War.

∾

My funeral proceeds on its own
moved by the power of darkness to the grave site.
I heard him ask: Where are they?
I recognized him by his clothes, his fear, his blue face,
the blood on the collar of his shirt,
by the bullets embedded in his flesh.
I recognized him, I did.
But the mourners were late.
So I said: Invite my killer …

Translated from the Arabic by Omnia Amin and Rick London.

Circle of Prey

Rick London

Hunted for the filament
of their beauty they
pierce their lips and

distend the eyes till
they bleed masking their
faces with mud and face

the full desert sun in
rhythmic display for days
to exalt the providers

of their magnificence
with a will to
convert it to power

Its First Smell

Sarah Menefee

they were torturing us

as though it was theater for them

that their sister had died: he was thirty-

seven: a fishmonger

he was forty: a father

of three

inconsolable brother

a river of tears flows out of the television

crumpled faces: oh my sister

nothing can bring ours back

someone selling fish from a burning river

that flows out of Eden

with back on fire

with scales of pain

all human all living pain

peeling the skin off the back of Oannes
whose cry:

writing in the dark

as it always is: dissolve with all

the ancient looted texts

Tigris runs red with blood

and black with slaughtered words

how they eviscerated her

the mother of all: split her apart

like a mussel

how many ways to tell

how they are knocked apart: child from parent

lover from beloved: here in the space

of violence

which war were you born into?

what was its first smell?

was it originary?

Automatize

Roberto Harrison

listen to the abused
they have no recourse
for the answers of your face

believe them for the silence
that the door of their city
will equate with your sadness

believe them as you no longer
can arrive
inside your name

see them as you will never stand
the days full of a single ocean
as the cells of your comfort

the absolute communication
of your mouth, the fortresses
of your open heart's laughing

for cash to arrive, will not erase. wrap them
as you would the most affectionate dog, the reception
that garbage makes for you

on a Saturday. believe them as you stand
for the unlimited light
of your ancient pyramids. they speak

with the same negations, the same blinding
mirrors, that because of the sun
will not reflect you. they speak with the arrival

of their own songs, the songs of a broken worm
a desert sends out with a million holes
to fill the sky with an eagle's carnage. their telephones

will no longer ring with your repeated
prayers. their children will never arrive

to the light of your swollen daydreams. they will not pierce

the flesh that holds you down
as you wake in the morning. their hammers
will not build your church, as the priest

of your meals will not look at you
to touch your soul
with the flesh of a thousand soldiers. their guns

will never press the circle
of the end of death
on your forehead. they will eat

your satisfactions and your responsible
gifts, as the rolling hills
of their abuses will blind the water

with blank beauties. they will not ask you what your name is
as you have already shattered
the day with names that unveil

the solitary bridge. they will not believe your thoughts, as they come
to them as trails in the Arctic, as a people
without the need for number. they will not believe

your actions, because there is no
way to believe the sand
in a world without a black and red spot on the sky. the problem

with the strings in your mind, is that they
can only see the motionless, and there is
no way, with them, to go past the cycles

of night and day. they leave you
with nothing
but the big computer of your sleep. believe the abused

as they are the river that the oceans need
to replenish the land
with bad weather. they are the hard times

that the comfort of your thoughts
will die in. they are the only hope
that you have for the world

as the world is always less
than those who communicate. as the world is always less
than the numbers of your feeding troughs, as they are

the heart that is sick
for you
to recover. they are the less, as the names of your gods

will know, as they will sound out
their own names for you
in the ocean in your satellite. they will not beg you

again for the right to speak, as their mouths
now have planted grains of sand in the circles
of your unknown answers.

they will remember, always, the crooked kisses
you planted on their warm bricks,
for the last coin of their holidays. they will bleed

the wars that you claim you repair
with a courage born of carnivals
that the diminutive assumption

of your friendship, the oil emergency
that promises the freedom
of your name, will endure. they will bleed it

for the pain you echo to the world
with accomplishment
and pleated pants that sing without prisons. they will arrive

when the televisions endure
your playground, as the forgotten children
that do not recover their muted obliterations

remember that another language, the sex
of its cruelty
will return. they will know again

why you know. they will make the knowledge of your cities
the last refuge
for a mathematics of reflective pain. the shimmering cars
that you shine on the highways, that you brutalize
with the encouragement of doctors
in the summer that the winter pearls itself

to see, will stop. they will call themselves another time
as the muted conversations, the erased
flesh of their attentions, in the rodeo that separates

the hat
from the sea
will be sentimental and intrusive. they will shoot

the love within hate
that the climb to the stars of the spirit of commerce
will be poor for. they will never stand

as the truth that any service will release
to make light of their dignity. believe the abused
as they will return by the very same treachery

that the politics of reason renounce
to darken the day
as it is light outside, as it sees

the truth of light in the pocket
of your amused
revolt—a towering head of Hosts

and is

Verses for Everyday Use

Fadhil al-Azzawi

The glory seeker begs for his daily bread in eternity.

∾

In History's Employment Agency there is always an unoccupied post
for the hangman

∾

Scarcely had he convinced himself that he had become the only
coachman of history's cart, then he found himself on the edge
of the abyss.

∾

There is nothing more ugly than a uniform, particularly when it is
dressed by beautiful thoughts.

∾

There are executioners that act out of passion and executioners that act
out of instinct.
The sage says, "If they all look like me even in my whims, how did it
happen that I came to be their victim?"

∾

Some of the dead lease their graves from the living without thinking of
how they are going to pay the rent.

∾

Words stick on the lips out of affection.

∾

Letting my feet carry me to where they like, I learn the pleasure of
my tired steps.

∾

Immortality said "Cover me with the wilting flowers!"

∾

We have to tell the king that he is naked, he might get cold.

❧

How strange ! Even the despots were children once.

❧

Much worse than the emperor who went naked into the street was his clown. It was he who carried the dirty clothes of his master to the marketplace and exhibited them for sale.

❧

No sooner had he met a dervish to be followed than he found him dead.

❧

A mouse hunted the cat that swallowed it.

❧

I asked autumn to sweep away the fallen leaves of his trees.

❧

To mankind I say: "You are too old to be my teacher!"

❧

People themselves pay the salaries of the police who clap them in irons.

❧

Even in his distant exile, he doesn't lose hope. The moon that the exiled poet sees from the windows of his room will soon shine over his homeland too.

❧

Ideologies are ID's carried by the angels who lost their way to paradise

❧

There is always an acrobatic clown who walks on a tightrope, performing his fantastic leaps. When he finally reaches the end of the rope, we thank the wind for being kind to him.

❧

We all stand up for the revolutions. They teach us how to applaud.

∾

Lions dream of prey that will believe in them.

∾

Theory said to life: "Come, I'll show you the way!"
Life laughed and replied: "But I am the way."

∾

A lie usually wears truth's shirt to fancy-dress parties.

∾

When we have nothing but our memory, life stops scolding us.
At the end of the day the fisherman always throws his torn net
into the river.

∾

To amuse his sparrow he carried it in its cage to the forest.

∾

We name our children after our ancestors to prove that the world
repeats itself.

∾

I wonder about a tyrant who licks the blood on his hands, then
refuses to be called a monster.

∾

Before getting on the train of history be sure that you already have
your ticket, lest midway the conductor throws you off.

∾

In front of every great poet march a thousand small poets who plough
the way for him, and behind every great poet march a thousand who
wipe out his tracks.

∾

In the labyrinth—the traveller will throw his guidebook into the fire
in order to be true to himself.

∾

In the desert wasteland of life, where there is no escape from ourselves, we hear the wolves howling in our dreams. So we close this last window in our exile, squat bored and weary in our dark cellar and continue our play until the end.

∾

We do not hear the roaring and the thunder as the eons dawn before our eyes, and of the planets as they plough their strange ways through the universe. Only my neighbor's dog, barking on the balcony, disturbs the night's serenity.

∾

The wolf howls in his distant desert to remind us of his intentions. The lamb will comfort himself with the knife carried by the shepherd at his waist.

∾

The truth goes out into the street wearing its new dress. Many people will see it, but not recognize it. O traveller, smear it with mud, so we can follow it.

Translated from the Arabic by Fadhil al-Azzawi and Beau Beausoleil.

Paper Elegy

Amaranth Borsuk

After flurry, flight,
I couldn't tell light
from shadow, lichtov
                  from cotev, couldn't write,
recalling, air knife,
             each paper slice. Pages
returned to pulp—
             headbox effluent—a fluent
slurry of words.
             I walked sightless over
beaten and cured,
             listened for fibrillation's breaking.
Lips' numb mutiny:
             too many slip into
darkness, throats circled
in censor's ruff, currency,
cigarettes—always surrounded,
sundered, drowned. Mute, any
mouth hungers. Our
books begin ground, pressed,
but never mention
this bruised history, erased.
Nothing else left
but metonymy's numb limb:
little distance distilled.
I can't get across.

311 and Counting

Lamees al-Ethari

As of May 3rd, 2007 the Brussels Tribunal has listed 311 Iraqi Academics killed, in addition to 74 others either kidnapped or arrested since the American invasion of the country in 2003. Unfortunately, the actual number is much higher.

no. 312

A white coat on a wooden hanger.

A photograph: 200 students in black robes.

A figure of a heart with red and blue veins.

One shot through the head.

no. 313

A desk pilled with last week's essays.

19th Century British Poetry.

Dark rimmed glasses silently folded.

Kidnapped and still missing.

no. 314

He didn't have a desk.

But he came anyway.

To give lectures while sirens flared.

So the students wouldn't give up.

Shot on the way home.
Mohammed Al Rawi, Alharith Abdul Hamid, Kamal Al Jarah, Ali Jassim,
Kamil Abdul Hussien, Ahmed Izaldin Yahya, Amir Kasim Al Kaisi,
Khalid Al Hassan, Hassan Ahmed, ...

This poem was printed as a broadside by Annemarie Munn for the Al-Mutanabbi Street
Broadside Project.

A Very Short Letter

Shayma' al-Saqr

"Dear Sabreen,
I was asked to be one of the editors of an English-language
anthology to commemorate al-Mutanabbi Street ... I would be happy
if you could contribute a short text and I will translate it.

Cordially and Respectfully"

Skirmish!

My thoughts grab my emotions by the hair in the room. At the
top of the stairs the twin talents of patience and coexistence are
warring. In the garden, I seethe and am ready for an immediate
combative reflex. When my father calls out "Sabreen," I show my
teeth and yell: why are you cursing me? When my child Wadee'a
cries, I scream: I will suffocate her and deliver her from all this
misery. I didn't want to read the e-mail again. Did he say that I was
invited? Did he write that my name is among the contributors? Was it
a poem or a short text? My head is a tight-shut cooking pot full of
eggplants, cauliflower, potatoes, bread, celery, pepper, leeks,
tomatoes, and liver meat, cucumbers, six eggs, boiling water, and the
buttery foam of tomato paste.

Attack!

At the borders of the pot, the spices are on their toes, ready to
jump. The genealogies of all the oils and liquids are mixing with what
my father bought before noon. The fate of this battle is probably clear
to the reader. It is the trash. Of course, had the professor not saddled
me with the responsibility of writing about al-Mutanabbi Street, the
vegetables would not have been ruined.

What a predicament!

Instead of the meeting of an egg in a womb, I find myself forced
to look for in vitro fertilization. To look for a fertility clinic where a
husband is let down by his ability to ejaculate and a wife is forced to
encourage her husband to win the cells of life in order to
compensate, in a desperate attempt, for past failures. The doctor is

behind the door repeating, like a priest, incantations about erections, but ones that are exonerated from ecstasy, because of the objective:

– Do you think it's milk Doc … and that I'm just a cow?

I know very well that the end result is one and the same: an embryo born by artificial insemination is no different from one born of love, but I also know that inorganic introductions are like the birthmark on my daughter's face.

What a predicament!

If I decline I will squander a historic opportunity to make up for my past mistakes.

What a predicament!

I must say yes, even though I do not know al-Mutanabbi Street outside of that tiny window provided by my college classmates' tales and my father's stories. My classmates were obsessed with the shiver of buying a banned book and the ecstasy of stealing books that were not banned. My father used to sneak out when it was close to 2 p.m. on a Friday and he would return with books, sandwiches, and exotic stories about what lies hidden in cellars or what issues from the one-jawed mouth of a bookseller who used to be called "al-Rijab's grandson." There were secrets, books, pamphlets, scandals, wine, and bootleg cigarettes.

My ambition wants to use this solicitation to make underground book warehouses whose keys are with the one-jawed grandson of al-Rijab. I want to create halls built back in the time of the Abbasids in old style and with giant stairways. It wants to put next to the shiver of buying banned books the explosion of a bookshop that resembles a mythic tome full of knowledge and secrets. A tome with its own floors, basements, and halls. Six of these halls are hexagonal. Four are windowless and twenty-eight with ceiling windows that are opened to receive the sun and become a space for long whispers and a treasure trove of secrets. It wants basement guards who only sleep when they die so they are buried standing, each on the floor he guarded. There must be allusions to postponed catastrophes or books surrounded with secrecy. Books that caused strange deaths during the days of al-Amin and la-Ma'mun, or after the Mongols left

Baghdad. I want a library in the shape of a labyrinth, boasting books that can only be sublime when they are stamped with the censors' various stamps. I want an old man who has become stone because he stood there for so long, but a mysterious power still inhabits him and he preserves the order of the library.

But my ambition breaks down when I remember how run down al-Mutanabbi street looks from al-Rusafi Square. "The ambitious path ornamented with Borges and Eco is not the path." That is what I told myself as I was consoling a colleague who went there with notions of liberty, but was taken into the cellars of the booksellers and she did not return with a book, but rather with a swollen belly. An illegitimate pregnancy in an Islamic country!

Of course Sir, al-Mutanabbi Street is a market for men, be they customers or sellers, and there is no trace for women whom the professor can ask for a commemoration! Way back, prior to the Ba'th's "Islamic Awakening" in 1991, there were two women in their sixties who used to sell fried food next to the alcohol shop owned by Hajj Muhammad al-Khashali. They were lifelong friends, coworkers in a profession that started in the days of Abd al-Karim Qasim. It was a friendship that takes a special path on Fridays, a path whose vocabulary is sighs and..

Irregular teeth are stacked according to a competition.

There is a black frying pan that resembles a cooking pot and a kerosene cooker. Eggplants, pumpkins, potatoes, breadcrumbs, cauliflower, leeks, pepper, six eggs, tomatoes, liver meat and cucumbers. One of the women used to put a half bottle of *araq* below her cart. The other used to put it in a kettle that appeared like a battered jug to al-Mutanabbi's customers.

The winds from the frying mixes with hot musk.

The woman on the right sidewalk wears a black headscarf and offers customers the same product, but the tomatoes are "tender" and drinking the araq is less scandalous, which gives the customers a security not provided by the fat one. The latter sings all day and moves about wearing no underwear and cannot arouse even the worst drunkards, the sexually oppressed, or those with exceptional desires. As soon as the fingers of the one on the left sense that the

alcohol bottle is getting light she goes insane and makes up a fight
with her competitor. The sweet lilting voice turns into curses. The
skirt leaves the hips exposing, for the millionth time, rows of
blackened fat that can only be covered when Qasim al-Rijab, from his
grave, covers them with a piece of his shroud and a punch to the
nose. She wakes up and covers as if nothing had happened. She
puts a large tray full of food on her head and her eyes wander and
gaze at al-Haj Muhammad al-Khishali who holds a hat with a mark
mixed with old clippings about the offices of doctors, lawyers, and
pharmacies at al-Mutanabbi.

"How many pharmacies are there in al-Mutanabbi? I wanted to ask
my father as he was buying from the "meat closet" three "mixed"
sandwiches and was taken by her singing style.

But …

Just a minute, Sir. Why did you ask me in particular to write
about al-Mutanabbi? Dare I say that you want to get an international
reputation and increase your sales? Or do you want to capitalize on
my anger after my husband's kidnapping and contribute to repeating
the slogan" a country built with skulls and blood will never be
destroyed"? You have no right to do this professor? You have no
right to abuse me and this is why I refuse to send a text for
publication? Didn't you say in your third e-mail that you considered
me your sister?

Fuck you!

Two Days Later

"I was asked to be one of the editors of an English language
anthology commemorating al-Mutanabbi Street… I would be happy
if you would contribute…"
Dear Professor,

I apologize for the delay in responding and I would like to
inform you that I would be delighted to contribute. I have decided to
respond positively, because I want quick fame, especially after my
husband was kidnapped, as you know, and the bind I'm in for having
to raise my daughter of one and a half years all by myself. I am a
woman, a man, and a child all in one body. Can you imagine how

one woman can bear three beings under her skin in the sweltering heat of August?

I have decided to sneak into al-Mutanabbi and rely on American films and the culture of Iraqi masks. I have decided to tell my father about your courageous invitation and the dreams of an instant move from not publishing in Iraqi literary outlets to international recognition. I'll tell him how that will make up for the years of deprivation given to me first by Saddam, and later the occupation, and now their offspring which, what a surprise, has an off-white skin, kinky hair and blue eyes. The offspring of two spouses who remained happy even after one of them killed the other. The first deserved the oil prize and the other prophecy.

A Week Later

"I was asked to be one of the editors of an English language anthology commemorating ... I would be happy if you would contribute

Sir, I have to decline. My father has refused your offer and considering my current circumstances I have to succumb to him. I wrote to you before in one of my e-mails that my father is an artist and a writer who refuses to belong to institutional cultural camps and thinks I should be loyal to his legacy. I brandished all my swords and explosives and "house fights" to make him agree, but he is as stubborn as an ox. His excuse was the loss of the man with one jaw, the grandson of al-Rijab who was killed in a car bomb. He fell silent when I suggested that he mend bridges with one of his friends who was thought to have died, or on a trip, or who immigrated.

Before he retired to his studio on Friday, I retrieved my acting talents, which I though I'd lost forever and I donned an Arab man's traditional garb with dark sunglasses and used some cotton to have a belly. I paraded myself before my father who had once made both me and my mother swear by the Qur'an – and mind you, he is an atheist not to publish his works until seventy years had passed after his death. He was surprised by the disappearance of a striking female face behind a fake moustache and a beard. He did not protest that much and laughed loudly like never before.

Quickly, let's go to al-Mutanabbi before you wake up from this madness.

His spirit was that of a film director and not a father. He locked his studio, stood on the sidewalk and hailed a taxi to which he pushed us both:

– To al-Rusafi Square! We are in a hurry.

He called a friend whose number was saved on his mobile:

– Would you like to meet? I'm on my way to al-Mutanabbi.

Reconnecting with a friend after ages left him giggling. At al-Mutanabbi, protected by my father, I played the role of a journalist. I spied on workers and engineers busy digging in the street. Workers who have no knowledge of al-Mutanabbi's old and new maps, or about the book cellars waiting for a revolution or a coup to restore their secrecy.
At the "al-'Asriyya Bookstore" there were many unbanned clippings. More pages at "al-Nu'man" and "al-Haydariyya" Stacks of paper at "al-Maktaba al-'Arabiyya" and mounds of books and book covers at the attic of "Abd Al-Hamid Zahid." Stench. Open sewage. Strange insects. There was my father who was about to explode of heat and anger for a trap he'd set for himself when he stood close to al-Muthanna to chat with a friend he loved, but avoided for decades.

Dear Sir,

These are the characters of the scene and nothing at al-Muthanna Bookstore has a hint of a tragedy! There are no stacks of books that are only shown to "trusted ones" or in drops as in Saddam's time, nor anything. It is just like any other explosion. The only difference is in the remains. Instead of watermelon peel, or slipping on tomatoes and having women's *abayas* become more like nooses, there are pieces of paper, covers, and shelves where stones and smoke have perched. I even miss the vomit which filled my mouth when I realized once that I had stepped on a crushed skull at the site of the last explosion at Bab al-Mu'azzam. There are crushed papers on the sidewalk.

Let's consider the situation, Sir. A woman who is promised by a man to be lifted to the international arena disguises herself. She forces her father to make up with a friend he's not seen for ages. She stands inside the destroyed al-Muthanna Bookstore, looks at the owner, Qasim al-Rijab as he walks up front. His literary assembly reminds her of Dr. Sa'ib Shawkat's house and the fire which stormed the bookstore at the end of the 1990's and left his sons to dust.

Setback!

Sir, there is nothing but disgusting books and papers whose only bond is cellulose and a threatening dust cloud.

Because of the headaches I've been having since my pregnancy I thought of collecting pieces of paper. I told myself: take five kilograms of these papers and try at home to put together what can and even what cannot be put together. Bring opposites closer or make harmony out of jarring tones. I took whatever I saw or came across. I started to pick things up from the ground and the shelves. "Don't touch the urinal," I reprimanded myself, but then I though: on the contrary, the urinal, too, might have an important text. Even if it's not important, I will bestow importance on it, because I found it at a destroyed urinal at al-Muthanna Bookstore in al-Mutanabbi after the bombing. The idea I got in the bathroom led me to think of variations in space, place, and color and even psychological variations. I saw a half burnt piece of cardboard, which reminded me of the classical style of representing war and how paper flies, or a line of poetry is severed into two. How the waters of the Tigris acquire two colors; red for blood and blue for ink. I remembered that people made a bridge out of mud, books, and blood to connect both sides of the city.

Then inspiration came all of a sudden; I saw a half erased piece of paper stuck between the wall and a shelf. I think the fat woman is the one who left the piece of paper like this before faking an explosion. When she was in heat she exploded and left pieces of cardboard flying in the dark cellar.

The dreams of visiting al-Mutanabbi told me that bookmakers wrote on yellowish sheets and 80 mm paper with black or red fonts, therefore they will be illegible. Because the ink of old presses was made of date juice, a hoopoe's blood. Garlic and glue made of okra, which disintegrates under the sun.

I said to myself that I must find a cellar where Babylonian and Assyrian tablets are preserved. Yes. I must also find texts written on reed, leather, or skulls. Then I though that even if I don't find any Sumerian tablets I can claim that I did in my story. Who will know the truth now that the one-jawed man is dead and even white ants have escaped from al-Mutanabbi?

Abdalrahman Afandi's photograph with his hat in hand in 1890 led me to Mulla Khdhayyir with a white turban in 1900, then Nu'man al-A'dhami in 1905 with a kiffiyyah. Were they themselves or their wet photographs in an album, which leads to a cave under al-Muthanna bookstore? King Faisal I was seen in 1921 flying to the cave where an explosion took place to celebrate his coronation. I saw Zakha Street, which was famous in the Abbasid period and which opens unto Musa Road. There are, on both sides, cultural and religious establishments, including the Sa'ada al-Rasa'illi School and the Urjuwan Sufi convent. This is where the Qishla district starts and where the Iraqi government in the Ottoman and Monarchic periods had its tomb!

I ended up in the deep cellar.

Qasm al-Rijab is burying the neck of the vestibule with shelves and sacks of books, but he becomes ash and a broken cement wall one meter wide is revealed. It leads to a tunnel that is lit despite the difficulty light would face reaching it.

I learned from my father later after going home that this secret cellar was connected to a network of tunnels leading to many libraries, including the famous al-Mustansiriyya which survived the Mongol's siege in the thirteenth century. It was at al-Mustansiriyya that a gay bookseller had invented a method for the blind to read by touching, five centuries before the West. His name was Zayn al-Din. This tunnel was also the target of a long search by the mukhabarat during Saddam's time. Their search failed, but ended up killing Qasim al-Rijab and his sons in that fire. I also learned from my father that the last person to carry the secret was that one-jawed grandson. Infinite thoughts gathered at that magical moment. I collected other pieces of paper with no clear idea, or just because I felt sorry for those who wrote those papers. I left all those tunnels after forty-five minutes like a woodcutter carrying a mound in a black plastic bag. My father screamed:

What's this? Are you mad?

I'm going to be the best writer. Just wait and see!

He laughed out loud.

At Home

I cut up all the papers and mixed them together. I traced the burned words and contexts began to emerge. Like a fortuneteller, I shut my eyes and started to pull certain pieces. Stories started to line up. I depended on a stream of consciousness, cutting and pasting, breaking some texts and making others succumb before prepositions and sentences. I followed Ibn al-Nadim and what he wrote about Baghdad's civil war more than a millennium ago when " books were erased and written on again and words were erased to be replaced with others."

I employed this last technique thinking that any ray is extinguished in erasure. "Words are erased and others are written in blood." Books are burned so that fish can be grilled. Words and their dots are altered. They are written and erased time and again." Thus, meaning dissolves like a piece of salt in a dead sea.

I decided to connect the various contexts, but this is impossible. I remembered what you'd said in your fifth e-mail about hybrid writing, so I made a hole in each context and brought a wire and put it through. The contexts are now hanging on the wire!

With my apologies,

Sabreen

Translated from the Arabic by Sinan Antoon.

An excerpt from this prose poem was printed by Robin Price for the Al-Mutanabbi Street Broadside Project.

The Street of the Poet

Jim Natal

When the Mongols overran Baghdad, the Tigris was said to have first
turned red with blood from the mayhem, and then black with ink from
the books of the Grand Library that were thrown into the river.

Fire and water to the same end, the same purpose, magnificent libraries
ransacked, ravaged, and gutted by any means at hand, no shortage
of edicts or fervored intention. Blood and ink lost
are lost not for good, but
forever.

∾

Baghdad, 1258: volumes are tossed and sunk, pulp in muddy Tigris
currents, pages and illuminated script like leaves and planks floating;
if there were candles instead of buildings
burning on the banks it would be
ceremony.

∾

Baghdad, 2007: a car bomb rips al-Mutanabbi Street, named for
the great poet. Bookstores burst unbound; presses warp; sweet tea,
blood, and coffee soak the ground. Nothing learned
in 700 years but more efficient destruction.

∾

Now, a museum displays a burned-out Iraqi vehicle salvaged from
the blast, unidentifiable except for four door frames and wells
for wheels. People pass with superficial glances, think it
abstract sculpture rather than another charred
messenger.

∾

When books become smoke, the words tend to drift. They crumble
into vowels and consonants, letters find the upper atmosphere
and jetstream global distances, disrupt flight patterns,
thought patterns, cover al-aalam.*

∾

---

* Arabic for "the world."

After a wildfire, hills must be reseeded or the fallen ash will harden,
crust over at the next rain. After a flood, the waters must go somewhere.
They join like favorite passages and every river—
brown or red or black—flows
holy.

Contributors

Wafaa Abdulaali holds a PhD in English from the University of Baghdad, Iraq, and an MA in English from the University of Mosul, Iraq. Dr. Abdulaali has taught English literature and translation at the University of Mosul since 1991. She was a visiting scholar at the Harvard Divinity School.

Elmaz Abinader is a writer, poet, and performer. Her works include *In Country of My Dreams*, winner of the PEN Oakland Award for poetry; a memoir *Children of the Roojme*; and several one-woman performance plays, including *Country of Origin* that won two Drammy awards. She is cofounder of the Voices of Our Nations Arts Foundation (VONA), which holds workshops for writers of color.

Mark Abley is a poet, journalist, editor, and nonfiction writer living in Montreal. His books include *Spoken Here: Travels among Threatened Languages* and *The Prodigal Tongue: Dispatches from the Future of English*.

Etel Adnan is an Arab-American poet, essayist, playwright, and artist. Her latest published works are *In the Heart of the Heart of Another Country, Master of the Eclipse & Other Stories*, and *Sea and Fog* (forthcoming from Nightboat Books, 2012). She has had plays produced in San Francisco, Paris, Caen, and Dusseldorf. Some of her poetry has been put to music by Tania Leon, Gavin Bryars, Henry Threadgill, Annea Lockwood, and Zad Moultaka, and performed at various concerts and festivals. As a painter who has been internationally exhibited, she has been invited to participate in DOCUMENTA 2012 in Kassel, Germany.

Meena Alexander has published six volumes of poetry including *Raw Silk* and *Quickly Changing River*. Her volume of essays, *Poetics of Dislocation*, appeared in the University of Michigan Poets on Poetry series. She is the author of the memoir *Fault Lines* and editor of *Indian Love Poems*. Her awards include those from the John Simon Guggenheim Foundation, Fulbright Foundation, Rockefeller Foundation, and Arts Council of England. She is distinguished professor of English at CUNY, teaching at Hunter College and the Graduate Center.

Kazim Ali has worked as a political organizer, lobbyist, and yoga instructor. His books include books of poetry, *The Fortieth Day* and *The Far Mosque*, the novels *Quinn's Passage* and *The Disappearance of Seth*, and the forthcoming mixed-genre work *Bright Felon: Autobiography and Cities*. He teaches at Oberlin College and in the Stonecoast MFA program.

Sonia Alland divides her time between New York City and her home in a village in Southern France. Alland's collaboration with the Iraqi poet Salah al-Hamdani began after their meeting at a poetry festival in France in 2004. Her translation of a selection of his poetry and prose, *Baghdad, Mon Amour*, was published in 2008.

Alise Alousi's poems have appeared in many journals and anthologies including *Poets Against War, Inclined to Speak: Contemporary Arab-American Poetry*, and *I Feel a Little Jumpy Around You*. She is the associate director of the InsideOut Literary Arts Project in Detroit.

Omnia Amin was born in Cairo, Egypt. She is an author, translator, and professor in the College of Arts and Sciences at Zayed University in Dubai, United Arab Emirates.

Ralph Angel is the author of four books of poetry: *Exceptions and Melancholies: Poems 1986–2006* (2007 PEN USA Poetry Award); *Twice Removed; Neither World*, (James Laughlin Award of The Academy of American Poets); and *Anxious Latitudes*; as well as a translation of Federico García Lorca's *Poema del cante jondo* (Poem of the Deep Song). Other awards include a gift from the Elgin Cox Trust, a Pushcart Prize, a Gertrude Stein Award, the Willis Barnstone Poetry Translation Prize, a Fulbright Foundation fellowship, and the Bess Hokin Award of the Modern Poetry Association.

Brother Anthony of Taizé was born in Truro (Cornwall, UK) in 1942 and is one of the foremost living translators of contemporary Korean poetry, with over twenty-six titles to his credit. He is currently professor emeritus, Department of English Language and Literature at Sogang University, Seoul, where he has taught since 1980.

Sinan Antoon is an Iraqi-born poet, novelist, and translator. He has been living and working in the United States since he left Iraq in 1991. His works include a collection of poems, *The Baghdad Blues*, and a novel *I'jaam: An Iraqi Rhapsody*. His poems and essays have appeared in *Iraqi Poetry Today*, *Banipal*, *World Literature Today*, *The Nation*, and *Ploughshares*. He teaches Arabic literature and culture at New York University.

Yassin "The Narcicyst" Asalman is an Iraqi MC/Media Master, born in the UAE, raised in Canada, and continually questioned by the powers that be. Yassin "The Narcicyst" Asalman's musical career was spawned through the collaborative work of the Euphrates family: a growing collective of Muslim visual artists, musicians, painters, filmographers, and photographers. Releasing two albums with Euphrates, *A Bend in the River* and *Stereotypes Incorporated*, the crew garnered worldwide attention from *Time* magazine to publications out of the Middle East and Europe. A graduate in political science and communication studies, Narcy went on to get an MA in media studies, focusing on the identity politics in Hip-Hop Poetics, specifically encountering and dissecting the Arab-American experience through a thesis project entitled "Fear of an Arab Planet." With a book being released under the same title, and a brand new album called *The Illuminarcy*, "The Narcicyst" is sure to make you see yourself through the proverbial mirror that is the current state of the world.

Raya Asee was born in 1970 in Maysan in Southern Iraq. After she graduated from the Academy of Fine Arts in Baghdad, where she studied textile design, she worked as a theatrical costume designer. Between 2004 and 2007, she worked in radio, television, and as a print journalist in Baghdad. The desperate security situation in Iraq forced Raya to leave the country in 2007. She was granted asylum in Sweden and is waiting for her thirteen-year-old son, Bashar, to be allowed to join her.

Fadhil al-Azzawi was born in Kirkuk in the North of Iraq. He studied English literature at Baghdad University, followed by further study in Leipzig University in Germany where he earned a PhD in cultural journalism. He edited a number of magazines in Iraq and abroad and founded the literary magazine, *Shi'r 69* (Poetry 69). He was arrested many times and spent three years in jail for his political and cultural activities. He left Iraq in 1977. In 1980, he and other Iraqi writers founded the Union of the Democratic Iraqi Writers in Exile in Beirut, Lebanon. He has published more than twenty books, including novels, poetry volumes, prose texts, and many literary works of translation from German and English into

Arabic. His poems and some of his books had been translated into many languages. He has lived in Berlin since 1983.

Tania Baban is a book artist, graphic designer, and the cofounder of Conflux Press. Her books find a home in many private, institutional, and museum collections, including those at the Getty Research Institute, USC, and Brown University.

Beau Beausoleil is a poet and bookseller in San Francisco, California. His latest book is *Concealed in Language*. He is the founder of the al-Mutanabbi Street Coalition.

Amaranth Borsuk is the author of *Handiwork*, winner of the 2011 Slope Books Poetry Prize, from which the poem in this volume is taken. Her other publications include *Tonal Saw*, a chapbook, and *Between Page and Screen*, an augmented poetry book completed with programmer Brad Bouse. Her poems, translations, and book reviews have appeared widely in print and online. She has a PhD in literature and creative writing from the University of Southern California and is currently a Mellon Postdoctoral Fellow in the Humanities at MIT, where she works on scholarly and creative projects at the juncture where print and digital media and modernist and contemporary poetics meet. A book artist and letterpress printer, her interest in material media informs her poetry and scholarship.

Sargon Boulus (1944–2007) was born in al-Habbaniyya, Iraq to an Assyrian family. He left Iraq in the late 1960s and lived in Beirut before settling in San Francisco. He published four collections of poetry, contributed significant translations, and is considered one of the major Arab writers of the last three decades.

Fran Bourassa is a poet, a workshop facilitator and a contributing writer to numerous anthologies. She was awarded a scholarship to Banff Wired Writing Studio, and has twice been a delegate for the BC Festival of the Arts. She is the recent First Prize Winner of the Vancouver International Writers Festival contest.

Summer Brenner's books for adults and children include *Nearly Nowhere*; *I-5: A Novel of Crime, Transport, and Sex*; and *Ivy, Homeless in San Francisco*. She lives in the San Francisco Bay Area.

Sarah Browning is director of Split This Rock Poetry Festival. She is also the author of *Whiskey in the Garden of Eden* and coeditor of *D.C. Poets Against* *the War*, an associate fellow of the Institute for Policy Studies, poetry coeditor of *On the Issues* magazine, and cohost of Sunday Kind of Love, a monthly poetry series at Busboys and Poets in Washington, DC. She has received fellowships from the DC Commission on the Arts & Humanities and the Creative Communities Initiative.

Julie Bruck is a Montreal-born, San Francisco–based poet and teacher. Her books include *Monkey Ranch* (2012), *The End of Travel*, and *The Woman Downstairs*.

Bushra al-Bustani is currently living in Mosul, one of the most heated cities in war-torn Iraq, where she is a professor of Arabic at the University of Mosul. She has published nine collections of poetry in addition to a book of critical essays, *Qira'a fil-nass el-shi'ri el-Hadith* (Readings in Modern Poetic Texts). She also has an unpublished collection of more than forty short stories titled *Hawatiful-Layl* (Night Calls). Her work now appears in *al-Adib*, a major weekly newspaper of literary criticism in Iraq.

Lewis Buzbee has been a bookseller and a publisher, and is the author of *The Yellow-Lighted Bookshop, After the Gold Rush*, and *Fliegelman's Desire*, as well as three novels for younger readers: *Steinbeck's Ghost, The Haunting of Charles Dickens*, and *Mark Twain and the River of Time*.

Eileen Grace O'Malley Callahan is a poet, printer, book designer, publisher, and teacher living and working in Berkeley, California. Her work has long been associated with Turtle Island Foundation and Hipparchia Press. A small chapbook of her poems, *The Uses of Grief*, was published in 1992.

Sita Carboni is cofounder of Pandora's Collective, a Vancouver-based charity established to promote literacy and self-expression. She has performed throughout Greater Vancouver in various events including the World Poetry Readings Series, Word on the Street, and the North Shore Writers Festival.

Hayan Charara is the author of two poetry books, *The Alchemist's Diary* (2001) and *The Sadness of Others* (2006) and editor of *Inclined to Speak: An Anthology of Contemporary Arab American Poetry* (2008). His honors include a literature fellowship from the National Endowment for the Arts, the Lucille Joy Prize for Poetry, and the New Voices Award Honor for his children's manuscript, *The Three Lucys*. He holds a PhD in literature and creative writing from the University of Houston and is the president of RAWI, the Radius of Arab-American Writers.

Amir el-Chidiac is strongly influenced by hip-hop and the traditions of Arabic poetry. Amir's poetry and prose explores issues of identity, the body, the social consciousness of political expression, the censored tongues and the bordered chorus of oppression. In 2007, Amir received an MFA in writing and consciousness from the New College of California. Amir's work has been published in *Riffrag, Mizna, Tea Party* magazine and the chapbook anthology *I Saw My Ex at a Party*.

Thomas Christensen is the author or translator of nineteen books, including *New World/New Words: Translating Latin American Literature*. His *1616: The World in Motion* will be published in January 2012 and his translation of *Selected Poems of José Ángel Valente* is similarly forthcoming. He is director of publications at the Asian Art Museum in San Francisco.

Jabez W. Churchill is a grandfather, father, Spanish/French instructor, retired peace officer, charter skipper, and poet. His works can be found online.

Dilara Cirit is studying English at UC Berkeley after three years of intensive poetics at Saratoga High School in California. Among her awards and publications in both teen and adult literary journals is the First Place Prize at the 2007 Pleasanton Poetry and Prose Contest for her poem "Descent."

Gloria Collins teaches composition in the English Department at San Jose State University. Her chapbook *Homage to Basilicata* was published in 1998. She coordinates the London Meadow Poetry Workshop, a collective of poets and writers in San Jose, California.

Mahmoud Darwish (1941–2008) was born in al-Birweh village in Galilee, Palestine. He published more than twenty books of poetry and ten books of prose. Until his death at the age of sixty-seven, he was the editor of the international literary journal *al-Karmel*, based in Ramallah. His many awards included the Lenin Peace Prize, the French medal for Knight of Arts and Letters, the Lannan Prize for Cultural Freedom, and the Prinz Claus Award from the Netherlands.

Kwame Dawes was born in Ghana in 1962 and spent most of his childhood and early adult life in Jamaica. He is the author of thirteen books of poems, and twenty of his plays have been produced in the past twenty-five years. He is Distinguished Poet in Residence, Louis Frye Scudder Professor of Liberal Arts, and founder and executive director of the South Carolina Poetry Initiative at University of South Carolina. He is also the director of the University of South Carolina Arts Institute and the programming director of the Calabash International Literary Festival, which takes place in Jamaica every May.

Steve Dickison directs the Poetry Center and American Poetry Archives at San Francisco State University and is a publisher at the small press Listening Chamber (with offshoots, Rumor Books and Parrhesia Press). With David Meltzer, he coedited and published the irregular music magazine *Shuffle Boil*. He is the author of *Disposed* (2007). He teaches, with a focus on San Francisco literary/cultural history, at SFSU and at California College of the Arts. He lives in San Francisco.

Diane di Prima lives and teaches in the San Francisco Bay Area. She is the author of forty-four books of poetry and prose, and her work has been translated into more than twenty languages. Her most recent work is *Opening to the Poem*, a book of essays and exercises on writing poetry. Di Prima was awarded the Fred Cody Award for Lifetime Achievement and Community Service in 2006, and the Reginald Lockett Award by PEN Oakland in 2008.

Lutfiya al-Dulaimi is an Iraqi fiction writer. She has published twenty-two books of fiction, essays, plays, and translations. She left Iraq in 2006 and now lives in Amman, Jordan.

Cornelius Eady's latest book of poetry, *Hardheaded Weather*, was published in April 2008. He teaches in the Creative Writing Program at the University of Notre Dame, and is cofounder with Toi Derricotte of the Cave Canem workshop.

Jordan Elgrably is an Arab Jewish writer with roots in Morocco and France. His work has appeared widely in four languages, in such publications as *The Paris Review*, *Salmagundi*, *Le Monde* and *El País*, and in numerous anthologies. He is the artistic director of Levantine Cultural Center in Los Angeles, which he cofounded in 2001 to present the arts and cultures of the Middle East and North Africa.

Daniela Bouneva Elza grew up on three continents and has crossed numerous geographic, cultural, and semantic borders. She has released more than a 150 poems into the wor(l)d in over fifty publications. In 2011, she completed her doctorate in philosophy of education at Simon Fraser University and launched her first e-book: *the book of It*. Her book of poetry, *The Weight of Dew*, was published in 2012.

Lamees al-Ethari was born in Iraq in 1976 and divides her time between her homeland and the United States and Canada. She is a writer and artist who has received the Graduate Creative Writing Award for Poetry from Kansas State University (2007), the Dorothy Shoemaker Literary Award for Poetry (2009), the Graduate Creative Writing Award from University of Waterloo (2011), and the Dorothy Shoemaker Literary Award in Prose (2011). She is currently a PhD student at the Department of English Language and Literature at the University of Waterloo in Canada. She specializes in Arab North American women's writing.

George Evans is the author of numerous works, including the poetry collections *The New World* and *Sudden Dreams*. He lives in San Francisco.

B.H. Fairchild is the author of *The Arrival of the Future, Local Knowledge*, and *The Art of the Lathe*, a finalist for the National Book Award and winner of the Kingsley Tufts Award, the William Carlos Williams Award, the California Book Award, the PEN Center West Poetry Award, and an award from the Texas Institute of Letters. He is the recipient of Guggenheim, Rockefeller/ Bellagio, and NEA Fellowships, and recently received the Arthur Rense Poetry Award from the American Academy of Arts and Letters. He lives in California.

Annie Finch's books of poetry include *The Encyclopedia of Scotland, Eve, Among the Goddesses, Calendars*, and a noted translation of the *Complete Poems of Louise Labe*. Her other books include *The Body of Poetry, The Ghost of Meter, A Poet's Ear*, and five anthologies on poetics. A professor of English at the University of Southern Maine, she directs the Stonecoast low-residency MFA Program in Creative Writing.

Gloria Frym's most recent books include *Mind over Matter* and *Any Time Soon*. She is associate professor of writing and literature at California College of the Arts in the San Francisco Bay Area.

Gary Gach was born in Los Angeles, 1947. He is editor of *What Book!? Buddha Poems from Beat to Hiphop* (winner of the American Book Award) and author of *The Complete Idiot's Guide to Understanding Buddhism* (winner of the Nautilus Book Award).

Amy Gerstler's most recent books of poetry include *Dearest Creature* (2009), *Ghost Girl* (2004), *Medicine* (2000), *Crown of Weeds* (1997). Her work has appeared in numerous magazines and anthologies, including the *New*

Yorker, Paris Review, American Poetry Review, several volumes of Best American Poetry, and the Norton Anthology of Postmodern American Poetry.

Erica Goss's poems, articles and reviews have appeared in many journals, most recently Hotel Amerika, Pearl, Main Street Rag, Rattle, Eclectica, Blood Lotus, Café Review, Zoland Poetry, Comstock Review, and Perigee. Her chapbook, Wild Place, was published in 2011 by Finishing Line Press. She won the first Edwin Markham Poetry Prize in 2007, judged by California's Poet Laureate Al Young, and was nominated for a Pushcart Prize in 2010. Goss teaches creative writing and humanities in the Bay Area and is a contributing editor for Cerise Press. She holds an MFA from San Jose State University.

José Luis Gutiérrez is a San Francisco–based poet and host of the BookShop West Portal Poetry Series. His work has appeared online on Spillway Review and Eratio and in print in the anthology San Francisco Poets II (2008): Sparring with Beatnik Ghosts vol. 3, Margie: The American Journal of Poetry 8, San Francisco Poets II (2010) and Letterbox 5: More to the Point).

Marilyn Hacker is the author of eleven books of poems and eight collections of translated poetry, including Desperanto and Marie Etienne's King of a Hundred Horsemen. She is the winner of the 2007 Robert Fagles Translation Prize and teaches English and French in New York. She studies Arabic in Paris.

Marian Haddad is the author of Wildflower. Stone. (2011), Saturn Falling Down, and Somewhere between Mexico and a River Called Home (2004). A recipient of an NEH grant, Haddad has taught creative writing at various colleges in the United States.

Husain Haddawy was born and grew up in Baghdad. He has taught English and comparative literature at various American universities, written art criticism, and translated numerous books from Arabic into English, including Mahmoud Darwish's Psalms, and The Arabian Nights. He is now living in retirement in Thailand.

Salah al-Hamdani was born into a poor family in Baghdad in 1951, and joined the workforce at age seven. He began to write poetry while imprisoned in the infamous Abu Ghraib prison for his anti-Saddam activities. Escaping from Baghdad, he made Paris his home for the past thirty years and has worked there as an actor and a writer. The poem in this collection is from his poetic memoir, Baghdad, Mon Amour, translated from French by Sonia Alland (2008).

Sam Hamill is an esteemed poet, translator, essayist, and editor. He was editor of Copper Canyon Press from 1972 to 2004. Hamill has taught in prisons for fourteen years, in artist-in-residency programs for twenty years, and has worked extensively with battered women and children. He is the author of more than forty volumes of poetry, poetry-in-translation, and essays including, *Almost Paradise: Selected Poems & Translations* (2005), *Dumb Luck* (2002), *Gratitude* (1998), and *A Poet's Work* (1998). He also founded *Poets Against War* in 2003.

Sam Hamod is the first American-born Muslim to publish a book of poetry, *Beaten Stones Like Memories* (1965). He has been nominated for the Pulitzer Prize in Poetry, published eleven books of poetry and work in dozens of anthologies in the world. His PhD is from the Writers Workshop of the University of Iowa. He is the only American-born Muslim to be director of the Islamic Center in Washington, DC. His poems appear in *Inclined to Speak: Arab American Poetry* and *We Begin Here: Poets on Palestine and Lebanon*.

Muhammad al-Hamrani (1971–2007) was an award-winning Iraqi novelist, short story writer, and journalist. He was born in al-Amara in Southern Iraq. He worked at al-Mutanabbi Street for many years as a bookseller before becoming a journalist. He died of complications following a surgery in 2007.

Nathalie Handal is an award-winning poet, playwright, and writer. She is the author of three poetry books: *The NeverField*, *The Lives of Rain*, and *Love and Strange Horses*; and two poetry CDs, *Traveling Rooms* and *Spell*. Handal is the editor of *The Poetry of Arab Women: A Contemporary Anthology* and coeditor of *Language for a New Century: Contemporary Poetry from the Middle East, Asia & Beyond*. Palestinian by heritage, she has lived in Europe, the United States, the Caribbean, Latin America, and the Arab world.

Gazar Hantoosh was born in al-Diwaniyah, Iraq, and began publishing poetry in the 1970s. Among his books are *The Red Forest* and *The Happiest Man in the World*.

Richard Harrison is the author of six books of poetry, among them the Governor-General's Award nominated, *Big Breath of a Wish*, poems about his daughter learning to speak, and *Worthy of His Fall*, a meditation on faith and violence. Harrison teaches English and Creative Writing at Mount Royal College in Calgary. His poetry on war has also appeared in *Poets Against the War*, and in *Babylon Burning*.

Roberto Harrison's most recent books include *Os* (2006) and *Counter Daemons* (2006). A chapbook, *reflector*, was published in the fall of 2008. Another chapbook, *Urrac*, was published in the Spring of 2009. He lives and works in Milwaukee, Wisconsin.

Mohammed Hayawi, an Iraqi bookseller, was killed by a car bomb on al-Mutanabbi Street on March 5, 2007.

Dima Hilal is a poet and writer, born in Beirut and raised in California, where she studied at UC Berkeley. Her work has appeared in the *San Francisco Chronicle*, *Aramco*, *Orion*, and *Poetry of Arab Women*, among others. She has been featured at Beyond Baroque, World Stage, Levantine Cultural Center, LA County Museum of Art, and the Alexandria Library in Egypt. Hilal resides in Dana Point, where she is completing a poetry collection.

Owen Hill is the author of seven small poetry collections and two mystery novels, *The Chandler Apartments* and *The Incredible Double*. He also reviews crime novels for the *Los Angeles Times*. Most recently, he was invited to read at the Frank O'Connor Short Fiction Festival in Cork, Ireland.

Jane Hirshfield's sixth poetry collection, *After*, was named a Best Book of 2006 by the *Washington Post*, *San Francisco Chronicle*, and England's *Financial Times*. Her work has appeared in the *Atlantic Monthly*, the *New Yorker*, *Poetry*, *Orion*, among others, and has been chosen five times for *The Best American Poetry* collection. In 2007, she traveled with a small group of writers through the Middle East, and met with a larger international group of writers for The New Symposium's inquiry into justice.

Jen Hofer is a Los Angeles–based poet, translator, interpreter, teacher, knitter, bookmaker, public letter-writer, and urban cyclist. Her recent books include the homemade chapbook *Lead & Tether*; *Ivory Black*, a translation of *Negro marfil* by Myriam Moscona; *The Route* (with Patrick Durgin); *sexoPUROsexoVELOZ* and *Septiembre*, a translation from *Dolores Dorantes* by Dolores Dorantes; and *lip wolf*, a translation of Laura Solórzano's *lobo de labio*. "less then more…" is from the book *one*, published by Palm Press in 2009.

Irada al-Jabbouri studied English language and media at Mustansiriya University in Baghdad, then gained a PhD in Media from Baghdad University. Her subject was the Image of Women in Iraqi Cinema, 1946–1994. She worked for many years as a journalist on cultural issues, and at present teaches in the Media College of Baghdad University. She has written six collections of short stories and one children's book, and she is a founding member of Iraqiyat, a women's research center in Baghdad.

Lena Jayyusi was born in Amman, Jordan, to Palestinian parents and obtained a PhD in sociology from the University of Manchester and an MS in Film Studies at Boston University. She is associate professor and graduate program coordinator for the College of Communication at Zayed University in Dubai.

Fady Joudah's *The Earth in the Attic* won the Yale series for Younger Poets in 2007. His translations of Mahmoud Darwish's poetry have earned him a PEN award in the United States and the Banipal prize in the UK.

Esther Kamkar is an Iranian-born poet who lives and works in Palo Alto, California. Her new book, *Hum of Bees*, was published in 2011.

Persis M. Karim is a contributing poet and editor of *Let Me Tell You Where I've Been: New Writing by Women of the Iranian Diaspora*, and coeditor of *A World Between: Poems, Short Stories and Essays by Iranian-Americans*.

Young-Moo Kim is a professor at Seoul National University, and well-known in Korea as a literary critic and poet with three published volumes of his own. Together with Brother Anthony, he translated and published poems by Chon Sang-Pyong, Kim Kwang-kyu, So Chong-Ju, and Shin Kyong-Nim, as well as Ko Un.

Ko Un is a former Buddhist priest, noted activist, and elder statesman of contemporary Korean literature and the author of over 140 books. Translators Brother Anthony, Young-Moo Kim, and Gary Gach have published his *Flowers of a Moment, Songs for Tomorrow: Poems 1961–2001*, and *Ten Thousand Lives*.

Tony Kranz is a writer, printer, and photographer living in Encinitas, California.

Josh Kun is associate professor in the Annenberg School for Communication and the Department of American Studies and Ethnicity at the University of Southern California. He is the author of *Audiotopia: Music, Race, and America* and coauthor of *And You Shall Know Us by the Trail of Our Vinyl*, an album cover history of Jews in America. He is currently finishing a book on Tijuana.

Joe Lamb is an arborist, writer, and applied ecologist living in Berkeley with his wife, Anna, their six-year-old daughter, Carson, and their dog, Xtra. Joe was a hospital corpsman during the Vietnam War, working mainly on psychiatric wards. He founded the Borneo Project, an NGO that works to promote rainforest preservation and indigenous rights. His writing has appeared in several journals and in the anthologies *Veterans of War, Veterans of Peace* and *The Rag and Bone Shop of the Heart.*

Genny Lim is a native San Franciscan poet and playwright. She is the author of the award winning play *Paper Angels* and several collections of poetry, *Winter Place, Child of War* and *ISLAND: Poetry and History of Chinese Immigrants on Angel Island, 1910–1940.* In 2007, she performed in Sarajevo, Bosnia-Herzegovina, and in 2005 at the World Poetry Festival in Caracas, Venezuela.

Elline Lipkin is the author of *The Errant Thread,* chosen by Eavan Boland for the Kore Press First Book Award. Her book *Girls' Studies* was published in 2009. She received her PhD in creative writing from the University of Houston and is currently a research scholar with the Center for the Study of Women at UCLA, where her work focuses on the lives of contemporary girls and feminist literary criticism.

Dana Teen Lomax is the author of *Disclosure, Currency,* and *Room,* and the coeditor of *Letters to Poets: Conversations about Poetics, Politics, and Community* (2008). She is currently working on a book of poems with the working title *Shhh! Lullabies for a Tired Nation.* She lives in Northern California with her family.

Rick London's latest publication is the poetry collection *The Materialist* (2008). He lives and works in San Francisco.

Niamh macFhionnlaoich is currently attending UC Davis as a chemical engineering student but she continues to enjoy poetry. Her friends continue to inspire her and help her through life.

Rachida Madani was born in Tangiers, Morocco, in 1951, and still lives there. Her first book, *Femme je suis,* was published in 1981. *Contes d'une tête tranchée,* from which this sequence of excerpts is taken, is her second poetry collection, published in Morocco in 2001. A collection of her poems was published in France in 2007, as well as an experimental prose narrative *L'Histoire peut attendre.*

devorah major served as Poet Laureate of San Francisco from 2002 to 2006. Her poetry books include *street smarts, where river meets ocean,* and *with more than tongue.* She has published two novels, *An Open Weave* and *Brown Glass Windows.* major collaborated with composer Guillermo Galindo to create Trade Routes, a symphony with spoken word and chorus, that premiered with the Oakland East Bay Symphony. A new collection of poems, teardrops in the mouth of the moon and speculative novel *Ice Journeys* are forthcoming. She performs her poetry nationally and internationally and is a poet-in-residence at San Francisco's Fine Arts Museums and adjunct professor at the California College of the Arts.

Nazik al-Malaika (1922–2007) is considered by many to be one of most influential contemporary Iraqi female poets. Al-Malaika is famous as the first Arabic poet to write in free verse and as the author of four volumes of poetry. Al-Malaika taught at a number of schools and universities, most notably at the University of Mosul.

Suzy Malcolm is a songwriter/poet for children and adults. Her often humorous writing has been published in several anthologies. She cohosts Word Whips North Shore Edition and loves that it's a writers' group open to the public. Suzy has three kids' music CDs to her credit and two upcoming CDs for grownups. One of her poems was chosen to be etched in glass at the new Lynn Valley Library and another was used by an international organization on a poster for peace. She lives in Vancouver, Canada.

Huda al-Marashi is an Iraqi-American poet and writer. She lives in Cleveland, Ohio, with her husband and two children.

Jack Marshall is the author of the memoir, *From Baghdad to Brooklyn* and several poetry collections. His many awards include a Guggenheim Fellowship, a PEN Center USA Award, two Northern California Book Awards, and a nomination from the National Book Critics Circle for his poetry collection, *Sesame.* He lives in the San Francisco Bay Area.

Khaled Mattawa is the author of three books of poetry. He has translated seven volumes of contemporary Arabic poetry and edited two anthologies of Arab American literature. Mattawa received a Guggenheim fellowship, an NEA translation grant, an Alfred Hodder Fellowship from Princeton University, and three Pushcart prizes. He teaches creative writing in the MFA program at the University of Michigan, Ann Arbor.

Sarah Menefee is a San Francisco poet. Her latest books are *Human Star* and *In Your Fish Helmet*. She is also an activist and organizer in the homeless and poor people's movements.

Philip Metres is the author of *To See the Earth* (poetry, 2008), *Come Together: Imagine Peace* (anthology, 2008), *Behind the Lines: War Resistance Poetry on the American Homefront since 1941* (criticism, 2007), *Catalogue of Comedic Novelties: Selected Poems of Lev Rubinstein* (translation, 2004), and *A Kindred Orphanhood: Selected Poems of Sergey Gandlevsky* (translation, 2003). He has also the author of four chapbooks, *abu ghraib arias* (2011), *Ode to Oil* (2011), *Instants* (2006), and *Primer for Non-Native Speakers* (2004). His work has appeared in *Best American Poetry* and *Inclined to Speak: Contemporary Arab American Poetry* and has garnered an NEA, a Watson Fellowship, two Ohio Arts Council Grants, and the Cleveland Arts Prize in 2010. He teaches literature and creative writing at John Carroll University in Cleveland, Ohio.

Deena Metzger, a poet, novelist, essayist, storyteller, teacher, healer, and medicine woman, has taught and counseled for over forty years. She is the author of many books, including most recently, *La Negra y Blanca; Feral; Ruin and Beauty: New and Selected Poems; From Grief into Vision: A Council; Entering the Ghost River: Meditations on the Theory and Practice of Healing; Doors: A Fiction for Jazz Horn; The Other Hand;* and *Tree: Essays and Pieces*. She is senior advisor to Everyday Ghandis, a peace-building NGO working in Liberia. She and her husband, Michael Ortiz Hill, introduced the way of Dar: Healing Communities Based on Spiritual Practice, Council, Energy Work, and Dream Telling, to North America.

Christopher Middleton is an English poet, essayist, and translator. He lives in Austin, Texas.

Dunya Mikhail is an Iraqi-American poet born in Baghdad in 1965 and living in the United States since 1996. She has published five books in Arabic and two in English. The Arabic titles include *The Psalms of Absence* and *Almost Music*. Her first book in English, *The War Works Hard*, won the PEN Translation Award, was shortlisted for the Griffin Prize, and was named one of the twenty-five best books of 2005 by the New York Public Library. Her latest, *Diary of a Wave Outside the Sea*, won the Arab American Book Award in 2010. The translation of both books was achieved in collaboration with Elizabeth Winslow. She was awarded the UN Human Rights Award for Freedom of Writing in 2001.

Peter Money was born in California in 1963. He was a student of beat generation poet Allen Ginsberg. He has published several books and a CD, including *To day—Minutes only* (a prose-poetic dialogue with Saadi Youssef) and the underground novella *Che*. He is the publisher of Harbor Mountain Press in Vermont.

Susan Moon's books include *The Life and Letters of Tofu Roshi; Not Turning Away: The Practice of Engaged Buddhism;* and most recently, *This Is Getting Old: Zen Thoughts on Aging with Humor and Dignity.* A lay teacher in the Soto Zen tradition, she lives in Berkeley, California.

A.E. Munn is a writer and letterpress printer in the San Francisco Bay Area. She contributed a broadside to the Al-Mutanabbi Street Project and is currently at work on a collection of short stories.

Muhsin al-Musawi is professor of Arabic and Comparative Studies at Columbia University, and is the editor of the *Journal of Arabic Literature*. He also taught in Tunisia and the Middle East and published widely in English and Arabic. His books in English include *Islam on the Street*, which was Choice Outstanding Academic Title for 2010; *The Islamic Context of the Thousand and One Nights; Reading Iraq: Culture and Power in Conflict; Arabic Poetry Trajectories of Modernity and Tradition; The Postcolonial Arabic Novel; Scheherazade in England;* and *Anglo-Orient*.

Nahrain al-Mousawi is a doctoral student of comparative literature at UCLA and a member of the American Academy of Poets. Her poetry and translations have been published in *Evergreen Review, Lana Turner, Nidus, Adirondack Review, Fireweed, Wolf Moon Press, Rattle,* and others.

Majid Naficy has published over twenty books in Persian. He fled Iran in 1983, a year and a half after the execution of his wife, Ezzat Tabaian, in Tehran. Majid has published two collections of poetry, *Muddy Shoes* (1999) and *Father and Son* (2003) as well as his doctoral dissertation, "Modernism and Ideology in Persian Literature" (1997, in English).

Azar Nafisi is best known for her memoir *Reading Lolita in Tehran: A Memoir in Books.* She is currently a visiting professor and Director of Cultural Conversations at the Foreign Policy Institute of Johns Hopkins School of Advanced International Studies. She has taught and lectured in Tehran, London, and the United States. Her most recent book is *Things I've Been Silent About,* a narrative about her life in Iran.

Musa al-Naseri was born in Baghdad in 1964. He holds a master's degree in history and was working toward his PhD at the time of his immigration to the United States. From 2001 to 2007 he worked as a sales representative for a Baghdad wholesale supplier of stationery and imported office supplies. His daily sales calls carried him along al-Mutanabbi Street, as well as many historic adjacent streets. He was on al-Mutanabbi Street on the day of the bombing.

Afaf Nash, born in Baghdad, Iraq, is a doctoral student in applied linguistics at UCLA. Her educational background includes a BA in English literature from the University of Baghdad and an MA in linguistics from California State University, Fullerton.

Ibrahim Nasrallah is a Palestinian poet, born in 1954 in the al-Wehdat refugee camp in Jordan, where his parents had taken refuge in 1948. He lived in the camp for thirty-three years, attending the school sponsored by the United Nations Relief and Works Agency for Palestinian Refugees (UNRWA), and later studying at the UNRWA Teacher Training College, in Amman. He is the author of fourteen books of poems and the recipient of numerous poetry awards, and has gained wide recognition as a novelist, photographer, and journalist.

Jim Natal is the author of three poetry collections, most recently *Memory and Rain*. His work has appeared in many journals and anthologies. The cofounder of Conflux Press, he teaches creative writing at Yavapai College in Prescott, Arizona.

Bonnie Nish is cofounder of Pandora's Collective, a Vancouver-based charity established to promote literacy and self-expression. Published widely, some of her poetry and book reviews can be found in the anthologies *Undercurrents* and *Quills*, and online at www.hackwriters.com, www.blueprintreview.de and www.greenboathouse.com. Nish is currently working on a Masters of Arts Education at Simon Fraser University.

Fred Norman was born in the days of Hitler, and he has lived in the days of Bush. When it comes to man's inhumanity to man, nothing much has changed. He continues to hope, however, that he might someday write the words that will make the human beast humane.

Linda Norton is the author of *The Public Gardens: Poems and History* and the chapbook *Hesitation Kit*. She has worked in libraries, bookstores, and publishing houses since she was sixteen. She is a senior editor at the Bancroft Library at UC Berkeley. Norton's collages have appeared on the covers of books by Claudia Rankine, Julie Carr, and Stacy Szymaszek, and are featured at Counterpath Press Online along with her essay, "The Great Depression and Me." "Landscaping for Privacy," her collaboration with composer Eve Beglarian, is available on iTunes.

Ayub Nuri is an award-winning Iraqi Kurdish journalist. He covered the Iraq war for European and American news organizations including Global Radio News in London, BBC World Service, and Public Radio International. His opinion articles have appeared in the *New York Times*, the *Washington Post*, and the *Toronto Star*. He has taught journalism at the Institute for War and Peace Reporting (IWPR) in Iraq and served as Journalist-in-Residence at Swarthmore College, Pennsylvania.

Naomi Shihab Nye lives in old downtown San Antonio. She is the author or editor of thirty-two books.

Susannah Okret grew up in Oxford, England, and read French and Spanish at the University of Leeds. She is managing editor of the *Jewish Quarterly*.

Maysoon Pachachi is a London-based filmmaker of Iraqi origin, whose documentaries include *Iranian Journey, Bitter Water, Return to the Land of Wonders*, and *Our Feelings Took the Pictures: Open Shutters Iraq*. She helped found Act Together: Women's Action for Iraq, and in 2004, a free-of-charge film-training center in Baghdad, whose students have produced sixteen short documentary films.

Robert Perry is a poet, book artist, and graphic designer living and working in Palo Alto, California.

Abd al-Rahim Salih al-Rahim was born in 1950. He teaches at Iraq's al-Qadissiya University.

Adrienne Rich (1929–2012) was the author of many books of poetry, including *Tonight No Poetry Will Serve* (2011) and *Telephone Ringing in the Labyrinth* (2007). She edited Muriel Rukeyser's *Selected Poems* for the Library of America. *A Human Eye: Essays on Art in Society*, appeared in April 2009. She was the 2006 recipient of the National Book Foundation's Medal for Distinguished Contribution to American Letters.

Katrina Rodabaugh is a writer and visual artist, living and working in the San Francisco Bay Area. Her work has appeared in journals, galleries, and theaters including the San Francisco Center for the Book, Columbia College, Chicago Center for Book & Paper Arts, the University of Alabama W.S. Hoole Special Collections Library, the Z Space Studio, CounterPULSE, The Thick House, *There* online journal, and ::thepressgang::, among others.

Janet Rodney is a digital artist, poet, and letterpress printer living in Santa Fe, New Mexico, where she runs the Weaselsleeves Press. Her most recent books of poetry are *Moon on an Oarblade Rowing* (2005) and *Terminal Colors, Selected Poems 1974–2005* (2006). Vox Audio has released recordings of her reading. Her limited edition books are in fine rare book and print collections across the country.

Rijin Sahakian (b. 1978, Baghdad) has developed multidisciplinary arts programs in the United States and internationally. Sahakian has presented work on contemporary Iraqi art and culture at universities and cultural institutions including the World Bank, Arizona State University, Stanford University, the Dubai Film Festival, and the Arab American National Museum. She has also consulted and acted as a producer on various film and exhibition projects, including the feature film *Detroit Unleaded*; the Iraq:Reframe project at Montalvo Arts Center in Saratoga, California; and the Desert Initiative at the ASU Art Museum. She received her MA in Contemporary Art and Cultural Policy from New York University. Recently awarded a graduate Fulbright Fellowship for her research on contemporary Iraqi art in Amman, Jordan, she is also a visiting scholar at the Columbia University Middle East Research Center. Sahakian is Founding Director of Echo for Contemporary Iraqi Art, a nonprofit whose mission is to support the generation, presentation, and preservation of contemporary Iraqi art.

Amina Said was born in Tunisia in 1952, and now lives in Paris. She is the author of nine collections of poetry, including *La douleur des seuils* (2002) and *Au Present du Monde* (2005). She has also published two books of tales and fables from Tunisia. Marilyn Hacker's translations of her poems have appeared in *Prairie Schooner, Modern Poetry in Translation, The Cimarron Review, Poetry Daily,* and *Mantis*.

Shayma' al-Saqr is an Iraqi writer born in Baghdad in 1978. She studied drama at the Academy of Fine Arts in Baghdad and acted in a number of productions, but stopped acting in 2002. She lives in Baghdad.

Aram Saroyan's *Complete Minimal Poems* received the 2008 William Carlos Williams Award from the Poetry Society of America. His other recent books are *Artists in Trouble: New Stories* and *Starting Out in the Sixties*, a selection of essays.

Badr Shakir al-Sayyab was one of the greatest poets in Arabic literature, whose experiments helped to change the course of modern Arabic poetry. At the end of the 1940s he and Nazik al-Malaika, along with Abdulwahab Albayati and Shathel Taqa, founded the free verse movement and gave it credibility with the many fine poems published in the 1950s. These included al-Sayyab's famous "Rain Song," which was instrumental in drawing attention to the use of myth in poetry. He revolutionized all the elements of the poem and wrote highly involved political and social poetry, along with many personal poems.

Roger Sedarat is the author of *Dear Regime: Letters to the Islamic Republic*, and the author of the chapbook, *From Tehran to Texas*. He teaches at the MFA program at CUNY, Queens in New York.

Anthony Shadid was born in Oklahoma City in 1968 and died on February 16, 2012, in Syria while covering the Syrian revolution. At the time of his death, he was working as the Beirut bureau chief for the *New York Times*, after serving as the newspaper's deputy bureau chief in Baghdad. Until December 2009, Shadid had been the Baghdad bureau chief of the *Washington Post*, where he had worked since 2003. He won the Pulitzer Prize for International Reporting in 2004 for his coverage of the U.S. invasion of Iraq and the occupation that followed, and was awarded again in 2010 for his coverage of Iraq as the United States began its withdrawal. Shadid was the author of three books, *Legacy of the Prophet: Despots, Democrats and the New Politics of Islam*, published by Westview Press in 2000; *Night Draws Near: Iraq's People in the Shadow of America's War*, published in 2005 by Henry Holt; and *House of Stone: A Memoir of Home, Family, and a Lost Middle East* published after his death.

Deema K. Shehabi is the author of *Thirteen Departures from the Moon*. Her work has appeared in various journals and anthologies including *Inclined to Speak: Contemporary Arab-American Poetry*, *The Kenyon Review*, *Drunken Boat*, *Literary Imagination*, *The Poetry of Arab Women*, *Poetry Review* (London), and *Wasafiri*. Her work has been nominated for the Pushcart prize four times, and she served as vice president for RAWI, the Radius of Arab-American Writers, Inc.

Gail Sher is a psychotherapist and teacher. She lives, works, and practices Tibetan Buddhism in the San Francisco Bay Area.

Zaid Shlah resides in the San Francisco Bay Area. His poetry has appeared in literary magazines, journals, and anthologies in both Canada and the United States. In 2005 he was awarded the American Academy of Poets Award. His first book of poetry, *Taqsim*, has been published in the United States and Canada. He teaches English literature and composition at Solano Community College.

Saadi A. Simawe, an Iraqi-American author, teacher and translator. He is the editor of an anthology of forty writers, *Iraqi Poetry Today*.

Evelyn A. So's poetry appears in *Reed Magazine* and *Caesura*, among others. In 2010, she won the Dorrit Sibley Poetry Award and served as a panelist on the Al-Mutanabbi Street Project at the annual meeting for AWP, the Association of Writers & Writing Programs. She is working on a poetry manuscript and essays and memoirs on art, culture, and travel.

Lilvia Soto lives in Casas Grandes, Chihuahua, Mexico. She has a PhD in Spanish-American literature from Stony Brook University in Long Island, New York. She has taught at Harvard and other American universities, and has published poetry in both English and Spanish, short stories and literary criticism in Spanish, as well as literary translations, in Spain, Canada, the United States, and several Latin American countries. She is working on an English-language collection of poems about the Iraq Wars and a bilingual collection on her Mexican roots.

Louise Steinman is a writer whose work often deals with war, memory, and reconciliation. She is the author of the award-winning memoir, *The Souvenir: A Daughter Discovers Her Father's War.* She has curated the ALOUD literary series for the Library Foundation of Los Angeles for the past eighteen years and codirects the Los Angeles Institute for Humanities at USC.

Janet Sternburg is the author of *Phantom Limb*, a memoir; *Optic Nerve: Photopoems*; and the landmark two volumes of *The Writer on Her Work*. Her photographic work has appeared in *Aperture* and been exhibited in one-person shows in New York, Los Angeles, Mexico, Berlin, and Korea. In 2003, she was chosen by the *Utne Reader* as one of forty creative people in all art forms whose work is "innovative, with depth and resonance, full of ideas and insights that challenge us to live more fully."

Judith Lyn Sutton has devoted her life to the written word. She has an MA in English and was once a private student of Diane di Prima's, and has won awards and publication in anthologies and journals nationwide. She ranks inclusion in a book of just twenty poets including Jack Kerouac, as well as her work with the al-Mutanabbi Street Coalition and her poetry students on the Iraq Reframe Project, as among her highest honors. As a playwright and producer, she spent twenty years directing a professional regional theater warmly received by Bay Area audiences and critics alike.

Terese Svoboda is the author of five books of poetry, including *Weapons Grade* (2009). Her poetry has been published in *Times Literary Supplement*, *Paris Review*, *New Yorker*, *Slate*, *Atlantic*, *Ploughshares*, *APR*, *Grand Street*, and *New Republic* as well as *Volt*, *88*, *Guernica*, *Jubilat*, and *Hotel Amerika*.

Laurie Szujewska is an artist, printmaker, and typographer in whose work the word is image. She makes prints using the medium of letterforms, words, oil paints, and inks on a Vandercook printing press. Her art and graphic work has been exhibited worldwide. Her studio, Ensatina Press, is in Sonoma County, California.

Habib Tengour was born in Mostaganem, Algeria in 1947. His father was a militant nationalist, and the family moved to France in 1952 to escape police persecution. Tengour studied anthropology and sociology in France, where he now teaches. He returns frequently to Algeria. He is the author of numerous novels and collections of poetry including *Le Vieux de la montagne*, *Le Maître de l'heure*, *Ce Tatar-là*, *Gravité de l'ange* and *L'Arc et la cicatrice*.

Brian Turner was an infantryman in Iraq with the U.S. Army. His debut book of poems, *Here, Bullet*, won the 2005 Beatrice Hawley Award, the *New York Times* Editor's Choice selection, the 2006 Pen Center USA "Best in the West" award, and the 2007 Poets Prize. His second collection, *Phantom Noise*, meditates on the soldier's return and was shortlisted for the T.S. Eliot Prize.

Ibn al-Utri was a poet of the early ninth century.

Suzanne Vilmain was born in Waterloo, Iowa, and has lived in Santa Fe, New Mexico, since 1973. She worked as a junior high school English teacher, artist, letterpress printer, bookmaker, and graphic designer before starting Counting Coup Press in 2006.

Sholeh Wolpé is the author of two collections of poetry, *Rooftops of Tehran* (2008), and *The Scar Saloon* (2004); a CD of poetry and music; and a book of translations, *Sin: Selected Poems of Forugh Farrokhzad* (2007), for which she was awarded the Lois Roth Translation Prize in 2010. She is a regional editor of *Tablet & Pen: Literary Landscapes from the Modern Middle East* edited by Reza Aslan (2010), and the editor of an anthology of poems from Iran, *Forbidden: Poems from Iran and Its Exiles* (2012). Sholeh's poems, translations, essays, and reviews have appeared in scores of literary journals, periodicals, and anthologies worldwide and been translated into several languages. Born in Iran, she now lives in Los Angeles.

Kenneth Wong is the author of *A Prayer for Burma* (2003). His writings have appeared in the *San Francisco Chronicle*, *Grain*, and *AGNI*.

Saadi Youssef is one of the leading poets of the Arab world. Born in 1934 in Basra, Iraq, he has published thirty volumes of poetry and seven books of prose. He left Iraq in 1979, and after many detours, he has settled in London.

Daisy Zamora is a Nicaraguan poet and the author of six poetry collections in Spanish. The most recent collection of her work in English is *The Violent Foam: New and Selected Poems*. She lives in San Francisco and Managua.

Acknowledgments

Abinader, Elmaz, "The Proper Purgation." Copyright by Elmaz Abinader. Printed with permission of the author.

Abley, Mark, "A Book of Remedies." Copyright by Mark Abley. Printed with permission of the author.

Adnan, Etel, "Country of Large Rivers." Copyright by Etel Adnan. Printed with permission of the author.

Alexander, Meena, "Fragment, in Praise of the Book," originally appeared in Pen America. Copyright by Meena Alexander. Reprinted with permission of the author.

Boulous Sargan, "The Letter Has Arrived," originally appeared in Azma Ukhra li-Kalbi al-Qabila, Another Bone for the Tribe's Dog (Dar al-Jamal, Beirut: 2007). Translated by Sinan Antoon. Reprinted with permission of the translator.

Bruck, Julie, "March 9, 2007, al-Mutanabbi Street, Baghdad," from Monkey Ranch (Brick Books, 2012). Copyright 2012 by Julie Bruck. Used with permission of the author.

Buzbee, Lewis, "Crossroads." Copyright by Lewis Buzbee. Used with permission of the author.

Christensen, Thomas, "Remembering al-Mutanabbi," originally appeared in the Asian Art Museum Newsletter. Copyright by Thomas Christensen. Reprinted with permission of the author.

Darwish, Mahmoud, "I Recall al-Sayyab" and "They Didn't Ask: What's After Death," from The Butterfly's Burden, translated by Fady Joudah. Copyright 2007 by Mahmoud Darwish. Translation copyright by Fady Joudah. Reprinted with the permission of the Permissions Company, Inc., on behalf of Copper Canyon Press, www.coppercanyonpress.org.

di Prima, Diane, "Revolutionary Letter #77, Awkward Song on the Eve of War," from Revolutionary Letters (Last Gasp Press, 2007). Copyright 2007 by Diane di Prima. Reprinted with permission of the author.

Eady, Cornelius, "The Blues Sat Down on al-Mutanabbi Street." Copyright by Cornelius Eady. Printed with permission of the author.

Finch, Annie, "Interpenetrate," from Calendars (Tupelo Press, 2003). Copyright 2003 by Annie Finch. Reprinted with permission of the author.

Hacker, Marilyn, "Ghazal: dar al-harb," from Names. Copyright 2010 by Marilyn Hacker. Used by permission of W.W. Norton & Co., Inc.

Hantoosh, Gazar, "Destinies," originally appeared in Poetry International. Copyright by Gazar Hantoosh. Translated by Saadi Simawe.

Hirshfield, Jane, "The Poet," from The Lives of the Heart. Copyright 1997 by Jane Hirshfield. Reprinted with permission of the poet and HarperCollins Publishers.

Joudah, Fady, "Proof of Kindness," originally appeared in Pen America. Copyright by Fady Joudah. Reprinted with permission of the author.

Madani, Rachida, "Tales of a Severed Head," from Tales of a Severed Head (Yale University Press, 2012). Translated by Marilyn Hacker. Printed with permission of the translator.

Malaika, Nazik al-, "Five Hymns to Pain," originally appeared in *The Poetry of Arab Women*, edited by Nathalie Handal (Interlink Books, 2001). Translated by Husain Haddawy. Reprinted with permission from the editor. Copyright by Nazik al-Malaika.

Marshall, Jack, "Close to God," reprinted with permission from *The Steel Veil* (Coffee House Press, 2008). Copyright 2008 by Jack Marshall.

Mattawa, Khaled, "Adolescence of Burnt Hands," from *Amorisco* (Ausable Press, 2008). Copyright 2008 by Khaled Mattawa. Reprinted with permission of the author.

Nasrallah, Ibrahim, "The Last Supper," "The Celebration," and "My Special Invitation," from *The Rain Inside* (Curbstone Books, 2009). Copyright 2009 by Ibrahim Nasrallah. Translated by Omnia Amin and Rick London. Reprinted with permission of the author and translators.

Norton, Linda, "Psalms and Ashes," originally appeared in *Denver Quarterly* 43, no. 3 (2009). Copyright by Linda Norton. Reprinted with permission of the author.

Rich, Adrienne, "Tonight No Poetry Will Serve," from *Tonight No Poetry Will Serve: Poems 2007–2010*. Used by permission of the author and W.W. Norton & Co. Inc.

Said, Amina, "I live here in the basement of the Gare de Lyon," from *The Present Tense of the World* (Black Widow Press, 2011). Translated by Marilyn Hacker. Reprinted with permission of the translator.

Sayyab, Badr Shakir al-, "Rain Song," from *Modern Arabic Poetry*, edited by Salma Khadra Jayyusi (Columbia University Press, 1991). Translated by Lena Jayyusi and Christopher Middleton. Reprinted with permission of the publisher. "For I Am a Stranger," from *Anthology of Modern Arabic Poetry*, edited by Mounah Abdallah Khouri and Hamid Algar (University of California Press, 1974). Reprinted with permission of the publisher.

Shadid, Anthony, "The Bookseller's Story, Ending Much Too Soon," from the *Washington Post*, March 12, 2007. All Rights Reserved. Used by permission and protected by the Copyright Laws of the United States. The printing, copying, redistribution, or retransmission of the material without express written permission is prohibited.

Shlh, Zaid, "Occident to Orient," originally appeared in *Taqsim* (Frontenac House, 2006). Copyright by Zaid Shlh. Reprinted with permission of the author.

Tengour, Habib, "In the Country of the Dead," originally appeared in *The Yale Anthology of 20th Century French Poetry*, edited by Mary Ann Caws (Yale University Press, 2004). Translated by Marilyn Hacker. Reprinted with permission of the translator.

Youssef, Saadi, "Night in Hamdan," "Attention," "April Stork," and "Solos on the Oud (#3)" from *Without an Alphabet, Without a Face: Selected Poems of Saadi Youssef*. Translated by Khaled Mattawa. Copyright 2002 by Saadi Youssef. Translation copyright 2002 by Khaled Mattawa. Reprinted with permission of The Permissions Company, Inc. on behalf of Graywolf Press, Minneapolis, Minnesota, www.graywolfpress.org.

Zamora, Daisy, "No Man's Land," from *The Violent Foam: New and Selected Poems* (Curbstone Press, 2002). Translated by George Evans. Copyright by Daisy Zamora. Reprinted with permission of the translator.

ABOUT PM PRESS

PM Press was founded at the end of 2007 by a small collection of folks with decades of publishing, media, and organizing experience. PM Press co-conspirators have published and distributed hundreds of books, pamphlets, CDs, and DVDs. Members of PM have founded enduring book fairs, spearheaded victorious tenant organizing campaigns, and worked closely with bookstores, academic conferences, and even rock bands to deliver political and challenging ideas to all walks of life. We're old enough to know what we're doing and young enough to know what's at stake.

We seek to create radical and stimulating fiction and non-fiction books, pamphlets, T-shirts, visual and audio materials to entertain, educate and inspire you. We aim to distribute these through every available channel with every available technology — whether that means you are seeing anarchist classics at our bookfair stalls; reading our latest vegan cookbook at the café; downloading geeky fiction e-books; or digging new music and timely videos from our website.

PM Press is always on the lookout for talented and skilled volunteers, artists, activists and writers to work with. If you have a great idea for a project or can contribute in some way, please get in touch.

PM Press
PO Box 23912
Oakland, CA 94623
www.pmpress.org

FRIENDS OF PM PRESS

These are indisputably momentous times—the financial
system is melting down globally and the Empire is
stumbling. Now more than ever there is a vital need for
radical ideas.

In the four years since its founding—and on a mere
shoestring—PM Press has risen to the formidable challenge of publishing and
distributing knowledge and entertainment for the struggles ahead. With over
175 releases to date, we have published an impressive and stimulating array of
literature, art, music, politics, and culture. Using every available medium, we've
succeeded in connecting those hungry for ideas and information to those putting
them into practice.

Friends of PM allows you to directly help impact, amplify, and revitalize the
discourse and actions of radical writers, filmmakers, and artists. It provides us
with a stable foundation from which we can build upon our early successes and
provides a much-needed subsidy for the materials that can't necessarily pay
their own way. You can help make that happen—and receive every new title
automatically delivered to your door once a month—by joining as a Friend of PM
Press. And, we'll throw in a free T-shirt when you sign up.

Here are your options:

- **$25 a month** Get all books and pamphlets plus 50% discount on all webstore
  purchases

- **$40 a month** Get all PM Press releases (including CDs and DVDs) plus 50%
  discount on all webstore purchases

- **$100 a month** Superstar—Everything plus PM merchandise, free downloads, and
  50% discount on all webstore purchases

For those who can't afford $25 or more a month, we're introducing **Sustainer
Rates** at $15, $10 and $5. Sustainers get a free PM Press T-shirt and a 50%
discount on all purchases from our website.

Your Visa or Mastercard will be billed once a month, until you tell us to stop.
Or until our efforts succeed in bringing the revolution around. Or the financial
meltdown of Capital makes plastic redundant. Whichever comes first.

I-5

Summer Brenner

ISBN: 978-1-60486-019-1
$15.95   256 pages

A novel of crime, transport, and sex, *I-5* tells the bleak and brutal story of Anya and her journey north from Los Angeles to Oakland on the interstate that bisects the Central Valley of California.

Anya is the victim of a deep deception. Someone has lied to her; and because of this lie, she is kept under lock and key, used by her employer to service men, and indebted for the privilege. In exchange, she lives in the United States and fantasizes on a future American freedom. Or as she remarks to a friend, "Would she rather be fucking a dog . . . or living like a dog?" In Anya's world, it's a reasonable question.

Much of *I-5* transpires on the eponymous interstate. Anya travels with her "manager" and driver from Los Angeles to Oakland. It's a macabre journey: a drop at Denny's, a bad patch of fog, a visit to a "correctional facility," a rendezvous with an organ grinder, and a dramatic entry across Oakland's city limits.

"Insightful, innovative and riveting. After its lyrical beginning inside Anya's head, I-5 shifts momentum into a rollicking gangsters-on-the-lam tale that is in turns blackly humorous, suspenseful, heartbreaking and always populated by intriguing characters. Anya is a wonderful, believable heroine, her tragic tale told from the inside out, without a shred of sentimental pity, which makes it all the stronger. A twisty, fast-paced ride you won't soon forget."
— Denise Hamilton, author of the *L.A.Times* bestseller *The Last Embrace*

"I'm in awe. I-5 moves so fast you can barely catch your breath. It's as tough as tires, as real and nasty as road rage, and best of all, it careens at breakneck speed over as many twists and turns as you'll find on The Grapevine. What a ride! I-5's a hard-boiled standout."
— Julie Smith, editor of *New Orleans Noir* and author of the Skip Langdon and Talba Wallis crime novel series

"In I-5, Summer Brenner deals with the onerous and gruesome subject of sex trafficking calmly and forcefully, making the reader feel the pain of its victims. The trick to forging a successful narrative is always in the details, and I-5 provides them in abundance. This book bleeds truth—after you finish it, the blood will be on your hands."
— Barry Gifford, author, poet and screenwriter

Ivy, Homeless in San Francisco

Summer Brenner
with illustrations by Brian Bowes

ISBN: 978-1-60486-317-8
$15.00   176 pages

In this empathetic tale of hope, understanding, and the importance of family, readers face the difficult issue of poverty and the many hardships of being homeless through an inspiring young heroine named Ivy. Ivy is the story of a young girl who finds herself homeless on the streets of San Francisco when she and her father, Poppy, are evicted from his artist loft.

Struggling to survive day to day, Ivy and Poppy befriend a dog who takes them to the ramshackle home of quirky siblings Eugenia and Oscar Orr, marking the start of some amazing adventures. Blending a spoonful of Charles Dickens' *Oliver Twist* with a dash of Armistead Maupin's *Tales of the City* and a few pinches of the *Adventures of Lassie*, Ivy's tale will appeal to young readers as well as give adults material to discuss with children.

"*Lolitas, Oliver Twists and Huckleberry Finns live on, and now, Ivy's tale of hope lives right alongside them.*"
— Robin Clewly, *San Francisco Chronicle*

"*A quirky, clever story about a young girl's journey through the streets and homeless shelters of San Francisco… Ivy is fictional, but her circumstances are honest reflections of life for the many homeless children.*"
— *San Jose Mercury News*

"*All the parts fit in so well that I almost forgot that I was reading a book. It was as if I was watching a movie and could hear their thoughts… I think this book is great for all ages. Ivy is both fun and moving.*"
— Anna Moss, age 12. Boston, MA

"*Ivy was one of the best books I have ever read. I liked it because it taught an important lesson of faith and trust.*"
— Rachel Hodge, age 13. Savannah, GA

The Incredible Double

Owen Hill

ISBN: 978-1-60486-083-2
$13.95   144 pages

Clay Blackburn has two jobs. Most of the time he's your average bisexual book scout in Berkeley. Some of the time he's . . . not quite a private detective. He doesn't have a license, he doesn't have a gun, he doesn't have a business card—but people come to him for help and in helping them he comes across more than his fair share of trouble. And trouble finds him seeking the fountain of youth, the myth of paradise, the pie in the sky . . . The Incredible Double.

Clay fights his way through corporate shills, Berkeley loonies, and CEO thugs on his way to understanding the secret of The Double. Follow his journey to a state of Grace, epiphanies, perhaps the meaning of life. This follow-up to *The Chandler Apartments*, red meat to charter members of the Clay Blackburn cult, is also an excellent introduction to the series. Hill brings back Blackburn's trusty, if goofy sidekicks: Marvin, best friend and lefty soldier of fortune; Bailey Dao, ex-FBI agent; Dino Centro, as smarmy as he is debonair. He also introduces a new cast of bizarre characters: drug casualty turned poet Loose Bruce, conspiracy theorist Larry Sasway, and Grace, the Tallulah Bankhead of Berkeley. Together—and sometimes not so together—they team up to foil Drugstore Wally, the CEO with an evil plan.

"Very well written, well paced, well time-lined and well-charactered. I chuckled seeing so many of my poetic acquaintances mentioned in the text."
— Ed Sanders

"Owen Hill's breathless, sly and insouciant mystery novels are full of that rare Dawn Powell-ish essence: fictional gossip. I could imagine popping in and out of his sexy little Chandler building apartment a thousand times and never having the same cocktail buzz twice. Poets have all the fun, apparently."
— Jonathan Lethem author of *The Fortress of Solitude*

"Guillaume Appollinaire and Edward Sanders would feast on this thriller of the real Berkeley and its transsexual CIA agents and doppelgangers staging Glock shoot-outs. A mystery of contingencies centering in the reeking Chandler Arms and the quicksand of Moe's Books."
— Michael McClure

The 5th Inning

E. Ethelbert Miller

ISBN: 978-1-60486-521-9
$15.95   176 pages

The 5th Inning is poet and literary activist E. Ethelbert Miller's second memoir. Coming after *Fathering Words: The Making of an African American Writer* (published in 2000), this book finds Miller returning to baseball, the game of his youth, in order to find the metaphor that will provide the measurement of his life. At 60, he ponders whether his life can now be entered into the official record books as a success or failure.

The 5th Inning is one man's examination of personal relationships, depression, love and loss. This is a story of the individual alone on the pitching mound or in the batters box. It's a box score filled with remembrance. It's a combination of baseball and the blues. The paperback has an additional chapter.

"*Traditionally, it's viewed as a female occupation, to strip away the layers and examine the experience of relationships with a partner, with children, within one's own interior emotional life. Here comes a strong, real male voice, exploring the terrifying territory of growing older—in a marriage, in a family, in one's body. Ethelbert Miller writes with naked honesty and courage about what it is to be a man no longer young. Youth may have left him. Passion has not.*"
— Joyce Maynard, author of *At Home in the World*

"*The 5th Inning is a poetic meditation as much as a memoir. Ethelbert brings his poet's eye to the game of baseball and transforms it into a metaphor for a life that knows strikes, groundouts, and errors as well as the beauty of a ball sailing straight across homeplate.*"
— Josephine Reed, WPFW

"*Ethelbert Miller brings an accomplished poet's stunning language to this important memoir, and no one writes more eloquently about the lives—the triumphs and dilemmas—of black American men than he does.*"
— Charles Johnson, author of *Middle Passage*, on *Fathering Words*

Wisdom Teeth

Derrick Weston Brown
with a foreword by Simone Jacobson

ISBN: 978-1-60486-417-5
$14.95   136 pages

To consider *Wisdom Teeth* is to acknowledge inevitable
movement, shift, and sometimes pain. There's change
hidden just below the surface and, like it or not, once
it breaks, everything has to make room. So goes the
aptly titled debut poetry collection from poet and educator Derrick Weston Brown.
Wisdom Teeth reveals the ongoing internal and external reconstruction of a poet's
life and world, as told through a litany of forms and myriad of voices, some the
poet's own.

Wisdom Teeth is a questioning work, a redefining of personal relationships,
masculinity, race, and history. It's a readjustment of bite, humor, and perspective
as Brown channels hip-hop, Toni Morrison, and Snagglepuss to make way for the
shudder and eruption of wisdom.

"This brilliant first effort is akin to a mixtape, filled with nostalgic hip-hop references—
MF Doom, A Tribe Called Quest, and J Dilla, among others—a love letter from a
grown man still much enamored of the youth culture today. Found here are playful
experiments with the eintou, bop, and brownku, African American forms seldom
approached with such mastery."
— Simone Jacobson, managing editor for *Words. Beats. Life: The Global Journal of*
Hip-Hop Culture

"We need more songs like this young man's right here. Truth cuts its way beneath the
unspoken like new teeth on their way to light. Son of Langston, come on through."
— Ruth Forman, author of *Prayers Like Shoes*

"Derrick Weston Brown ventures into the canon to echo the voices of Morrison's Sweet
Home Men, *then bends his ear to the streets of DC to render the shouts and whispers*
of corner brawls and slapped down dominoes—all the while balancing the bridge
between Ellington and the sacred tribes of hip-hop."
— Tyehimba Jess, author of *Leadbelly*

"Full of wit and whimsy, Wisdom Teeth *postulates a poetics of heart-whole*
appreciation and honesty—for love and life, for family and friends, for literature and
history, for pop culture and the poet's ever-cognizant powers of observation."
— Tony Medina, author of *My Old Man Was always on the Lam*

Suspended Somewhere Between:
A Book of Verse

Akbar Ahmed
with a foreword by Daniel Futterman

ISBN: 978-1-60486-485-4
$15.95   152 pages

Akbar Ahmed's *Suspended Somewhere Between* is a
collection of poetry from the man the BBC calls "the
world's leading authority on contemporary Islam." A
mosaic of Ahmed's life, which has traversed cultural
and religious barriers, this book of verse is personal with a vocal range from
introspective and reflective to romantic and emotive to historical and political. The
poems take the reader from the forbidding valleys and mountains of Waziristan
in the tribal areas of Pakistan to the think tanks and halls of power in Washington,
DC; from the rustic tranquility of Cambridge to the urban chaos of Karachi.

The collection spans half a century of writing and gives the reader a front row seat
to the drama of a world in turmoil. Can there be more drama than Ahmed's first
memories as a boy of four on a train through the killing fields of North India during
the partition of the subcontinent in 1947? Or the breakup of Pakistan into two
counties amidst mass violence in 1971? Yet, in the midst of change and uncertainty,
there is the optimism and faith of a man with confidence in his fellow man and in
the future, despite the knowledge that perhaps the problems and challenges of the
changing world would prove to be too great.

Ahmed's poetry was a constant source of solace and renewal to which he escaped
for inspiration and sanity. He loved poetry of every kind whether English, Urdu
or Persian. Ahmed was as fascinated by Keats and Coleridge as he was by Rumi
and Ghalib. For us, he serves as a guide to the inner recesses of the Muslim world
showing us its very heart. Through the poems, the reader gets fresh insights into
the Muslim world and its struggles. Above all, they carry the eternal message of
hope and compassion.

*"Anyone wanting to understand Islam today must read Akbar Ahmed's collection. We
are given rare glimpses into the dilemmas, pain, and despair but ultimately love and
hope of Muslims through the verses of this true renaissance man."*
—Greg Mortenson, author of *Three Cups of Tea*

*"Akbar Ahmed is a national treasure. Allow him to lead you through his tumultuous,
thrilling life in this gorgeous collection of poems, written across five decades and three
continents—a life of loss, despair, child-like wonder, and love."*
—Daniel Futterman, actor (*A Mighty Heart*, as Daniel Pearl, 2007) and Oscar-
nominated screenwriter (*Capote*, 2005).

Vida

Marge Piercy

ISBN: 978-1-60486-487-8
$20.00   416 pages

Originally published in 1979, *Vida* is Marge Piercy's classic bookend to the Sixties. *Vida* is full of the pleasures and pains, the experiments, disasters, and victories of an extraordinary band of people. At the center of the novel stands Vida Asch. She has lived underground for almost a decade. Back in the '60s she was a political star of the exuberant antiwar movement—a red-haired beauty photographed for the pages of *Life* magazine—charismatic, passionate, and totally sure she would prevail. Now, a decade later, Vida is on the run, her star-quality replaced by stubborn courage. She comes briefly to rest in a safe house on Cape Cod. To her surprise and annoyance, she finds another person in the house, a fugitive, Joel, ten years younger than she, a kid who dropped into the underground out of the army. As they spend the next days together, Vida finds herself warming toward a man for the first time in years, knowing all too well the dangers.

As counterpoint to the underground '70s, Marge Piercy tells the extraordinary tale of the optimistic '60s, the thousands of people who were members of SAW (Students Against the War) and of the handful who formed a fierce group called the Little Red Wagon. Piercy's characters make vivid and comprehensible the desperation, the courage, and the blind rage of a time when "action" could appear to some to be a more rational choice than the vote.

A new introduction by Marge Piercy situates the book, and the author, in the times from which they emerged.

"Real people inhabit its pages and real suspense carries the story along... 'Vida' of course means life and she personifies it."
— Chicago Tribune

"A fully controlled, tightly structured dramatic narrative of such artful intensity that it leads the reader on at almost every page."
— New York Times Book Review

"Marge Piercy tells us exactly how it was in the lofts of the Left as the 1960s turned into the '70s. This is the way everybody sounded. This is the way everybody behaved. Vida bears witness."
— New York Times

"Very exciting. Marge Piercy's characters are complex and very human."
— Margaret Atwood

Send My Love and a Molotov Cocktail: Stories of Crime, Love and Rebellion

Edited by Gary Phillips
and Andrea Gibbons

ISBN: 978-1-60486-096-2
$19.95   368 pages

An incendiary mixture of genres and voices, this collection of short stories compiles a unique set of work that revolves around riots, revolts, and revolution. From the turbulent days of unionism in the streets of New York City during the Great Depression to a group of old women who meet at their local café to plan a radical act that will change the world forever, these original and once out-of-print stories capture the various ways people rise up to challenge the status quo and change up the relationships of power. Ideal for any fan of noir, science fiction, and revolution and mayhem, this collection includes works from Sara Paretsky, Paco Ignacio Taibo II, Cory Doctorow, Kim Stanley Robinson, and Summer Brenner.

Full list of contributors:

Summer Brenner
Rick Dakan
Barry Graham
Penny Mickelbury
Gary Phillips
Luis Rodriguez
Benjamin Whitmer
Michael Moorcock
Larry Fondation

Cory Doctorow
Andrea Gibbons
John A. Imani
Sara Paretsky
Kim Stanley Robinson
Paco Ignacio Taibo II
Ken Wishnia
Michael Skeet
Tim Wohlforth

The Wild Girls

Ursula K. Le Guin

ISBN: 978-1-60486-403-8
$12.00   112 pages

Ursula K. Le Guin is the one modern science fiction author who truly needs no introduction. In the forty years since *The Left Hand of Darkness*, her works have changed not only the face but the tone and the agenda of SF, introducing themes of gender, race, socialism, and anarchism, all the while thrilling readers with trips to strange (and strangely familiar) new worlds. She is our exemplar of what fantastic literature can and should be about.

Her Nebula winner *The Wild Girls*, newly revised and presented here in book form for the first time, tells of two captive "dirt children" in a society of sword and silk, whose determination to enter "that possible even when unattainable space in which there is room for justice" leads to a violent and loving end.

Plus: Le Guin's scandalous and scorching *Harper's* essay, "Staying Awake While We Read," (also collected here for the first time) which demolishes the pretensions of corporate publishing and the basic assumptions of capitalism as well. And of course our Outspoken Interview which promises to reveal the hidden dimensions of America's best-known SF author. And delivers.

"Idiosyncratic and convincing, Le Guin's characters have a long afterlife."
— *Publishers Weekly*

"Her worlds are haunting psychological visions molded with firm artistry."
— *The Library Journal*

"If you want excess and risk and intelligence, try Le Guin."
— *The San Francisco Chronicle*

"Her characters are complex and haunting, and her writing is remarkable for its sinewy grace."
— *Time*

"She wields her pen with a moral and psychological sophistication rarely seen. What she really does is write fables: splendidly intricate and hugely imaginative tales about such mundane concerns as life, death, love, and sex."
— *Newsweek*

Byzantium Endures: The First Volume of the Colonel Pyat Quartet

Michael Moorcock
with an introduction by Alan Wall

ISBN: 978-1-60486-491-5
$22.00   400 pages

Meet Maxim Arturovitch Pyatnitski, also known as
Pyat. Tsarist rebel, Nazi thug, continental conman, and
reactionary counterspy: the dark and dangerous anti-hero of Michael Moorcock's
most controversial work.

Published in 1981 to great critical acclaim—then condemned to the shadows and
unavailable in the U.S. for thirty years—*Byzantium Endures*, the first of the Pyat
Quartet, is not a book for the faint-hearted. It's the story of a cocaine addict, sexual
adventurer, and obsessive anti-Semite whose epic journey from Leningrad to
London connects him with scoundrels and heroes from Trotsky to Makhno, and
whose career echoes that of the 20th century's descent into Fascism and total war.

This is Moorcock at his audacious, iconoclastic best: a grand sweeping overview
of the events of the last century, as revealed in the secret journals of modern
literature's most proudly unredeemable outlaw. This authoritative U.S. edition
presents the author's final cut, restoring previously forbidden passages and deleted
scenes.

*"What is extraordinary about this novel. . . is the largeness of the design. Moorcock has
the bravura of a nineteeth-century novelist: he takes risks, he uses fiction as if it were
a divining rod for the age's most significant concerns. Here, in* Byzantium Endures, *he
has taken possession of the early twentieth century, of a strange, dead civilization and
recast them in a form which is highly charged without ceasing to be credible."*
— Peter Ackroyd, *Sunday Times*

*"A tour de force, and an extraordinary one. Mr. Moorcock has created in Pyatnitski a
wholly sympathetic and highly complicated rogue. . . There is much vigorous action
here, along with a depth and an intellectuality, and humor and color and wit as well."*
— *The New Yorker*

*"Clearly the foundation on which a gigantic literary edifice will, in due course, be erected.
While others build fictional molehills, Mr. Moorcock makes plans for great shimmering
pyramids. But the footings of this particular edifice are intriguing and audacious enough
to leave one hungry for more."*
— John Naughton, *Listener*

Lonely Hearts Killer

Tomoyuki Hoshino

ISBN: 978-1-60486-084-9
$15.95   232 pages

What happens when a popular and young emperor suddenly dies, and the only person available to succeed him is his sister? How can people in an island country survive as climate change and martial law are eroding more and more opportunities for local sustainability and mutual aid? And what can be done to challenge the rise of a new authoritarian political leadership at a time when the general public is obsessed with fears related to personal and national "security"? These and other provocative questions provide the backdrop for this powerhouse novel about young adults embroiled in what appear to be more private matters—friendships, sex, a love suicide, and struggles to cope with grief and work.

PM Press is proud to bring you this first English translation of a full-length novel by the award-winning author Tomoyuki Hoshino.

Since his literary debut in 1997, Tomoyuki Hoshino has published twelve books on subjects ranging from "terrorism" to queer/trans community formations; from the exploitation of migrant workers to journalistic ethics; and from the Japanese emperor system to neoliberalism. He is also well known in Japan for his nonfiction essays on politics, society, the arts, and sports, particularly soccer. He maintains a website and blog at http://www.hoshinot.jp/.

"A major novel by Tomoyuki Hoshino, one of the most compelling and challenging writers in Japan today, Lonely Hearts Killer deftly weaves a path between geopolitical events and individual experience, forcing a personal confrontation with the political brutality of the postmodern era. Adrienne Hurley's brilliant translation captures the nuance and wit of Hoshino's exploration of depths that rise to the surface in the violent acts of contemporary youth."
— Thomas LaMarre, William Dawson Professor of East Asian Studies, McGill University

"Since his debut, Hoshino has used as the core of his writing a unique sense of the unreality of things, allowing him to illuminate otherwise hidden realities within Japanese society. And as he continues to write from this tricky position, it goes without saying that he produces work upon work of extraordinary beauty and power."
— Yuko Tsushima, award-winning Japanese novelist

Calling All Heroes: A Manual for Taking Power

Paco Ignacio Taibo II

ISBN: 978-1-60486-205-8
$12.00   128 pages

The euphoric idealism of grassroots reform and the tragic reality of revolutionary failure are at the center of this speculative novel that opens with a real historical event. On October 2, 1968, 10 days before the Summer Olympics in Mexico, the Mexican government responds to a student demonstration in Tlatelolco by firing into the crowd, killing more than 200 students and civilians and wounding hundreds more. The Tlatelolco massacre was erased from the official record as easily as authorities washing the blood from the streets, and no one was ever held accountable.

It is two years later and Nestor, a journalist and participant in the fateful events, lies recovering in the hospital from a knife wound. His fevered imagination leads him in the collection of facts and memories of the movement and its assassination in the company of figures from his childhood. Nestor calls on the heroes of his youth—Sherlock Holmes, Doc Holliday, Wyatt Earp, and D'Artagnan among them—to join him in launching a new reform movement conceived by his intensely active imagination.

"Taibo's writing is witty, provocative, finely nuanced and well worth the challenge."
— *Publishers Weekly*

"I am his number one fan. . . I can always lose myself in one of his novels because of their intelligence and humor. My secret wish is to become one of the characters in his fiction, all of them drawn from the wit and wisdom of popular imagination. Yet make no mistake, Paco Taibo—sociologist and historian—is recovering the political history of Mexico to offer a vital, compelling vision of our reality."
— Laura Esquivel, author of *Like Water for Chocolate*

"The real enchantment of Mr. Taibo's storytelling lies in the wild and melancholy tangle of life he sees everywhere."
— *New York Times Book Review*

"It doesn't matter what happens. Taibo's novels constitute an absurdist manifesto. No matter how oppressive a government, no matter how strict the limitations of life, we all have our imaginations, our inventiveness, our ability to liven up lonely apartments with a couple of quacking ducks. If you don't have anything left, oppressors can't take anything away."
— *Washington Post Book World*

Fire on the Mountain

Terry Bisson
with an introduction
by Mumia Abu-Jamal

ISBN: 978-1-60486-087-0
$15.95   208 pages

It's 1959 in socialist Virginia. The Deep South is an independent Black nation called Nova Africa. The second Mars expedition is about to touch down on the red planet. And a pregnant scientist is climbing the Blue Ridge in search of her great-great grandfather, a teenage slave who fought with John Brown and Harriet Tubman's guerrilla army.

Long unavailable in the US, published in France as *Nova Africa*, *Fire on the Mountain* is the story of what might have happened if John Brown's raid on Harper's Ferry had succeeded—and the Civil War had been started not by the slave owners but the abolitionists.

"*History revisioned, turned inside out... Bisson's wild and wonderful imagination has taken some strange turns to arrive at such a destination.*"
— Madison Smartt Bell, Anisfield-Wolf Award winner and author of *Devil's Dream*

"*You don't forget Bisson's characters, even well after you've finished his books. His* Fire on the Mountain *does for the Civil War what Philip K. Dick's* The Man in the High Castle *did for World War Two.*"
— George Alec Effinger, winner of the Hugo and Nebula awards for *Shrödinger's Kitten*, and author of the Marîd Audran trilogy.

"*A talent for evoking the joyful, vertiginous experiences of a world at fundamental turning points.*"
— *Publishers Weekly*

"*Few works have moved me as deeply, as thoroughly, as Terry Bisson's* Fire on the Mountain*... With this single poignant story, Bisson molds a world as sweet as banana cream pies, and as briny as hot tears.*"
— Mumia Abu-Jamal, prisoner and author of *Live From Death Row*, from the Introduction.

with PM Press

Low Bite

Sin Soracco

ISBN: 978-1-60486-226-3
$14.95   144 pages

Low Bite Sin Soracco's prison novel about survival,
dignity, friendship and insubordination. The view
from inside a women's prison isn't a pretty one, and
Morgan, the narrator, knows that as well as anyone.
White, female, 26, convicted of night time breaking and
entering with force, she works in the prison law library,
giving legal counsel of more-or-mostly-less usefulness to other convicts. More
useful is the hootch stash she keeps behind the law books.

And she has plenty of enemies—like Johnson, the lesbian-hating warden, and
Alex, the "pretty little dude" lawyer who doesn't like her free legal advice. Then
there's Rosalie and Birdeye—serious rustlers whose loyalty lasts about as long
as their cigarettes hold out. And then there's China: Latina, female, 22, holding
US citizenship through marriage, convicted of conspiracy to commit murder—a
dangerous woman who is safer in prison than she is on the streets. They're all
trying to get through without getting caught or going straight, but there's just one
catch—a bloodstained bank account that everybody wants, including some players
on the outside. *Low Bite*: an underground classic reprinted at last and the first title
in the new imprint from The Green Arcade.

"*Vicious, funny, cunning, ruthless, explicit… a tough original look at inside loves and
larcenies.*"
— Kirkus Reviews

"*Where else can you find the grittiness of girls-behind-bars mixed with intelligence,
brilliant prose, and emotional ferocity? Sin Soracco sets the standard for prison writing.
Hardboiled and with brains!*"
— Peter Maravelis, editor *San Francisco Noir* 1 and 2

"*Tells a gripping story concerning a group of women in a California prison: their crimes,
their relationships, their hopes and dreams.*"
— Publisher's Weekly

"*Sin Soracco is the original Black Lizard. Low Bite will take a chunk out of your leg if not
your heart. Read it, it will devour you.*"
— Barry Gifford, author *Port Tropique*, Founder Black Lizard Books